DECODING CEO-SPEAK

DECODING CEO-SPEAK

Russell Craig and Joel Amernic

UNIVERSITY OF TORONTO PRESS
Toronto Buffalo London

Rotman-UTP Publishing
An imprint of University of Toronto Press
Toronto Buffalo London
utorontopress.com

Library and Archives Canada Cataloguing in Publication

Title: Decoding CEO-speak / Russell Craig and Joel Amernic.
Names: Craig, Russell (Professor of business), author. | Amernic, Joel H.
  (Joel Henry), 1946–author.
Description: Includes bibliographical references and index.
Identifiers: Canadiana (print) 20210193042 | Canadiana (ebook) 20210193093 |
  ISBN 9781487505950 (cloth) | ISBN 9781487533021 (EPUB) |
  ISBN 9781487533014 (PDF)
Subjects: LCSH: Chief executive officers – Language – Case studies. | LCSH:
  Discourse analysis – Social aspects – Case studies. | LCSH: Corporate culture –
  Case studies. | LCGFT: Case studies.
Classification: LCC HD30.3 .C73 2021 | DDC 306.44088/6584 – dc23

ISBN 978-1-4875-0595-0 (cloth)
ISBN 978-1-4875-3302-1 (EPUB)
ISBN 978-1-4875-3301-4 (PDF)

We acknowledge the financial support of the Government of Canada, the Canada
Council for the Arts, and the Ontario Arts Council, an agency of the Government of
Ontario, for our publishing activities.

Canada Council
for the Arts

Conseil des Arts
du Canada

ONTARIO ARTS COUNCIL
CONSEIL DES ARTS DE L'ONTARIO

an Ontario government agency
un organisme du gouvernement de l'Ontario

Funded by the   Financé par le
Government   gouvernement
of Canada   du Canada

Canadä

Contents

List of Exhibits

Foreword

Business leaders may be revered or reviled, but they are never ignored. When Jack Welch, former CEO of General Electric, died in March 2020, his passing made headlines throughout the world. Instinctively, most of us are fascinated by powerful authority figures and pay close attention to what they say and do. The organizational theorist Yiannis Gabriel has argued that many "ordinary" employees experience an encounter with a CEO as akin to meeting God, a supreme judge who holds their destiny in his or her hands. CEOs are well aware of the power this gives them.

This fascinating book shows that CEOs pay close attention to the words they use – in letters to shareholders, on Twitter, in press releases – to create narratives that frame themselves and their companies in the best possible light.

In a series of compelling case studies, Russell Craig and Joel Amernic demonstrate that the tone at the top also frames reality for people *within* organizations and those *external* to it, for good or ill. For example, they show how the language of BP's CEO Tony Hayward stressed the importance of cost savings as a top company priority. Absent was any consideration of what effect this would have on safety in what is one of the most dangerous industries in the world. In April 2010, BP's *Deepwater Horizon* drilling rig exploded, with the loss of eleven lives. It also inflicted incalculable damage on the environment. The safety shortcuts leading up to this have at least some of their roots in a tone at the top that showed BP's principal priority was neither safety nor the environment. In exposing this to forensic analysis, Craig and Amernic offer us invaluable new insights into how we can "read" company cultures to understand what has gone wrong, and perhaps anticipate what might go wrong in the future.

Like all of us, CEOs today use multiple forums to spread their messages. Twitter is an unfiltered form of social media, along with Facebook, Snapchat, and Instagram. They give CEOs practically unlimited opportunities to share information and misinformation. Richard Branson, we learn, had 12.6 million Twitter followers in 2020. He and his fellow CEOs have more opportunities for image and brand management than at any other time in history. We would be wise to study more closely how they use words to communicate.

Craig and Amernic take us on many journeys in the pages that follow. We see how CEO language can constitute propaganda, strategic self-disclosure, and deception, as well as a medium to share information straightforwardly. But communication can conceal as much as it reveals. We choose words to tell stories, and we prefer these stories to show us as heroes who save the day rather than as villains responsible for disaster. In that sense, business leaders are no different from the rest of us. However, they differ in the power that they possess. As the management academic Sydney Finkelstein once noted, being a CEO today is the nearest thing that many of us can get to being king or queen of our own country. Despite this, CEOs often use confessional tales, parables, and homespun stories to suggest that they are one of the common people, imbued with modesty and bearing only good intentions. Their communications rarely admit to greed, narcissism, or hubris, all of which also proliferate in companies.

I found Craig and Amernic's analysis of this particularly fascinating. They expose the telltale linguistic tropes that show a grandiose sense of self-importance and that suggest CEOs are somehow uniquely qualified to deliver on fantasies of unlimited success. Enron remains a powerful warning of this to us all. More recently, the fatal crashes of two Boeing Max 737s were accompanied by bumbling assurances that there really was no cause for concern. After reading this book, none of us will ever again take the words of powerful people at face value.

Love them or loathe them, what CEOs do and say matters. This important book burrows beneath the bombast and the trite platitudes to show that their language – *CEO speak* – often tells us much more than its authors could ever have intended.

Dennis Tourish
Professor of Leadership and Organization Studies
University of Sussex Business School
Brighton, UK

Acknowledgments

This book has emerged from a collaboration between the two authors that spans three decades. Russell Craig is grateful for the privilege of working with a co-author of vibrant intellect and a seemingly unbounded tolerance and patience. Joel Amernic is grateful for the privilege of working with a co-author of sterling creativity and dedication to the highest standards of research. Both authors are mutually grateful for the warm *bonhomie* that has sustained their longstanding collaboration.

We thank our wives (Annette Craig and Lilly Amernic) and our extended families for their patience and tolerance as we labored on this book, distracted, often at odd hours. We also thank our respective universities (Faculty of Business, Durham University, UK, and the Rotman School of Management, University of Toronto, Canada) for providing the facilitative research environments that have enabled us to complete this book.

We are grateful also to Jennifer DiDomenico of the University of Toronto Press (UTP) for her skill, patience, and good counsel in guiding this book through UTP's rigorous approval process. We have benefited too from the perceptive feedback provided by Jessica Ross related to social media and from many helpful suggestions from the copy editor, Susan Bindernagel.

Parts of the following chapters have been sourced in material alluded to, or adapted and extended from, joint scholarly papers we have published between 2004 and 2020. In the list below, we acknowledge any additional authors of those papers in parentheses. Thus, we express thanks for the collaborative contributions of Dennis Tourish, Tony Mortensen, Shefali Iyer, Rebecca Nicolaides, Richard Trafford, and Rofiat Alli.

In addition to calling upon the "back catalog" of our scholarly publications that are listed below, this book also comprises much new material that has not been published previously. We also canvass "breaking issues" that arose at the time of writing (such as exploring the features of CEO language in the early stages of the COVID-19 pandemic).

The following of our joint research papers are drawn upon:

The deployment of accounting-related rhetoric in the prelude to a privatization. *Accounting, Auditing & Accountability Journal*, 17(1), 2004: 41–58.

"9/11" in the service of corporate rhetoric: Southwest Airlines' 2001 letter to shareholders. *Journal of Communication Inquiry*, 28(4), 2004: 325–41.

The mobilization of accounting in preening for privatization. *Accounting, Auditing & Accountability Journal*, 19(1), 2006: 82–95.

The tyranny of single performance measures: Financial accounting's operating ratio and the privatization of Canadian National Railway. *Studies in Political Economy*, 77, 2006: 177–194.

Improving CEO-speak: The CPA as communications advisor. *Journal of Accountancy*, 203(1), January, 2007: 65–6.

Making CEO-speak more potent: Editing the language of corporate leadership. *Strategy & Leadership*, 35(3), 2007: 25–31. Synthesised in "Leading in language: What the CEO should and should not say," *Strategic Directions*, 24(2), 2008: 24–5.

The charismatic leader as *pedagogue, physician, architect, commander* and *saint*: Five root metaphors in Jack Welch's letters to shareholders of General Electric. *Human Relations*, 60(12), 2007: 1839–72 (with D. Tourish). This paper is also featured in the *Wharton Leadership Digest*, April 2008.

A privatization success story: Accounting and narrative expression over time. *Accounting, Auditing & Accountability Journal*, 21(8), 2008: 1085–115.

Understanding accounting through conceptual metaphor: Accounting IS an instrument? *Critical Perspectives on Accounting*, 20(8), 2009: 875–83.

Exploring the public accountability communications of a CEO through "close reading" analysis: A teaching primer. *International Journal of Management Education*, 8(2), 2009: 75–82.

Accounting as a facilitator of extreme narcissism. *Journal of Business Ethics*, 96(1), 2010: 79–93.

Measuring and assessing tone at the top using Annual Report CEO letters. The Institute of Chartered Accountants of Scotland, Research Monograph, 2010 (with D. Tourish).

Detecting linguistic traces of destructive narcissism at-a-distance in a CEO's letter to shareholders. *Journal of Business Ethics*, 101(4), 2011: 563–75.

Reflecting a company's culture in "fairly presented" financial statements: The case of BP. *CPA Journal*, April 2012: 6, 8–10 (with D. Tourish).

Leadership discourse, culture, and corporate ethics: CEO-speak at News
Corporation. *Journal of Business Ethics*, 118(2), 2013: 379–94.

Exploring top management language for signals of possible deception:
The words of Satyam's chair Ramalinga Raju. *Journal of Business Ethics*,
113(2), 2013: 333–47 (R. Craig with T. Mortensen & S. Iyer).

Exploring signs of hubris in CEO Language. In R.P. Hart (ed.)
Communication and language analysis in the corporate world. IGI-Global,
Austin, TX, Chapter 5, 2014, pp. 69–88.

The lingo of leadership. *Communication Director*, 2, 2015: 76–9
(with D. Tourish).

Are there language markers of hubris in CEO letters to shareholders?
Journal of Business Ethics, 149(4), 2018: 973–86.

CEO speeches and safety culture: British Petroleum before the *Deepwater
Horizon* disaster. *Critical Perspectives on Accounting*, 47, 2017: 61–80.

Helping auditors identify signs of deception through psycholinguistics.
Journal of Financial Crime, 25(4), 2018: 1062–76 (R. Craig with
R. Nicolaides & R. Trafford).

Autobiographical vignettes in annual report CEO letters as a lens to
understand how leadership is conceived and enacted. *Accounting,
Auditing & Accountability Journal*, 33(1), 2020: 106–23.

Benefits and pitfalls of a CEO's personal Twitter messaging. *Strategy &
Leadership*, 48(1), 2020: 43–8.

The language of leadership in a deadly pandemic. *Strategy & Leadership*,
48(5), 2020: 41–7.

"'Fake' promises? Evaluating a CEO's assertions of a 'return to ethical
conduct.'" Under review.

DECODING CEO-SPEAK

chapter one

Introduction

We have been critical observers of corporate accountability for many years. Our focus has been on the oral and written language of CEOs of major companies – or what we refer to as *CEO-speak*. The speeches of CEOs, together with their letters to shareholders and their use of company websites, press releases, interviews, and social media (such as Facebook and Twitter), are powerful means of storytelling. We highlight that power in this book.

An editorial in the *Toronto Star* dated August 10, 2019 ("The raw power of language") eulogized Toni Morrison, recipient of the Nobel Prize in Literature, by contrasting her positive, life-affirming use of words with those of persons who used words "to slash and wound and even kill."[1] The editorial is consistent with a core message in this book: for better or worse, language is potent and has a "raw power." This power becomes even more potent when uttered by powerful people.

The focus of this book is on the public language of a powerful class of people – the CEOs of major companies. Influential management thinker Elliott Jaques emphasized the power of CEOs when he wrote that

> during the century just past, a new class of people has emerged with enormous power, for social good or for social harm, over the status and quality of life in our free enterprise democratic nations. This class is not a social nor a political class in the ordinary sense. It is a rather more amorphous group, members of which meet each other in many different business, professional, and technical settings … This class is the class of CEOs.[2]

Monitoring the language of CEOs (their CEO-speak) by all corporate stakeholders is a highly important task because those who exercise power in society (as CEOs do) must be held accountable for the "raw power" of their language. Any text prepared by CEOs, or written for them, should be assessed carefully because analysis of CEO-speak can yield many insights to important aspects of business endeavor, such as company policy, strategy, and ethicality. Analysis of CEO-speak can also provide insights to the priorities and personality of a CEO. Thus, the way CEOs use language merits ongoing scrutiny and careful assessment.

As the title of this book suggests, the following chapters seek to facilitate decoding the language of CEOs by explaining ways of mining meaning from written and oral CEO-speak. This is a critical task because CEO-speak can have a profound effect in fashioning perceptions, explaining strategy, shaping knowledge, and influencing social cognition and cultural relations.

The language CEOs use is especially important in the current era of heightened corporate accountability. Increasingly, companies and their CEOs are subject to higher levels of scrutiny by audit committees, regulatory authorities, journalists, and the public. Many CEOs strive to attain legitimacy through political correctness and virtue signaling. All of this renders a compelling case for the need to analyze CEO-speak in order to understand how CEOs make sense of the world and to appreciate why the corporations they lead behave as they do.

Many CEOs exploit the possibilities of language opportunistically. For example, they strategically place negative and positive words in their written communications to elicit more positive perceptions by readers. Further, CEOs often use language to exude personal commitment and authenticity and to portray a close relationship with followers. Transformational leaders, for example, use inspirational communications to generate high expectations and sacrifices by followers. Their language aims to convince followers that the CEO-leader possesses extraordinary insight to the economic, social, and political situation confronting the organization, can diagnose organizational and societal ailments accurately, prescribe effective treatments, and transform an organization beneficially.

The words CEOs use in their various communications are not neutral but are instrumental in enacting leadership. A CEO's words can spark action, enhance branding, share knowledge, transmit values, foster collaboration, and lead people into the future.[3] They can help "create and recreate particular worlds of understanding,"[4] "get people to do things,"[5] "make impressions on other people,"[6] and "sculpt reality."[7] The words of a CEO can influence the strategic positioning of a firm in the community and marketplace.

This book has two broad objectives. The first is to raise consciousness of the power CEOs' language has in shaping how we view companies and how we deal with them. The second objective is to reveal how the language of CEOs can be analyzed to expose its deeper meaning and purpose. We pursue these objectives through chapter-based case examples that focus variously on such matters as tone at the top, ethicality, reputation, deception, social media use, and personality.

This book aims to appeal to two broad audiences. First are CEOs and senior managers; the public relations, media, and communications consultants who advise them; plus the broad audience of corporate stakeholders (comprising investors, employees, lobbyists, activists, and the general public) who are keen to understand, through analysis of language, why CEOs and companies behave the way they do. This book will help them improve their scrutiny and interpretation of the words of business leaders.

The second intended audience comprises business school and communications studies students and academics who are interested in language and leadership. Readers in this interest group may be studying discourse analysis, leadership, linguistics, communications, public relations, strategy, accounting, financial analysis, and/or corporate signaling – or they might be interested in conducting research using close reading and computer-aided text analysis methods. Several of the company examples we discuss seem ideally suited for use as case studies in MBA or communications studies courses.

We draw together, and update and extend, the broad body of research we have conducted since the publication in 2006 of our book *CEO-Speak: The Language of Corporate Leadership* (McGill-Queen's University Press). The "back catalog" of research work that we draw on is listed in the Acknowledgments. In the following chapters, we provide a reflective and condensed overview of this prior work and juxtapose it with a large volume of our hitherto unpublished material. The intent is to develop a powerful coursing narrative that shows the power and capabilities of CEO-speak and ways of interpreting it.

Close Reading Analysis

The principal method we use to analyze the words of CEOs is known simply as "close reading." This involves slowing down the pace of reading of any source text, scrutinizing the words and metaphors used, and linking the text under investigation to the CEO's context. Our close reading analyses have emerged principally from multiple readings by both authors of a chosen text or speech transcript of a CEO. In these readings, we search for assumptions, ideology, silences, techniques of argumentation, and literary tropes (such as metaphor). This approach involves rereading sentences and paragraphs, exploring the sequence and frequency with which words and ideas are used, and reading a source text phrase by phrase to discern meaning. We reflect on how various facts, text, or arguments are co-related. We investigate the meaning of individual words, look for apt and inapt juxtapositions, seek insights to authorial intent, and try to understand a text's "inner workings."[8] We also develop ideas about pervading themes and seek to identify critical silences in any text analyzed.

In the following close readings, each author separately read the target text several times and made working notes. These notes were exchanged and reviewed until a consensus developed between the authors over several iterations. The close reading method we adopt is interpretive and is not an exact science. Although it produces many useful insights, it can also lead to contestable conclusions. This is because the social phenomena being analyzed are complex and there is usually a "plurality of plausible explanations" for the matters being considered.[9]

Nonetheless, close reading generates rich, story-based, sense-making understandings that are sensitive to the power of language. The close readings we conduct contextualize the environment in which entities operate. They are informed by the historical, social, and psychological forces that impel CEOs to lead companies in the ways that they do.

In several of the following chapters we complement our close reading analysis with results obtained from applying DICTION text analysis software. This software has been used across many disciplines by many researchers over many years, including, to a limited extent and cautiously, by us.[10] We briefly explain the key features of DICTION in appendix A.[11]

Reflections on CEO-Speak

Writing this book has prompted us to reflect again on the various forms and contexts of CEO-speak. The analyses we have conducted since the early 1990s lead us to conclude that CEOs often write as if they were visionaries, messiahs, or ruthless trail bosses. However, such a self-styled view on the part of CEOs needs tempering. Although CEOs seem at times charismatic and are culturally and socially revered, their words can display a self-constructed image of infallibility, narcissism, and/or hubris.

There is a wide variety of publicly available oral and written language of CEOs of major companies (their CEO-speak). This includes, but is not limited to, the following:

- Letters addressed to various stakeholders, such as the annual letter to shareholders published in a company's annual report. Another important variety of letter is the CEO's letter published in a corporate sustainability report. There are also letters published on important occasions, such as the letter Uber CEO Dara Khosrowshahi published in that company's initial public offering (IPO) registration document in May 2019. As well, there are "open letters" such as the one published online in February 2020 by BlackRock Chairman and CEO Larry Fink in which he asserted, "sooner than most anticipate … there will be a significant reallocation of capital as a result of climate change"[12]
- Speeches delivered by CEOs at a company's annual general meeting or at an industry association function
- Transcripts of earnings announcement conference calls with financial analysts
- Interviews with journalists
- Testimony before government committees
- Press releases
- Social media posts, such as on Twitter

The power of CEO-speak should not be underestimated. CEO-speak can win support for a corporation's policy on governance, accountability, management control, and measures of performance. For example, Jack Welch, CEO of General Electric (GE) from 1981 to 2000, used his CEO letters to stockholders to enlist support for his strategic positioning of GE, his view that bureaucracy was wholly distasteful, his conclusion that financial accounting numbers were appropriate indicators of GE's success, and his vision of a desirable management control system.[13]

Not all CEOs personally compose the written communications that appear above their signature or that are otherwise attributed to them. Some (such as Rupert Murdoch, News Corporation) say that they personally write their communications (see chapter 3). Many (such as Warren Buffett, Berkshire Hathaway) publicly acknowledge their strong role in drafting the CEO's letter to shareholders. However, it does not particularly matter whether CEOs are involved actively in *personally* drafting such communications. Their CEO letters in annual reports are "indicative of the CEO's mind-set – irrespective of whether or not [they] are crafted entirely by the CEO personally or by a 'ghost writer.'"[14] Although "Some CEOs brief professional letter writers and investor relations staff about the tone and content they want reflected in their letters to stockholders ... few delegate responsibility to others for determining the thoughts and issues that will comprise their completed letters."[15] Our view is that the words for which CEOs are responsible (by virtue of their signature or attribution) are symbolic and emblematic. Most readers take them to be the CEO's own words.

Although this book draws on a wide range of publicly available sources of CEO-speak, there is a strong focus on CEO letters to shareholders. This focus was influenced by the following four factors.

First, CEO letters to shareholders contain a personal accountability narrative that is not bound by formal rules or regulations: the CEO's "entitlement to narrate" a story is largely unfettered.[16] Thus, CEOs exert narrative dominance over their letter to shareholders by deciding what to tell and how to tell it.

Second, CEO letters provide a year-by-year history or "social account"[17] of a corporation from the privileged perspective of a CEO. They provide a dominant narrative that "lends consistency to otherwise fragmented experiences ... allows [assessment of] what is happening ... [and] ... is also community-building."[18] Most CEOs presume that readers will subscribe to the story parlayed.[19]

Third, because CEO letters often are closely affiliated with audited financial statements and other legally required documents, they provide an opportunity for the CEO to exercise management control and to espouse a vision, strategy, ideology, personality, and leadership style. This makes the CEO letter an important resource for engaging followers and other stakeholders, offering insight to corporate ethicality and accountability, helping understand the leadership process, and constructing leader identity.

Fourth, CEO letters contain important sources of information about top management,[20] including about a CEO's "mental model" of leadership. Our analysis of the metaphors used by Jack Welch in his CEO letters over 20 years as leader of GE between 1981 and 2000 concluded that Welch's language self-constructed his identity as leader by imagining he was the metaphoric equivalent of a person who had the characteristics of a pedagogue, physician, architect, commander, and saint.[21]

CEO letters reflect managerial attributions,[22] indicate framing strategies,[23] and act as a device for "communicat[ing] implicit beliefs about the organization and its relationship with the surrounding world."[24] CEO letters also offer a means for CEOs to identify personally with the corporations they lead. Often, "corporate personhood" is embodied in the CEO as "a human face that is frequently enlisted in public relations materials to counter the perceptions of corporations as impersonal and inhumane."[25] Rhetorically, a CEO letter can constitute a CEO metonymically and have subtle conditioning effects on the attitudes of observers. Metonymy occurs where the name of one thing, the CEO, is used for that of another thing the CEO is closely associated with, the company. The CEO's name becomes the embodiment of the company. Examples include Bill Gates (Microsoft Corporation),[26] Sir Richard Branson (Virgin), and Elon Musk (Tesla).

Although CEO letters are the most widely read part of company annual reports,[27] rarely are CEOs brought to account sharply for the words they choose to use. However, there are winds of change. CEOs must be much more conscious of their CEO-speak in the present era of heightened corporate accountability – one that has been prompted, for example, by the *Sarbanes-Oxley Act, 2002*, and the establishment in 2003 of the Public Company Accounting Oversight Board in the USA (and similar legislation and regulatory bodies in other countries).

Many benefits are likely to accrue from a close reading of CEO-speak. Such reading can help to identify precursors, or justifications, of socially (un)acceptable corporate and personal behavior. As a society, we should not be blasé about the potential for CEO-speak to inflate expectations (e.g., by distorting assessment of reported profits) or to assist CEOs in exploiting their positions for personal, financial, and/or psychological gain. Although recent corporate law reform might have dissuaded CEOs (for the moment at least) from inflating their assessments of financial performance, the potency of recent financial accounting, auditing, and corporate governance reforms has yet to be tested strongly. If reforms are diluted or rolled back, there will be further reason to subject CEO-speak to critical scrutiny.

Auditors need to be conscious that words matter. They should be alert to the prospect that executives and company directors exercise a patina of accountability through multiple channels, including through their language in annual report letters to stockholders, in speeches, and in social media. Auditors should be more conscious of their responsibility to monitor whether the words uttered and written by CEOs about financial affairs correspond with the numbers appearing in financial statements. As part of this monitoring, auditors should understand that there is an implicit "figurative script" often hidden beneath the surface of the actual words used.

Society in general, and regulators and legislators in particular, need to reflect on whether opportunities for questioning CEO-speak have become overly ritualized and, consequently, ineffective. They need to be more alert to the power of CEO-speak and to the importance of developing skills to analyze it critically. This book is directed to raising such alertness.

CEOs themselves must be more conscious that the words they choose when discharging their accountability to stakeholders are highly likely to be scrutinized. Recent accounting and corporate governance scandals have prompted audit committees, regulatory authorities, and others involved in oversight of CEOs to be more aware of a legal and moral obligation to "blow the whistle" on errant CEOs and any of their dubious written and/ or spoken narratives.

This book unfolds as follows. The next five chapters are devoted prin- cipally to exploring how written and oral communications by CEOs can fashion the "tone at the top" of a company. In chapter 2 we elaborate on what we mean by "tone at the top" and show ways we might assess it, using material drawn from letters to shareholders of major companies,[28] such as BP. Chapter 3 conducts a close reading of the 2010 "letter to fellow stock- holders" of Rupert Murdoch, CEO of News Corporation. This provides insights to the ethical character and tone at the top of News Corporation *before* the phone-hacking scandal of 2011 became widely known in the UK.

In chapter 4, we explore tone at the top and the language of ethical leadership. We conduct a fine-grained analysis of the opening statement of Wells Fargo's CEO, Timothy Sloan, to a US Senate committee in Octo- ber 2017. Sloan's intent was to persuade the committee and the American public that Wells Fargo was on a path back to ethical conduct. Chapter 5 outlines some techniques that can reveal traces of deception in written discourse. We closely analyze six CEO letters to shareholders that were issued prior to the collapse of the major Indian company Satyam in 2009. In chapter 6, we explore the rhetorical influence of CEOs on a company's safety culture by analyzing the speeches of several CEOs of BP. We show how this reveals the ambient tone at the top with respect to safety at BP prior to the *Deepwater Horizon* disaster in 2010.

The four chapters that then follow focus more on the medium of commu- nication: Twitter (two chapters), autobiographical vignettes, and *accounting- speak*. In chapter 7, we explore the benefits and pitfalls of a CEO's use of a private Twitter account. This analysis is developed further in chapter 8 where we investigate how Uber CEO Dara Khosrowshahi used his personal Twitter account as a propaganda tool to promote a better image for Uber. Chapter 9 analyzes letters of CEOs of Canadian National Railway (CN) over the period 1992 to 2018. The aim is to explore how CN used accounting-speak to sustain the strategic wisdom of management's decision to privatize CN. In chapter 10, we highlight how autobiographical vignettes by a CEO can help to sustain a company's strategic agenda.

Then, in chapter 11, we focus on the hints CEO-speak can contain about the personality of a CEO. Specifically, we explore the capacity for analysis of CEO-speak to identify traces of narcissism and/or hubris. In chapter 12, we offer some broad advice, in addition to that proffered in previous chapters, on ways to monitor CEO-speak effectively.

We conclude with an epilogue that focuses on the use of CEO-speak in the early stages of the COVID-19 pandemic. This book was submitted for publishing in the early spring of 2020, just as the pandemic began to take a firm hold globally. In the epilogue, we critique many of the uses of language by CEOs (or what we call *pandemic-speak*) that occurred as the pandemic progressed. Thereby, we provide contemporary insights to how CEOs communicate during a profound crisis.

For empirical support of the various views expressed, we draw principally from the CEO-speak of the leaders of major international companies, such as News Corporation, British Petroleum, Wells Fargo, Uber, Canadian National Railway, and Satyam. To a lesser degree, we also explore examples of the CEO-speak of Amazon, American International Group, Boeing, General Electric, IBM, JPMorgan Chase, Tesla, Walmart, Southwest Airlines, Starbucks, General Motors, and Enron. The selection of this case material is opportunistic and is not based on scientific sampling procedures. The conclusions we draw and the interpretations we make should be read with this caveat in mind.

The themes we address go to the heart of the role of a company CEO. They are matters that should be of keen interest to all who engage with, or are students of, business endeavor. Those themes deal with the potential for analysis of CEO-speak to inform understanding of a company's tone at the top, ethical behavior, reputation, attitude to safety, possible deceptive conduct, and to the personality of the CEO. The source texts for these analyses (mainly CEOs' letters to shareholders, written submissions to governmental enquiries, speeches, autobiographical vignettes, and personal tweets) provide a rich inventory to draw upon in decoding the language of corporate leaders and in mining the meaning in CEO-speak.

chapter two

Tone at the Top

The CEO sets the tone – good or bad.[1]

This is the first of five chapters that are broadly intended to show how close analysis of CEO-speak can help to develop better understanding of a company's tone at the top. Such analysis is important because the tone at the top has a strong effect on how companies function and project themselves internally and externally. The tone at the top can take many forms: for example, it might be one of resilience, or of confidence, or of aggression. In this chapter, we provide a broad foundation for more targeted analyses in following chapters of the tone at the top of major companies (News Corporation, chapter 3; Wells Fargo, chapter 4; Satyam, chapter 5; and BP, chapter 6).

The tone at the top is strongly influenced by the CEO because it is the CEO who "impos[es] his or her beliefs, values, and assumptions"[2] on a company. We regard CEO letters to shareholders as particularly fruitful sources for developing understanding of the tone at the top because of their capacity to bring to light a CEO's mindset, approach to leadership, and ideological disposition.

Understanding the tone at the top can reveal much about the personality and strategic outlook of a company's leaders: for example, by drawing attention to language that suggests hubris, implies intention to deceive, or reveals important aspects of a company's strategy. Understanding the tone at the top can also help in assessing whether CEOs will accept responsibility for the consequences of their previous decisions or whether they will deflect responsibility to others. Thus, knowledge of the tone at the top can help to predict how senior managers will respond to important external challenges and how they will view their company's trajectory and prospects. Such understanding will be beneficial in identifying whether organizational cultures are overly partial to risk or too risk averse.

The tone at the top can have critical consequences. A CEO who sets a tone at the top of "can do, nothing is impossible" seems likely to condone, implicitly or otherwise, contempt for formality, disregard for administrative propriety, and disrespect for regulation. The outcome of this might be to encourage playing loose with regulatory compliance rules and adopting dubious or aggressive accounting techniques.

Tone at the top can be set in non-language ways too. A case in point was the visit by the CEOs of the three major US car manufacturers (General Motors, Ford, and Chrysler) to Washington, DC in late 2008, seeking financial assistance to help their companies cope with the global financial crisis. At that time, "Politicians and the media noted the CEOs' reluctance to acknowledge that past strategic decisions concerning car designs had played a key role in their predicament."[3] The CEOs were miffed by such a suggestion. In choosing to stress the impact of the (then) credit crunch, the CEO's physical demeanor and general conduct set a tone of self-assuredness and over-confidence. This tone helped convince government policy makers that each of the CEOs had misdiagnosed their company's problems and would therefore be unlikely to make good use of government-supported financial assistance to correct past mistakes. By exuding a tone of over-certainty, the CEOs contributed significantly to the failure of their visit.

An *in*appropriate tone at the top can be very damaging; it can, for example, increase the risk of fraudulent financial reporting. In extreme cases, it can promote corporate collapse. As we explain later in this chapter, the letters to shareholders of Lord Browne as CEO of BP, from 1998 to 2006, proclaimed triumphant results in the face of unyielding adversity. Browne's triumphalism invited readers to believe in the high quality of his leadership. However, his letters gave little attention to major safety issues confronting BP. This set a tone at the top of possible neglect of safety – a tone that plausibly contributed to several subsequent disasters at BP installations (outlined in chapter 6).

Similarly, the Boeing MAX 737 airliner crashes of October 29, 2018 (in Indonesia) and March 10, 2019 (in Ethiopia) have led to accusations of a potent relationship between tone at the top and the safety culture at Boeing:

> How can you tell if Boeing's executives are focused on safety? … start by analyzing the words in Boeing's annual reports [looking] for key words that reveal

the underlying beliefs and values that define the company's culture. Why is this important? Because corporate culture inspires actions that determine results. And the quality of that culture starts at the top.[4]

The importance of tone at the top was also emphasized in 2004 in a speech titled "Tone at the Top: Getting it Right" by the Securities and Exchange Commission (SEC) Director, Division of Enforcement, Stephen Cutler.[5] He viewed tone at the top as being constituted by the words and deeds of top management. In 2006, considerable prominence was given to the tone at the top in postmortems following the failure of the Federal National Mortgage Association (known as "Fannie Mae"). For example, the US government's Office of Federal Housing Enterprise Oversight (OFHEO) reported that "decisions by Mr. Raines [Fannie Mae's CEO] shortly after he became CEO in 1999 set an inappropriate tone at the top that permeated the enterprise throughout his chairmanship."[6]

The tone at the top of Enron in the late 1990s implied that the company's written code of ethics did not need to be followed. The "culture of the organization almost encouraged breaking the rules and pushing the envelope – anything to keep the stock price propped up."[7] A process described as "ethical drift" set in. This was manifest in Enron's top leadership openly encouraging an atmosphere of hubris, narcissism, and indulgence, thereby untethering Enron from the real world.[8]

Tone at the top can be defined as a "company's 'integrity DNA,'" where integrity means "the possession and consistent adherence to high moral principles or professional standards that one refuses to change."[9] Thus, tone at the top is "the ethical (or unethical) atmosphere" created in the workplace by an organization's leaders that "trickle[s] down" to employees.[10] For example, a senior manager intent on establishing a tone at the top of fiscal prudence or frugality can do so by complying with the same budget allowances as subordinate staff (e.g., for economy class travel).

Exemplary work ethic cues that prompt expectations of employee behavior emerge from a company's tone at the top. "Good" cues might encourage behaviors that apply zero tolerance to fraud; uphold ethical values of honesty, loyalty, responsibility, and fairness; and encourage transparency and openness in financial reporting. "Bad" cues might lead to a culture of arrogance, combativeness, and intractability; an attitude of passivity or complacency; a culture of deception and misrepresentation; and an acceptance of intimidating behavior toward employees (especially whistleblowers).[11]

Determining the Tone at the Top through CEO Letters

CEOs "work with words."[12] They enact leadership largely (though not exclusively) through language. CEOs' letters to shareholders can help them to construct corporate culture and a tone at the top. Their words help them to chart the agenda they expect all persons connected with the company to follow. Their words define the values to which the company will aspire and can be chosen in a way that will help convince all stakeholders of the CEO's virtues.

A study of 200 CEO letters of *Fortune* 1000 companies concluded that their content reflected the credibility, efficacy, commitment, and responsibility of the CEO.[13] However, CEO letters can vary considerably in tone. They can reflect a wide range of leadership styles, personalities, commercial contexts, and cultural settings.[14] The language used can activate people's emotions and commitment, secure their compliance, and produce devoted believers in a company's ideology.[15]

We now outline two broad approaches to identify tone at the top. The first of these is a close reading approach involving nine "angles of vision"[16] or "lenses for seeing." We briefly explain each of these nine angles of vision and suggest how they can help assess the tone the top. In the ensuing case illustration, we focus on two of these nine lenses only: themes and metaphor. The second approach for identifying tone at the top involves the use of DICTION text analysis software. The principal benefit of DICTION is its capacity to indicate overall trends and themes in word use, rather than to offer definitive conclusions.

Angles of Vision[17]

Patterns

A patterns lens seeks to identify the patterns that occur regularly in a CEO's text. The supporting rationale is that insights will arise when there is a breach in the pattern. For example, a recurrent feature of the letters signed by Jack Welch during his 20-year tenure as CEO of General Electric (GE), 1981 to 2000, was that he began by reciting the financial results for the preceding year. However, in 1983, his letter began with a discussion of GE's strategy. Thus, Welch directed the audience's (and his own) attention to strategy (a proactive theme) rather than past financial results (a passive theme).

Time

Analysis of text over time will help to "grasp meaning." This is likely to be particularly useful over the long-term tenure of a single CEO and for a set of companies over time. Application of this lens shuns the "arrogance of presentism."

Emic

The emic lens involves imagining the motivations of the CEO for writing in a particular way. By adopting this perspective, we can learn "by taking seriously what [CEOs] say, what they think they are doing, what they make of things." This will help dispel "pre-conceived notions ... that preclude careful, serious listening [reading]."

Positionality

Valuable insights can be obtained by adopting the position, roles, or mindsets (as we perceive them) of other corporate stakeholders, such as shareholders, employees, and competitors. This enables us to "do justice to how someone can think and feel and conclude the way they do when all of this is, possibly, antithetical to how we ourselves think and feel!"

Ideology

Ideological stances of CEOs (whether implicit or explicit) require reflective consideration. For example, if a CEO's language reflects a "strict father" ideology,[18] the tone will most likely endorse conservative values, strict reward and punishment systems, and a top–down management style. In such an ideological context, tone at the top would be imposed without genuine consultative processes.

Themes

The themes pursued in CEO letters are likely to indicate attitudes to power and "adaptation, transition, and change." Of particular interest are binary themes, such as conflict and cooperation, order and confusion, success and failure, and resistance and compliance.

Metaphors

Metaphors link abstract concepts to concrete things. They tie the familiar to the unknown by providing a "cognitive bridge between domains."[19] Metaphors are often embedded in the deep structure of a text but are not stated overtly. They challenge analysts to tease out their implied and explicit inferences, paradoxes, and contradictions. The metaphors evident in CEO letters and other genres of CEO-speak can reveal how CEOs reason and perceive their company's place in the world.

In his 1991 CEO letter to shareholders of GE, Jack Welch invoked the metaphor THE MARKETPLACE IS BRUTALLY DARWINIAN. This metaphor structured Welch's thinking, guided his behavior as CEO, and helped create the tone at the top of GE. The image of brutal competition and survival of the fittest is depicted as beneficial irrespective of its immediate unpleasant effects. By invoking Darwinism metaphorically, Welch subtly framed aggressive action by GE as a natural and inescapable phenomenon – and as a process that went beyond the mediating power of human volition.

Irony

Irony enhances perception by enabling greater awareness of something through seeing "the viewpoint of its antithesis." From irony, we can learn about "that which is contradictory; and incongruity or paradox." Thus, if a CEO claims "our people are our most important asset" in the midst of a major corporate downsizing, the attendant irony suggests the CEO is disconnected from reality.

Silence

We can learn from "detecting silence [because this] opens us to an institution's injustices, and missed opportunities." Quite often what analysts miss "is disappointment, apathy, alienation, or sadness" or "those silences … that tell us we are somewhere worth being, that success is happening, that goals are being achieved." Although high-performing companies tend to cultivate a climate in which the "brutal facts of reality" are confronted head on,[20] much CEO rhetoric avoids frank discussion of difficulties.

Each of these nine focal points or lenses can assist in understanding the tone at the top. By applying them, a picture might emerge of a company that (for example)

- maintains the same organizational values from year to year (*patterns, time*);
- promotes a culture that reflects the social construction of the CEO (*emic, positionality*);
- obsesses with the virtues of a free market and survival of the fittest (*ideology*);
- resists change, is pro-conflict, and is success-obsessed (*themes*);
- is motivated by the BUSINESS IS WAR metaphor and becomes overtly aggressive, lacks compassion, and is non-conciliatory (*metaphor*);
- pleads for cost cutting and wage restraint while substantially increasing the remuneration benefits of directors and senior executives (*irony*); and
- declines to disclose the ramifications of a pending class action lawsuit (*silences*).

Analyzing Leadership Language Using Angles of Vision

Below we illustrate how applying two of the angles of vision (themes and metaphor) can enhance understanding of the tone at the top. We explore the CEO letters to shareholders of BP from 1998 to 2006. The temporal start point and endpoint are significant. 1998 was the year BP and the American petroleum company Amoco merged to create a dominant company in the industry. 2006 was the last CEO letter to shareholders of long-time BP Chief Executive Lord Browne of Madingley (previously known as Sir John Browne) before his departure from BP in 2007.

Themes

This angle of vision helps in recognizing what things a CEO regards as important. Our close readings of the nine CEO letters identified the 29 themes displayed in the left-hand column of exhibit 2.1.[21] The themes are listed according to the order in which they appear in the 1998 letter.

The text ascribes a "heroic" persona to BP, its management, and its leadership. The heroic theme appears in each letter. For example, in the 1998 letter,

> [t]he merger of BP and Amoco was announced on 11 August, and completed on 31 December. To have secured full regulatory approval in just 99 working days is a tremendous credit to all those involved and gives us an excellent opportunity to proceed rapidly with the process of integration.[22]

Exhibit 2.1 Themes in the letters to shareholders of BP's CEO, 1998 to 2006

Themes in the 1998 Letter that Recur in Later Years	1998	1999	2000	2001	2002	2003	2004	2005	2006
Heroic	X	X	X	X	X	X	X	X	X
Size	X			X		X			
Leadership is realistic	X				X			X	X
Making size acceptable	X							X	
Leadership is adaptive	X	X				X			X
Standard of care	X	X	X	X	X	X	X	X	X
Trust	X	X	X	X			X	X	X
Business environment is difficult	X	X	X	X	X	X	X	X	X
Business achievement	X	X	X	X	X	X	X	X	X
We have great strength	X	X	X						
Real value is in potential	X		X	X		X			X
Speed is good	X	X	X						
Management's enduring financial framework	X	X		X			X		X
The future is risky	X	X	X	X	X	X	X	X	X
Leadership is prudent	X	X	X	X	X	X	X	X	X
Key performance measures	X		X				X		X
Additional Themes in the Letters, 1999 to 2006									
Great strength is an enabler		X	X	X	X	X	X		
Strategy evolves long-term		X	X	X	X	X	X	X	X
Business philosopher			X	X	X	X	X	X	X
New is good		X				X	X	X	X
Growth is good			X	X	X		X		
People are human capital				X		X	X	X	
Success depends on adaptation and evolving strategy		X		X					
Size and diversity create strength				X				X	
Maximize productivity					X	X	X		
Leaders learn					X			X	X
Clarity in management control					X	X	X		
CEO as pedagogue							X		X
CEO as guiding eminence							X		

The first row of exhibit 2.1 reveals the enduring nature of the heroic theme across the corpus of Lord Browne's CEO letters from 1998 to 2006. However, resort to the heroic theme as a central feature of the letters is leader-centric, emphasizes size and growth, and dramatizes the heroic nature of leadership.

The themes that appear to be most important for any CEO can be determined by identifying the topic that occupies the most space or appears first (or at least early) in each letter. The "business philosopher" theme appears as the first theme at the beginning of the letters for 2001, 2002, 2003, 2005, and 2006. To understand important aspects of the tone at the top using this theme, we should answer the following four questions. What is the specific content of the business philosophy theme espoused? Is this theme pursued consistently over time? Does it occur concurrently with other contextual events? What does the CEO publicly "philosophize" about?

The themes that attract the attention of the CEO provide indicators of the tone at the top. The more attention a CEO devotes to a topic, the more important the topic is, or is intended to be, in the culture of the firm. The themes that are the most prominent in a CEO's letter signal to internal and external stakeholders what it is that *they* should be devoting *their* attention to, as a priority.

We assess the locus of attention of BP's CEO by assuming the topics that appeared first in each CEO letter had captured the CEO's attention and were matters the CEO intended readers to notice. The first theme in each letter, year by year, is shown in exhibit 2.2.

Browne's letters for 1998, 1999, 2000, and 2004 are introduced with words that resonate with a heroic leadership theme. For example, Browne explains the apparently epic achievement of melding two companies, BP and Amoco, along with other acquired companies, into the "great success" of 2000. Five letters (2001, 2002, 2003, 2005 and 2006) begin with a business philosopher theme. This suggests he shifted attention to broader, philosophical issues in what, for various reasons, were crisis years for BP. All nine letters reveal Browne's willingness to heroically claim credit for achievements.

The practice of CEOs eulogizing their achievements, while deflecting attention from crises and failures, underscores the need to question the construction of tone at the top.

Metaphors

The *metaphor* angle of vision can help to reveal a CEO's mindset. Through interpretative devices such as metaphor, a CEO can attribute responsibility,

Exhibit 2.2 First theme of each BP CEO letter to shareholders, 1998 to 2006

Year	First Theme	First Paragraph of Each CEO Letter
1998	Heroic leadership	1998 was a momentous year for the oil industry and for BP Amoco in particular. Despite the fact that oil prices ended the year 34% below their December 1997 level, we improved our underlying performance and delivered on our promises. We also took a crucial first step in the restructuring of the oil and gas sector.
1999	Heroic leadership	1999 was an exciting, dynamic and very successful year for BP Amoco. We combined two great companies into one, unifying our operations and processes, and our team of people. As a result, we were able to deliver the financial benefits of the merger in full and well ahead of schedule.
2000	Heroic leadership	2000 was a year of great success for BP. Record results were delivered, targets were met and a new group was established, bringing together the people and assets of a number of different businesses – including ARCO, Vastar and Burmah Castrol, as well as BP itself. Each element strengthens our portfolio and helps us to fulfill the strategic objectives we have been pursuing for the last five years.
2001	Business philosopher	2001 was a year that reminded us, in the most dramatic and tragic way, that events shape the lives of individuals and of companies. No one could have predicted the events of 11 September and very few expected the economic recession that ended a long period of growth in the USA.
2002	Business philosopher	Our strategy is to create value from a distinctive set of opportunities, biased toward the upstream, which through a disciplined approach to long-term investment growth can produce returns that are secure and highly competitive.
2003	Business philosopher	When I wrote to you last time, my team and I had as many questions as answers about the forthcoming year. Would our strategy endure a weak global economy, impending war in Iraq, continuing uncertainty over terrorism, increasingly complex regulation and a groundswell of anti-corporate sentiment? How would our competitors respond to the challenging position we had worked so hard to achieve?
2004	Heroic leadership	2004 was a great year for BP. In terms of overall performance, it was the best since the recent series of mergers and acquisitions.
2005	Business philosopher	We start from the view that the purpose of business is to satisfy human needs and, in doing so, to generate profits for investors. For BP, that means providing energy to fuel human progress and economic growth. It also means satisfying the need for a sustainable environment.
2006	Business philosopher	BP's purpose is a progressive one. That means we aim to generate returns for our investors by providing the energy for basic human needs such as light, heat and mobility and to do so in a safe, sustainable and environmentally responsible way. Our financial results were very strong in 2006. However, we fell short of our expectations in certain areas, notably with two oil spills in Alaska and the inability to start up the Thunder Horse platform as soon as we had hoped.

blame, and credit and establish causal connections and agency.[23] As leaders, CEOs use "words, phrases, and literary constructions [such as metaphors] to better and more convincingly communicate their vision of their organization."[24] Metaphors can trigger images, stir emotions, and emphasize and obscure things.[25]

In the following analysis, we identify the link between the metaphors and the themes in Browne's CEO letter to shareholders of BP for 1998 following the company-altering acquisition of Amoco. We query whether the metaphors Browne used developed specific arguments and positions to support the reasoning related to the themes. We also explore whether enthymemes (unstated assumptions) are evident, and if so, ponder their likely implications.

Metaphors provide a conceptual vocabulary to help identify legitimate problems and arrive at acceptable solutions. When used by CEOs, metaphors become a public language for communication. The more powerful and influential the CEO, the more the CEO's language affects how people (inside and outside the company) think and act. Use of particular metaphors in specific contexts renders the entailments of such metaphors more natural and uncontroversial.[26] Thus, much is to be gained by being sensitive to metaphors and the metaphor-related entailments, implications, contexts, and cognitive models involved.

Exploration of the "deeper level" of CEO text can help to identify fundamental root metaphors that are implicated in the practice of leadership.[27] Those pursuing such exploration should acknowledge that interpretations of texts, stories, and narratives are informed also by their own frame of reference.[28] Thus, the text of a CEO letter is affected by the constructions readers place on them.[29] We should be mindful that metaphors evoke multiple meanings in everyday language and in the minds of those who use them and perceive them.[30] Metaphor "is not an ornament. It is an organ of perception."[31]

Themes and Metaphors

Below, we explore the metaphor structure of the *heroic* theme in Browne's CEO letter for 1998 by linking the *metaphor* and *theme* angles of vision. We show the capacity for these two angles of vision to supplement and reinforce each other. We identify 45 instances of the word "we" in the letter, using the word "we" as a sort of probe to identify instances in which the collective BP leadership – "we" – was allegedly functioning in a heroic manner, and capture the surrounding context. However, for space purposes, we focus on examining the metaphor features of the first six instances of "we" (shown in bold). Each instance is numbered sequentially. For example, **we[2]** refers to the second instance of "we."

> **Paragraph 1**: 1998 was a momentous year for the oil industry and for BP Amoco in particular. Despite the fact that oil prices ended the year 34% below their December 1997 level, **we[1]** improved our underlying performance and delivered on our promises. **We[2]** also took a crucial first step in the restructuring of the oil and gas sector.[32]

Although both highlighted uses of "we" refer primarily to BP, a human-like agency is ascribed to the inanimate corporation, BP. This agency is reinforced three times: "we improved … [we] delivered … We … took …." In the life of a modern corporation, only corporate leaders can exercise such agency. Thus, these instances of "we" stand for the top leadership. The language choices made, including the structure "Despite X, we Y," makes agency both salient and potent. The intended message appears to be that top management has overcome natural impediments, improved underlying performance, and kept promises. This is heroic. Consequently, the metaphor TOP MANAGEMENT IS A HERO seems apt.

> **Paragraph 2**: The merger of BP and Amoco was announced on 11 August and completed on 31 December. To have secured full regulatory approval in just 99 working days is a tremendous credit to all those involved and gives us an excellent opportunity to proceed rapidly with the process of integration.

Since no instance of "we" appears in this paragraph, it is analyzed below, along with paragraph 3, in which **we[3]** appears.

> **Paragraph 3**: Although the merger creates one of the world's largest industrial organizations, **we[3]** are very aware that size alone is no guarantee of success.

Paragraph 2 uses the passive tense when announcing, and subsequently reporting, the completion of the merger. This absence of agency permits top management to share praise with "all those involved." Management then quickly reasserts agency by claiming this "gives us an excellent opportunity to proceed rapidly with the process of integration." The "we" referred to in paragraph 3 are wisely "aware that size alone is no guarantee of success." However, in an extraordinarily short time top management secures merger approval, shares praise, leads "one of the world's largest industrial

organisations" and is wise. Again, the metaphor TOP MANAGEMENT IS
A HERO seems an apt characterization of the leadership.

> **Paragraph 4**: All the available evidence suggests that big companies are com-
> monly regarded with suspicion, and that mergers are often considered to be
> simply about the accumulation of market power.

Since no instance of "we" appears in this paragraph, it is analyzed below
along with paragraph 5, in which **we[4]** appears.

> **Paragraph 5**: To be acceptable to the consumer and to society in general, merg-
> ers must be progressive – enhancing rather than reducing the range of choices
> available to the customer, by combining the skills and know-how to achieve
> things which neither company could have delivered on its own. That means
> **we[4]** have to listen with great care and be continuously responsive to the
> changing pattern of customer needs and desires.

The metaphoric nature of the text in which **we[4]** is embedded suggests the writer is alert to the need to "listen with great care" and "be
continuously responsive" "to the changing pattern of customer needs and
desires." Since no one person could literally "listen" or "be continuously
responsive" to so many customers and their "changing pattern of ... needs
and desires" (and indeed would be hard-put to identify these "needs and
desires"), **we[4]** is symbolic, or metonymical, in standing for the whole
company. Importantly, a link to **we[1]** and **we[2]** arises since **we[4]** might
also be interpreted as continuing the TOP MANAGEMENT IS A HERO
theme, especially if there is a vestige of literal intent in paragraph 5.

> **Paragraph 6**: In our sector, in particular the challenge is to ensure that hydro-
> carbons can be found, produced, refined, distributed and used without damaging
> the natural environment. BP Amoco will aim to provide consumers with the
> choices that make that aspiration achievable.

No instance of "we" appears in this paragraph. This may be deliberate
to avoid accountability because it is unlikely anything can be done with
hydrocarbons without risk to the natural environment.

> **Paragraph 7**: Secondly, **we[5]** have to organize and manage a huge world-
> wide company in a way which excites and empowers the people who work for
> us. **We[6]** have to avoid rigidity and bureaucracy and ensure that, within clear

boundaries and standards, individuals have the freedom to fulfil their potential and to make a difference.

We[5] and **we[6]** suggest a strong top-down approach to leadership. Top management must "organise and manage," set "clear boundaries and standards," and do so while also ensuring employees are excited, empowered, free, and make a difference. Again, a heroic mantle is evident. Who but a hero could do such things?

Thus, the first seven paragraphs reveal a coursing fundamental root metaphor, TOP MANAGEMENT IS A HERO. Since this metaphor appears so strongly, one might ask whether such portrayal by top management is intentional. The leadership approach signaled is that top management exercises leadership in a top-down fashion; knows best; knows all there is to know; has little regard for followership; is imbued with extraordinary insight, wisdom, and other abilities; and might not appreciate criticism, even if it is constructive and respectful. Thus, the tone at the top signals a perverse leadership approach.

Using DICTION to Assess Tone at the Top

Here we report briefly on a DICTION-based assessment of tone at the top in two sets of CEO letters to shareholders for 2006.[33] The first was a set of letters for UK-based companies comprising the Financial Times Stock Exchange (FTSE) 100 index of companies according to market capitalization (89 letters, comprising 156,702 words). The second was a set of letters of US-based companies in the *Fortune* 100 listing of America's largest corporations according to annual revenues (94 letters, 203,040 words).[34]

Each letter was downloaded from the company's website, converted to a text file, and formatted for DICTION processing.[35] Then, scores for the 40 DICTION variables were determined for the first 500 words of each letter. We chose the first 500 words because the initial paragraphs of written text have stronger rhetorical impact and are likely to be more influential in reflecting tone at the top. The comparative word usage norm applied was the Company Annual Report dictionary. For each company in both databases, the DICTION variable scores that were more than +2 or −2 standard deviations from expected values were designated as being out of range. In non-statistical parlance, they were extreme observations. The out-of-range extreme observations for FTSE 100 companies were compared against those for *Fortune* 100 companies.

Some FTSE 100 companies used common language to express a tone of cocky confidence in their (alleged) outstanding performance in a competitive, globalized business environment. Such a tone goes beyond simply a matter-of-fact reporting of success or expressing simple pride in achievement. It extends into smugness and self-glorification along with disdain for the efforts of competitors. Generally, there was no trace of humility. Rather, there was a narcissistic air of "look at me. Look how great I am." Matthew Emmens, CEO of Shire Pharmaceuticals, proposed that his company is a beacon and a unique and exemplary model because it "set its sights high, and then delivered on its promises." Such "setting of sights" reinforced his company's "reputation as a beacon" among its competitors. This was presumably due to two factors. First was the company's innate ability to "know what it takes to both shape and realize a vision." Second was the company's possession of a "unique business model that sets [it] apart from the competition, [together with] a disciplined and focused growth strategy, an achievement-oriented culture, and a high quality team of employees willing to meet extraordinary goals and get the job done."

In the *Fortune* 100 sample, the letter of Stan O'Neal, chairman and CEO of Merrill Lynch, dated February 22, 2007, touches on the angles of vision of "irony" and "ideology." This is apparent when his statements are juxtaposed against the company's precipitate sale at a grossly discounted price in September 2008. O'Neal's message is one of achieving success through hard work, discipline, and being strategically smart. O'Neal sees the maximization of shareholder wealth as arising from work that has a strong basis in Protestant values of "integrity, dedication, discipline" and a focus on others (clients). O'Neal is evangelical in extolling the virtues of global capitalism and the benefits of embracing it. He rejoices in the "remarkable position" of his company

> at the center of global capitalism – the most powerful force for improving lives and creating wealth that the world has ever known. All of us are proud of what we do and excited by a future that is literally brimming with opportunity … Together, we can and will continue to grow our business, [and] lead this incredible force of global capitalism.[36]

O'Neal's ideological endorsement of the "incredible force" of global capitalism is highly ironic given that Merrill Lynch would most likely have imploded during 2008 had it not been for the strong financial and regulatory intervention of the US Treasury and Federal Reserve. That intervention sustained the operational viability of many of global capitalism's key players in the USA.

Generally, the FTSE 100 and *Fortune* 100 company letters to shareholders featured a tone of exultation at the top. A company-by-company analysis revealed ambient tones of resigned frustration (William Hill plc); satisfaction and accomplishment (Reed Elsevier plc); confidence, triumphant affirmation, and success (United Health); and detachment and affirmation (JPMorgan Chase).

Although the tone at the top evidenced in the FTSE 100 and *Fortune* 100 letters was broadly similar, the FTSE l00 letters had a stronger tone of conservatism and matter-of-factness. In contrast, the *Fortune* 100 letters were more editorial, conversational, hyperbolic, and less cautious or equivocal. Nonetheless, many of the letters in both sets had a smug and confident tone of assurance, suggesting a general lack of humility. There was frequent brash boasting about products and a lack of perspective about the priority of various products in customers' lives.

The DICTION results broadly indicated a growing mood of optimism and a reluctance to acknowledge potential difficulties. They revealed that the CEO letters were more than a neutral mirror. Rather, they validated a particular worldview of the CEO and a preferred method of doing business.

Concluding Comments

Typically, a CEO places a strong premium on constructing a coherent tone at the top. While this is necessary to some degree, it can also create stifling organizational norms that facilitate corporate malfeasance and chicanery.

The LEADER AS HERO metaphor appears to have taken deep root in the rhetoric (and, hence, presumably in the practice) of BP's CEO and other top CEOs. The financial crisis of 2007–8 exemplified the perils of this leadership approach. Powerful leaders, with an apparently exaggerated view of their prowess and their business models, often did not recognize the value of competing views and input from other sources. Rather, they focused on asserting, arguing, and imposing their vision of the way forward – often in a tone of exaggerated certainty. We need to be alert to the possibility that the construction of an organization's tone at the top by means of a leader's CEO-speak can lead to a perverse tone at the top – or suggest narcissism and hubris on the part of the CEO (see chapter 11).

chapter three

Ethicality

This chapter explores the leadership language of global media mogul Rupert Murdoch in 2010. This was the year before a phone-hacking scandal involving journalists and senior managers employed by News Corporation came to public attention in the United Kingdom. In 2011, public enquiries in the UK exposed unethical conduct by some staff of News Corporation. Murdoch was the company's chairman and CEO. Did he set an appropriate ethical tone at the top *before* the scandal?

We focus on ethical implications of Murdoch's "Letter to Fellow Stockholders" that appeared in News Corporation's annual report for the year ended June 30, 2010. Did Murdoch's language in that letter help to condition the inapt and unethical conduct of News Corporation staff in hacking the phones of prominent citizens? We draw attention to the ethical signs embedded in Murdoch's letter and how they reflected the company's tone at the top and ethical values.

CEOs of global media conglomerates play a strong role in helping "to shape the social world by exerting control over issue-framing and information gatekeeping."[1] Mindful of this role, we assess Murdoch's leadership of News Corporation in the prelude to the phone-hacking scandal. What crucial links were there between the company's tone at the top, culture, and ethical behavior? We make a case that perverse leadership thinking helped to explain the inappropriate cultural values and poor ethical behaviors that were exposed subsequently about News Corporation.

Some statements in Murdoch's CEO letter for 2010 are highly ironic in view of subsequent revelations that the News Corporation newspaper, *News of the World*, was implicated in phone hacking. News Corporation was accused of abusing privacy and engaging in unprincipled and unethical activities. The phone hacking at issue allegedly was done at the behest of, or was condoned by, News Corporation executives. Several high-profile former executives of News Corporation were among about 100 persons arrested and/or charged with criminal offenses. These included Andy Coulson and Neil Wallis (respectively the former editor and executive editor of *News of the World*); Rebekah Brooks (former editor of *News of the World* and chief executive of News International); and Stuart Kuttner, Greg Miskiw, James Desborough, and Dan Evans (respectively former managing editor, former news editor, former show business reporter, and former reporter of *News of the World*).

Murdoch has described Tuesday, July 19, 2011, as "the most humble day of my life."[2] On that day, he appeared before the UK Parliament *House of Commons Culture, Media and Sport Committee* in his role as chair and CEO of News Corporation. The committee was investigating allegations of phone hacking involving journalists and management of *News of the World*. As was the case when four bank CEOs appeared several years earlier before the UK Parliament's *Banking Crisis Inquiry*, Murdoch engaged in "a language exercise" by attributing blame and avoiding responsibility.[3]

In 2011, News Corporation was a prominent diversified global media company controlled by the Murdoch family, headquartered in New York, and incorporated in Delaware. In addition to *News of the World*, the company owned Twentieth Century Fox, *Fox News*, and the *Wall Street Journal* in the US and *The Times*, *The Sunday Times*, *The Sun*, and 39 percent of the satellite broadcaster *BSkyB* in the UK.[4] The company's shares were listed on NASDAQ with a secondary listing on the Australian Securities Exchange. In 2010, annual revenues were approximately US$33 billion and assets approximately US$54 billion.[5]

In its report released on April 30, 2012, the UK parliamentary committee pulled no punches in concluding bitingly that

> if at all relevant times Rupert Murdoch did not take steps to become fully informed about phone-hacking, he turned a blind eye and exhibited willful blindness to what was going on in his companies and publications. *This culture, we consider, permeated from the top throughout the organisation* and speaks volumes about the lack of effective corporate governance at News Corporation and News International. We conclude, therefore, that Rupert Murdoch is not a fit person to exercise the stewardship of a major international company.[6]

This blunt and damning conclusion about Murdoch's leadership ("not a fit person to exercise the stewardship of a major international company") stemmed from the committee linking an inapt corporate culture at News Corporation to the tone at the top set by the company's leaders. The report emphasized that the tone at the top was a shaper of corporate culture and an important matter for broader attention. Mindful of this, we explore Murdoch's leadership language *before* the phone-hacking scandal reached full pitch in the (northern) summer of 2011. Did the annual report letter Murdoch signed as chair and CEO for the year ended June 30, 2010, contain embedded cultural and ethical linguistic signs of potentially scandalous behavior?

Murdoch was a dominant individual who exercised extreme power at News Corporation. He held the positions of chair and CEO concurrently. This practice is widely considered to be inconsistent with effective monitoring by a board of directors.[7] However, quite a few major companies in addition to News Corporation (such as JPMorgan Chase, Disney, and Facebook) have resisted appointing a separate chair.[8] Because Murdoch held these two roles, critical analysis of his discourse assumes greater importance.[9]

Murdoch's testimony before the UK parliamentary committee on July 19, 2011, and the Leveson Inquiry on April 25 and 26, 2012, involved two types of public utterances. First was his prepared testimony. This was presumably crafted with the help of public relations, legal, and management assistants. He most likely would have reviewed this carefully in advance. Second were unscripted, impromptu responses to questions posed by interrogators (although presumably he was coached in these responses). These two types of public utterances have the potential to reveal important aspects of Murdoch's intended corporate leadership through language.

Since our interest is in the tone at the top *before* the phone-hacking crisis, the example of Murdoch's CEO-speak that we have chosen to analyze is from that period. This was his signed annual report letter to "fellow stockholders" published in the opening pages of News Corporation's annual report for the year ended June 30, 2010, and titled "A Letter from Rupert Murdoch." News Corporation has made a full version of this letter publicly accessible at https://materials.proxyvote.com/Approved/65248E/20100816/AR_65901/HTML2/news_corp-ar2010_0010.htm.[10] To facilitate reading the following analysis of Murdoch's letter, we cite approximate line numbers to help readers locate the source text we refer to. (The full letter comprises about 225 lines).

We examine instances of Murdoch's singular first-person self-attributions in that letter and conduct a "close reading" of it. We highlight how Murdoch's use of language and metaphors displayed signs of a perverse tone at the top. Prior alertness to such language might have helped predict (and prevent) the inapt and unethical phone-hacking behavior that arose subsequently.

CEO letters to stockholders in annual reports have an important institutionalized, periodic, and calendared role in our socio-economy.[11] They are a showcase rhetorical event, offering leaders who are prone to narcissistic excess a stage upon which to proclaim their superiority.[12] These letters have been scrutinized widely in management and related areas because of their revelatory potential.[13] Although we examine only one of Murdoch's letters, we do so very closely within its context. Such an approach is consistent with the view that in studying human discourse, "any part implies a larger whole, which is in turn part of a still larger whole, and so on … [and that we should move] back and forth between small concrete parts, and even larger abstract wholes."[14] Thus, far from existing as an atom of disconnected discourse, Murdoch's CEO letter is embedded within a complex social context in which it can potentially reflect (and help constitute) a grander overarching discourse.

The undated letter is signed by Murdoch as chair and CEO. It was almost certainly prepared before August 6, 2010 (the date of that year's auditor's report) and before the phone-hacking scandal came to public prominence. Letters such as this are an annual accountability narrative by the CEO. Although we have no way of knowing how much of this letter he crafted personally, we accept the statement within the letter that he "sits down" each summer to write the letter and "to reflect upon [News Corporation's] performance" (line 56). What is highly relevant in this context is that Murdoch had a background as a journalist. As such, he is more likely than most CEOs to have written the letter largely, or perhaps entirely, by himself.

Our analysis reveals a CEO who set a less-than-savory tone at the top. Murdoch's text differs stylistically from CEO letters published by most corporate leaders. There are traces of the linguistic attributes of the tabloid press: an excessive use of pronouns, contractions, and repetitions, including "call-outs" or sidebars, and recourse to biased and emotive language. These features are unsurprising given Murdoch's journalistic background and his claimed authorship of the letter. However, the tabloid style seems inconsistent with the purpose of a CEO letter as a mechanism for corporate accountability. As we explain below, Murdoch's tabloidism is contemptuous, boastful, gloating, hubristic, patronizing, and reveals traces of vacuous hyperbolic nonsense.

We begin by discussing Murdoch's 15 uses of the first-person pronoun "I" and the context in which each use occurs. This allows us to explore the claims, ideas, and values Murdoch states directly and personally.[15] A CEO uses the word "I" to claim personal, intimate attribution. Thus, our exploration provides insight to the corporate culture Murdoch intended to build.

The value of assessing a leader's use of "I" is supported by prior studies of leaders' self-serving attributions.[16] Individuals who use relatively
more first-person singular pronouns (I, me, mine, my, myself) and fewer
first-person plural pronouns (we, us, our, ours, ourselves) score higher on
measures of narcissism.[17] The use of "I" in an important annual communication document such as a CEO letter can reveal what the claimant (the
CEO) feels, intends, and values — or at the least, what the CEO wishes to
portray is felt, intended, and valued.

Murdoch's use of "I" seems excessive in comparison to his industry
peers. For example, Disney's CEO, Robert Iger, used "I" four times in
his 2010 letter of 1,946 words (a rate of about one "I" per 486 words). In
2010, Time Warner's CEO, Jeff Bewkes, used "I" once in a letter of 1,257
words.[18] A broader comparison using the "self-reference" measure in the
DICTION text analysis software[19] indicates that Murdoch's self-references
in his 2010 CEO letter were significantly greater (in a statistical sense) than
the norm calculated from a corpus of corporate financial reports.

Murdoch begins by humanizing himself in the first sentence of his
CEO letter for 2010 by writing "I am pleased to report …." Thus, like
every human, he relishes in being "pleased." But his pleasure is perverse,
since it is made more vivid by his assertion that News Corporation is being
"renewed" and is "fundamentally stronger" in spite of "world economies
remain[ing] fragile." Murdoch boasts in expressing his pleasure. However,
the UK parliamentary committee subsequently contradicted his assessments by concluding that the corporate culture and ethical fabric at News
Corporation were neither "renewed" nor "stronger." Murdoch's use of "I"
in the following line further humanizes him because he is *writing* to "you,"
his fellow stockholders. *Writing* is more intimate than emailing or many
other forms of communicating. Murdoch reminds us that he writes yearly
and apparently enjoys such an annual ritual.

The two uses of "we" in the next paragraph are ambiguous. Do they
refer to shareholders *and* Murdoch? Do they refer to shareholders, Murdoch, and all employees of News Corporation? Or do they refer just to
members of the senior management group? Interpretation is left for the
reader. Different audiences are likely to have different interpretations. The
ambiguity of the pronoun "we" is a rhetorical mechanism: it is a "wander-
ing 'we'" with a "shifting reference point."[20]

The use of "I" in line 20 is framed by Murdoch's strong assertion: "But,
let me be clear." Murdoch is setting the stage for a crucial revelation: he
does not believe "we are out of the turmoil yet." The absence of equivocation in "I do not believe" is rhetorically potent. His use of "we" is an

inclusive, astute rhetorical move because it signals his apparent intent to portray shareholders, employees, perhaps customers, and everyone else in the world (including himself) as being in the same terrible situation, caught in "the turmoil." Despite such "turmoil," News Corporation's alleged feats of being "renewed" and "being stronger," as Murdoch asserted earlier, are inescapable and remarkable accomplishments.

In lines 20 to 23, Murdoch is a pedagogue presenting a tutorial in macroeconomics. He lists three "key obstacles" to "the global economic recovery": sovereign debt pressures, soaring deficits, and unacceptable US unemployment levels. Together these factors constitute the "turmoil" and the cause (according to Murdoch) of the unpredictability. His tutorial is simplistic and verges on arrogance. Cause and effect are muddled. The setting is vague and conveys little information about News Corporation. Murdoch's use of "I" to assert belief and non-belief suggests a strong, perhaps hubristic, personality. Murdoch-the-CEO wants his audience to be clear about his prescription for economic recovery. The emerging metaphoric persona is dual-faceted: MURDOCH IS A PHYSICIAN and MURDOCH IS A PEDAGOGUE. Both metaphors evidence traces of hubris and a "Father knows best" mentality.[21]

In line 28, Murdoch's assertion "…upon which I will reflect more later" seems professorial (MURDOCH IS A PEDAGOGUE). The entailments of this metaphor are that there has been full and objective consideration of issues and their context ("the long-term opportunities" resulting from "this disruption"). But such sober consideration seems inconsistent with displays of Murdoch's highly assertive language elsewhere.

Murdoch asserts belief in a "logical and disciplined plan…" (line 45). *Logic* and *discipline* are desirable qualities in (Western) corporate leadership. Murdoch is laying personal claim to these qualities. There is no linguistic equivocation.

In line 56, a "father knows best" or "strict father" metaphor again seems apparent.[22] Murdoch "sit[s] down to write this letter to you and reflect on our performance." This is paternalistic and consistent with his earlier statement that he "wrote to you at this time last year." It is consistent too with what we have observed about the Disney company founder Walt Disney: "CEOs hold power over many others and often behave as if they know what is right for those who do not hold power – that is, they seem to adopt the moral conceptual system of a 'Strict Father.'"[23] Moreover, Murdoch's use of "reflect" seems inapt. The cerebral implications of "reflect" are at odds with the "bold, strategic moves" that result in "us" (Murdoch?) being "put squarely in the news spotlight" (line 54). His use of "reflect" is at odds also with the claim that "the consistency of our Company's core strategy" "brings [clarity] to our operations." Being so sure of one's path seems antithetical to any reasonable interpretation of reflection as a mental activity.

Even if Murdoch is "half-joking" as he says, readers are left to ponder whether Murdoch is serious or delusional in wondering, "Is there anyone left on this planet who has yet to see [his company's movie] *Avatar?*" (lines 136–7). Or does this comment smack of deliberate "outgroup polarization"?[24] An implication is that anyone who has not seen the film is a lesser person and should somehow be devalued. An earlier example of a similar form of "outgroup polarization" occurred at line 22: "*Others* may see more positive signs." By themselves, these examples may just be instances of CEO hype. However, when combined with all other instances of grandiose language in the letter, they offer a linguistic hint of hubris.[25] Other examples of grandiose language are "renaissance," "global meritocracy," and "at any time in human history" (lines 180–1).

Indeed, Murdoch's assertion that "a digital renaissance ... is bringing us closer to a global meritocracy than at any time in human history" is highly contestable because it ignores a more chilling outcome. The "digital renaissance" that Murdoch mentions is not so much "bringing us closer to a global meritocracy" as it is enabling an immense accumulation of capital and power – such as by News Corporation.

In line 196, Murdoch uses the verb "glance." This suggests a "peek" or "glimpse" or less-than-thorough observation. This less-than-rigorous look "over the horizon" combines on the same line with "suspect[s]." The two tentative, informal first-person pronoun statements (lines 196 to 200) are at odds with other very definitive and assertive statements elsewhere in the letter. The inconsistency is curious and contrary to the earlier claims of "let me be clear" (line 20).

The "killer app" (line 198) and the assessment "far from killing us off" (line 202) evoke images of brutality and hint of a persecution complex. Murdoch's view that entities ("us") may be "kill[ed] off" suggests there is a vicious, hostile environment in which just a select few companies ("like News Corporation") will survive in "the prelude to a new golden era." The text here promotes a feeling of resentment on the part of News Corporation and Murdoch on the grounds that they are arraigned against the world ("planet"). The text implies that others have caused problems for News Corporation by disrupting[26] and putting "obstacles" in the company's way.

In his concluding paragraphs, Murdoch displays a hyperbolic sense of optimism ("boundless opportunities ... the world's leading content provider") (lines 205–6). Thereby, he possibly reflects a hubristic or narcissistic personality – at least insofar as text may suggest such a condition.[27] Superficially, his use of "I" at line 210 seems to co-opt empty words that lack substance. How can anyone, in the real world of "turmoil" that Murdoch describes as unpredictable and disruptive, be "certain" the company one leads "will maintain our leadership position for decades to come"?

Murdoch's self-assertions represent linguistic signs of several underlying or extended root metaphors:[28]

THE CORPORATE ENVIRONMENT IS BRUTAL, HOSTILE, DISRUPTIVE, UNPREDICTABLE, AND DEADLY.
ONLY A LOGICAL, DISCIPLINED, AND STRONG ENTITY CAN SURVIVE AND FLOURISH IN AN ENVIRONMENT THAT IS BRUTAL.
NEWS CORPORATION IS A LOGICAL, DISCIPLINED, AND STRONG ENTITY.
RUPERT MURDOCH IS NEWS CORPORATION.

Given the absence of equivocality in this metaphor schema, Murdoch's claim to be "reflective" is confounding.

Murdoch's language yields an overriding impression that he is a supremely confident and arrogant CEO who regards himself as the all-seeing leader of a forever-successful company. He basks in having led the company (by his own assessment) brilliantly during a "digital renaissance" (line 180).

Murdoch views News Corporation and its constituent companies as "vast," "well-run," "vibrant," and as collectively possessing the capabilities required to lead markets and their industry (lines 93, 49, 74, 95, 165). News Corporation makes "bold" moves and is resilient, able to "endure" economic downturns and survive them to "thrive" (lines 53, 30–1). Numerous action words portray News Corporation as a high-energy, hyperactive, dynamic company – one that engages in "negotiating," "delivering," "ushering," "mov[ing] forward," "harness[ing]," "re-imagin[ing]," and "reinventing" (lines 37, 41, 42, 52, 53, 174–6). All of this energy is (metaphorically) expended while remaining "logical and disciplined," flexible, and financially "well managed" despite "fac[ing] continued economic and competitive challenges" (lines 45, 71–2, 114).

The fondness of Murdoch for several keywords is revealing too. He states persistently that News Corporation is "strong." Indeed, he seems obsessed with this word and the image it conveys. Words with the stem root of "strong" or "strength" appear 14 times in his letter of 1969 words. Murdoch appears to be obsessed with "growth" too. Words with the stem root "grow" appear 17 times, preponderantly in connection with financial growth and profitability. There are mentions of "operating income growth," "revenue growth," "ratings [and advertising revenue] growth," "profit growth," and "advertising [revenue] growth" (lines 80, 124, 82, 131, 85, 95). Perhaps, by asserting the company's strength and growth, there were important image and impression management advantages for Murdoch.

Murdoch claims that News Corporation has the "right leadership" and that its staff are variously capable of "clear vision," dedication, and innovation and are "talented and committed" with "extensive expertise" (lines 111, 14, 15, 49–51). His staff's "capacity to develop market leading capabilities" arises presumably because they possess "talent, vision and initiative" (lines 95, 210).

Murdoch stresses the company's use of "rapid advances in technology" and mentions the "tremendous opportunity" the company sees with mobile phone technology (lines 154, 159). He claims the company aims to "harness the power of technology" and what "quality journalism requires" (lines 175, 167–8). One wonders whether his reference to the "killer app" (line 198) is a reference to the technology that was used in the unscrupulous phone-hacking practices News Corporation journalists engaged in or commissioned.

Although several revealing metaphors are featured, the popular metaphor THE COMPANY IS ON A JOURNEY is absent.[29] The major coursing metaphor is BUSINESS IS WAR. This metaphor is consistent with one that emerged from earlier analysis of Murdoch's use of the pronoun "I": THE CORPORATE ENVIRONMENT IS BRUTAL, RAW, HOSTILE, DISRUPTIVE, UNPREDICTABLE, AND DEADLY.

Thus, Murdoch's view seems to be that to survive in such a hostile, changing environment, an entity must be in a permanent state of war. Despite this, Murdoch seems unperturbed. He makes it clear that News Corporation can "win" in spite of adversity, economic turmoil, obstacles, and unpredictability (lines 20–3). The company can "capture growth," operate in an environment in which there are "winners," triumph over economic and market adversities, and outperform its competitors (lines 190, 98, 150, 9–11, 81–83). All this can be done while suffering the risk of being "killed off" (line 202). Murdoch concludes that News Corporation will be a clear winner: it "will maintain [its] leadership position for decades to come" (lines 210–11).

Like many seemingly self-obsessed CEOs, Murdoch sees himself as a great visionary. Indeed, implicitly, perhaps he is calling for recognition of his remarkable powers and of his nurturing of a supporting cast of managers who are prescient visionaries too (line 14). Murdoch proclaims to be the arbiter of what is an acceptable level of unemployment in the USA (lines 21–2). He can "see boundless opportunities" ahead (line 205). Remarkably, he has superhuman powers as a visionary – he is capable of the impossible (for lesser or any mortals) of being able to "glance over the horizon" (line 196).

Murdoch uses folksy condescension to preach to his audience: "When you have been in business as long as we have…" (line 68). Perhaps Murdoch is trying to emulate Warren Buffett, whose letters to stockholders of Berkshire Hathaway resonate with folksiness and attract keen interest. Murdoch teaches the world how News Corporation copes with adversity through asset diversification (line 69). He gives a lesson about the need to innovate to survive (line 192). Thus, the metaphor mentioned earlier remains apt: MURDOCH IS A PEDAGOGUE.

Hyperbole also features strongly in Murdoch's claims that a subsidiary, FOX News channel, is "simply unstoppable" (line 81). The company's cable TV presence includes launching "one of the most successful programs" (lines 86–87; 91). In film production, the company has produced "the most successful film of all time" and it has "ushered in a new era" of film and television (lines 41–2). There are no half measures with News Corporation: it "provide(s) the highest quality and the broadest array of content to the greatest number of people, whenever and however they want it" and it is "the world's leading content provider" (lines 156–7, 206, 219–21).

Murdoch revels in the BUSINESS IS WAR metaphor. When this is combined with the metaphor THE CORPORATE ENVIRONMENT IS BRUTAL, RAW, HOSTILE, DISRUPTIVE, UNPREDICTABLE, AND DEADLY, it sets the ethical tone at the top of News Corporation. Murdoch's language suggests that he and his senior staff believe they are gifted visionaries who possess the special abilities needed to succeed in such an environment. They can usher in a new era and provide winning answers in a "dog-eat-dog" competitive business world. Such a tone at the top likely encouraged a view that it was acceptable for newspaper journalists and managers to flout societal mores and ethical standards by using that "killer app" (phone-hacking technology?) to get their stories, no matter what, and beat competitors.

The language and metaphors Murdoch uses contain many signs that they will enable, if at least partly, a perverse culture. There are signs of their potential to lead to inapt ethical behavior in the absence of a countervailing power (such as an independent board of directors) spotting the dysfunction and acting to remediate it. While Murdoch's text is not an overtly manic screed, his rhetoric is tantamount to a perversion of a human-centered society. He praises extremism in competition and markets. He asserts outlandish claims of almost superhuman leadership abilities. His lack of humility is striking.

Concluding Comments

CEOs of major companies, especially those of mega-media conglomerates such as News Corporation, wield "enormous power to frame organizational reality for their internal and external stakeholders [and to craft] … organizational cultures that reflect shared values, expectations and behaviours."[30] In the case of News Corporation, Murdoch exercises power as CEO and chair to set his organization's culture. One outcome of this is "the potential to create stifling organizational norms that facilitate corporate malfeasance and chicanery."[31] The language used by a CEO should be recognized broadly for its capacity to help develop a questionable and potentially troublesome tone at the top.

As demonstrated here, close readings of CEO letters to shareholders can provide a countervailing discourse in an environment characterized by high ownership concentration of global media enterprises. Close readings can promote (both inside companies and in the broader community) an "awareness of the role of CEO text in creating, often subtly and unobtrusively, a shared social world … and [in] defining the public interest in a narrow, self-serving and perverse way."[32] This is ever more important if we accept that "all language is manipulation"[33] and that the language of an influential CEO, such as Murdoch, can possess this characteristic.

Given the growth in CEO power in recent decades, what type of moral and ethical code should persons such as Murdoch be accountable to? Is there a need for "an ethics of public language, which is necessarily an ethics of public manipulation-through-language …"?[34] These are important questions. The expansion of CEO power has led to the growth of "heroic" models of leadership as we have revealed in this and the previous chapter. These models have "encourage[d] many CEOs to use language to exaggerate their proficiency, level of insight, and ability to command events (many of which are beyond their control)."[35]

Murdoch's apparent hubris seems to render him and News Corporation impervious to broader society-based values. Conceivably, the tone Murdoch set at the top of News Corporation was one in which his minions regarded the "killer app" (phone-hacking technology?) as an acceptable weapon to use to increase circulation and profit in the "war" raging in a highly competitive business environment.

chapter four

Reputation

From an ethical perspective, stakeholders should critically monitor CEO-speak continuously. Mindful of this, here we explore the language Timothy Sloan used when he was CEO of Wells Fargo to sustain claims that Wells Fargo would behave in an ethically appropriate way in the future. These claims were prompted by numerous scandals involving the company.

We explore the opening written statement Sloan delivered to the Committee on Banking, Housing and Urban Affairs of the United States Senate on October 3, 2017. Our intent is to demonstrate how Sloan used framing, ideology, metaphor, and rhetoric to impress the committee that Wells Fargo was committed to better ethical behavior. Sloan's statement was intended to salvage Wells Fargo's reputation, which had been savaged by widespread allegations of unethical conduct.

On March 5, 2020, the majority staff of the US House of Representatives Committee on Financial Services concluded that Wells Fargo had failed over a 15-year period "to correct serious deficiencies in its infrastructure for managing risks to consumers and complying with the law" and had exposed customers "to countless abuses, including racial discrimination, wrongful foreclosure, illegal vehicle repossession, and fraudulently opened accounts."[1]

A close reading of Sloan's opening statement to the Senate committee yields insight to him as a person and as a leader. It also helps to better understand the important role a CEO's language can play in devising and embedding a desirable culture of ethical conduct.[2] Our close reading reveals how Sloan discharged his role as the company's "chief truth officer."[3] Sloan's appearance sought to draw attention to an epiphany in the managerial mindset at Wells Fargo. The statement he presented was based on superficial assumptions about leadership and followership and clouded responsibility for ethical lapses at the company. Ultimately, Sloan was unconvincing in enlisting belief that Wells Fargo would "return to ethical conduct."

CEO-speak is an important enabler of trust, especially when (as with Wells Fargo) trust is seriously impaired.[4] Although repairing trust requires more than mere words, nonetheless, a corporate leader's words are crucial, particularly in a high-profile public setting such as a US Senate committee hearing. A CEO's language has strong capacity to facilitate ethical and unethical impressions, attitudes, and behaviors among followers and other corporate stakeholders.

Sloan's prepared testimony asserted that "Wells Fargo is a better bank today than it was a year ago ... [and] next year, Wells Fargo will be a better bank than it is today ... because we have spent the past year determined to earn back the public's trust."[5] This assertion was hollow rhetoric. The failure to achieve this noble aim of being "a better bank" was exposed pointedly in a public letter written on October 4, 2018 (one year after Sloan's appearance) by Senator Sherrod Brown, ranking member of the US Senate Banking Committee, and ten Democrat colleagues.[6] The senators drew attention to evidence that in the year since Sloan's appearance before the committee "... yet more scandals have mounted at the bank, despite claims by Mr. Sloan and other executives that Wells Fargo [would] remediate its problems."

A further six months later, on March 28, 2019, Wells Fargo announced that Sloan would retire as CEO effective on June 30, 2019. In a press release announcing his retirement, Sloan acknowledged that he had "focused on leading a process to address past issues and to rebuild trust" and admitted "there remains more work to be done."[7] Sloan confided that "it has become apparent to me that our ability to successfully move Wells Fargo forward from here will benefit from a new CEO and fresh perspectives." This was tantamount to a confession of failure by Sloan in his major task of rebuilding trust in Wells Fargo. Indeed, Wells Fargo's problems endured into 2020. On March 10, 2020, the (then) CEO Charles W. Scharf admitted, "We have not yet done what is necessary to address our [ethical] shortcomings."[8]

Before analyzing Sloan's opening written statement to the Senate committee on October 3, 2017, we first provide some context. Wells Fargo is an American international banking and financial services company founded in 1852 and headquartered in San Francisco. The company has about $1.9 trillion in assets[9] and provides banking and associated services at approximately 8,600 locations, 13,000 ATMs, and offices in 42 countries. The company has approximately 269,000 full-time equivalent staff serving one in three households in the USA. In 2015, Wells Fargo was the world's twenty-second most admired company and the seventh most respected company. In 2016, Wells Fargo was ranked twenty-seventh on *Fortune*'s list of America's largest corporations and third in assets among all US banks. Despite such accolades and size, in early February, 2018, the US Federal Reserve Bank barred Wells Fargo from increasing its asset base until it fixed "internal problems."[10]

Timothy Sloan had previously held major leadership positions in the bank, including as chief administration officer (from 2010 to 2011), chief financial officer (2011 to 2014), head of wholesale banking (2014 to 2015), and chief operating officer (2015 to 2016).[11] His colleagues describe him as a "no-nonsense professional," a very hard worker, and someone who will "go anywhere, do anything" but has "little time for leisure."[12] Sloan was noted for his political influence, "commitment to the community," and his "won't back down" attitude in the face of political pressure.[13]

Thus, Sloan was a long-serving, highly experienced leader at Wells Fargo at the time he appeared before the Senate committee on October 3, 2017. He would have been very aware of the importance of leadership-through-language and of the political importance of what was at stake. He knew Wells Fargo and its recent scandal-ridden history very well. He had been CEO for almost one full year and, in that time, had engaged in intensive effort to redeem the company's reputation. Indeed, in a Wells Fargo news release dated October 12, 2016, announcing his appointment as CEO, Sloan said,

> It's a great privilege … to lead one of America's most storied companies at a critical juncture in its history. My immediate and highest priority is to restore trust in Wells Fargo. It's a tremendous responsibility, one which I look forward to … We will work tirelessly to build a stronger and better Wells Fargo.[14]

Thus, from commencement of his appointment as CEO, Sloan was deeply aware that his "immediate and highest priority [was] to restore trust in Wells Fargo."

The language skills of leaders such as Sloan can enable them to "set the tone, to lead, to be reasonable."[15] However, these skills can also be misused if they "present information or anecdotes that make their visions appear more realistic or more appealing than they actually are … [and help them] … to screen out problems or to foster an illusion of control when … things are quite out of control."[16] The present example of Wells Fargo explores the pertinence of these cautions about misuse of language.

How did CEO Sloan use language to "screen out problems" and offer an illusion of control?

Sloan's opening written statement to the Senate committee was a follow-up to the appearance before the same committee, a year earlier, by Wells Fargo's previous CEO, John Stumpf. The principal purpose of Stumpf's appearance had been to respond to concerns of senators and the public about "phony" accounts Wells Fargo set up for customers without the customers' knowledge. The Senate committee's interest stemmed from information that pointed to Wells Fargo's "high-pressure sales environment ... [that] ... drove employees to create as many as two million fake accounts ... and to reach extreme sales goals, some by breaking the law."[17]

On December 21, 2013, the *Los Angeles Times* alleged that because of "relentless pressure to ... meet quotas, employees [of Wells Fargo] have opened unneeded accounts for customers, ordered credit cards without customers' permission, and forged client signatures."[18] The (then) CEO Stumpf apologized very publicly before the Senate committee in 2016. He admitted that Wells Fargo had failed to fulfill its responsibility to customers, staff, and the American public and that it had violated the trust of customers by not doing "more sooner to address the causes of this unacceptable activity."[19]

Thus, the scandal that prompted the invitations to Stumpf and (one year later) Sloan to appear before the Senate committee arose from a violation of trust by Wells Fargo. Sanger, the (then) chair of Wells Fargo's board of directors, described the violations as "opening accounts for certain retail banking customers that they did not request or in some cases even know about."[20] Sanger continued by asserting "this behavior is unacceptable, not only to the Board but also to the overwhelming majority of our people who are hard-working and highly ethical." The unacceptable behavior mentioned was apparently just a small part of Wells Fargo's troubles. Many claims of further inappropriate behavior by Wells Fargo were made after the *Los Angeles Times* exposé in 2013.

On September 20, 2016, Stumpf was "grilled"[21] by the committee in a "stuttering" appearance.[22] He was castigated widely for saying, "I care about outcomes, not process."[23] He resigned as CEO a week later. Sloan was appointed his successor on October 12, 2016. In the following year, further highly dubious ethical practices at Wells Fargo were uncovered. For example, on August 31, 2017, Wells Fargo reported that a third-party review of its retail sales practices had increased the potentially fake customer accounts it held from 2.1 million to 3.5 million.[24] These fresh revelations set the scene for Sloan's testimony to the Senate committee on

October 3, 2017. What Sloan would say to the committee was a matter of keen media anticipation and public attention.[25] His appearance was a high-profile display of public rhetorical leadership by a CEO.

We analyze the 2211 words of Sloan's opening *written* statement. Our source is a transcript (reproduced in appendix B, with line numbers added) that covers the part of the hearing in which Sloan read his opening written statement.[26] This transcript is part of a 181-page document posted to the US government website.[27] This larger document also contains responses to written questions from the Senate committee and other supporting material. We focus on the framing of the written testimony and the way metaphor and ideology were used for rhetorical effect.

We do not explore the oral evidence or the verbal exchanges between Sloan and committee members. Journalists and politicians who have done so have been very critical of Sloan's rhetoric of good intent. They have dismissed the claim that restoration of trust would ensue from "the journey" on which Sloan said he was taking the company. This is apparent in the request on October 4, 2018, one year after Sloan's appearance, by Democrat members of the committee for a further hearing with Sloan and the chair of Wells Fargo's board of directors, Elizabeth Duke.[28] They cited "a history of inadequate response on behalf of Wells Fargo's senior leadership, and continued reports of misconduct." Their request was prompted by "rampant consumer abuses revealed over the last year [and by] more than a dozen widespread and persistent failures by the bank … since Tim Sloan last appeared before the Committee."

We now assess the ethicality of Sloan's CEO-speak in his statement and whether it was likely to be convincing and persuasive in projecting the claimed reality of Wells Fargo's situation. This is an important task because a leader is "responsible for the whole organization's approach to truth-telling."[29] We conclude that, contrary to Sloan's intention, his statement would have had a net negative effect on external perceptions of the ethical environment at Wells Fargo.

High-Profile Rhetorical Events

Appearing before a US Senate (or similar government) committee is a serious, high-profile endeavor with major reputational consequences. This seriousness was apparent in 2010 when five major bank CEOs appeared before investigatory committees established by the Troubled Asset Relief Program and the Financial Crises Inquiry Commission. The CEOs' carefully crafted testimonies "paint[ed] their banks' actions in the best light possible and minimize[d] any potential consequences, ranging from increased regulatory scrutiny to criminal charges ... [and preserved] their own best interests ..."[30]

The appearance of the CEO of a bank before a congressional or other high-profile committee is not limited to the USA. On February 10, 2009 four senior executives of major banks appeared before the Banking Crisis Inquiry of the Treasury Committee of the U.K. House of Commons to explain the failures of their banks.[31] Such appearances attract intense media and public attention.[32] Sloan's appearance on October 3, 2017, was no different. Indeed, it was rendered even more pressure-laden by his predecessor's lackluster performance before the same committee in the previous year, and by fresh Wells Fargo scandals that had been revealed in the intervening year. One of these was that up to 570,000 car loan customers of Wells Fargo had been charged inappropriately for failing to maintain qualifying insurance on their cars.[33] The spotlight was clearly on Sloan. The ethical status of his CEO-speak should have been irreproachable.

We now explain how we assessed whether this was the case by exploring aspects of the framing, ideology, metaphor, and rhetoric in Sloan's written statement.

Framing, Ideology, Metaphor, and Rhetoric

Framing. The framing of any argument is important since "[a]n audience's interpretation of and reaction to a person, event, or discourse can be shaped by the frame in which that information is viewed."[34] Framing makes "some aspects of a perceived reality ... more salient in a communicating text."[35] Bill Clinton's metaphorical frame of "A Bridge to the Future" was very effective in his Democratic Party presidential nomination acceptance speech in 1996. This symbolic and linguistic framing helped him to construct meaning, influence how events were perceived, and encourage acceptance of one meaning over another. Similarly, Donald Trump's framing metaphor of "Drain the Swamp" was effective in energizing his political base in the 2016 US presidential election campaign.

Frames function in one or more of four locations: "the communicator, the text, the receiver, and the culture."[36] The frames in a text "are manifested by the presence or absence of certain keywords, stock phrases, stereotyped images, sources of information, and sentences that provide thematic ... reinforce[ment]."[37]

Ideology. Exploration of the ideology in any text can benefit from responses to the nine questions outlined below.[38]

Q1: What are the assumptions about what is natural, just, and right?
Q2: What (and whom) do these assumptions distort or obscure?
Q3: What power relations are made to appear as if they are normal or good?
Q4: Which of the binary opposites (good/evil, natural/unnatural, tame/wild, young/old) is privileged, repressed, or devalued?
Q5: What people, classes, areas of life, and experiences are "silenced"?
Q6: What cultural assumptions and "myths" shape experience and evaluation?
Q7: What enthymemes are in the "logic" of the text?
Q8: How does the style of presentation contribute to the logic of the text?
Q9: What vision of human possibility lies at the heart of the ideology?

Answers to these questions can reveal the potential for language to hide ideology. Although CEOs should strive to make the ideology in their text transparent, this is not easily achieved. The nine questions above are a good practical starting point to help them do so.

Metaphor. Metaphor is important in the practice of leadership.[39] However, there is growing alertness to the dangers of unprincipled use of metaphor by leaders.[40] Metaphor can be a powerful and nuanced device in constructing ideology[41] because it "structures inquiry, establishes relevance, and provides an interpretive system."[42] Some metaphors "transport especially powerful biases, because they camouflage the social underpinnings of the reality to which they refer [and because] different metaphors have different ideological attachments."[43] Other metaphors are "a shadowy image for communicating only dimly perceived realities."[44]

Our analysis draws on four tests of the ethicality of metaphor use. These are

1. *History test.* "How closely does the metaphor correspond to the facts of the case?"
2. *Resonance test.* Does the metaphor "have a unique cultural power to incite?"
3. *Proportionality test.* "Is the metaphor's seriousness proportional to that which it is applied?"
4. *Quiet room test.* "Deep down, we know … [whether] we are arguing to incite or to enlighten."[45]

CEOs should be aware of their intentional or unintentional use of metaphor. This is important because many CEOs are moral role models.[46] Thus, they should be principled in their use of metaphors, particularly in high-profile rhetorical events. They should use metaphors proportionally and recognize that metaphors can help to set an organization's ethical tone at the top.[47] Metaphors should not be regarded merely as "linguistic decoration or verbal artistry [but as] indicative of leaders' thinking and … a basis of their actions."[48]

Rhetoric. Here we discuss rhetoric in its non-pejorative, classical sense[49] of constituting "the study of how people persuade."[50] Thus, we regard rhetoric as the process of seeking to have another person "look at things from our point of view" and share our "attention-structure."[51]

Word choice is an important aspect of rhetoric. This includes the strategic choice of language euphemisms "to approach unsettling, embarrassing, or distasteful … topics without appearing inconsiderate to peoples' concerns."[52] Another purpose of euphemisms is to "disguise" stories told about our unethical actions[53] so that they help turn unacceptable behaviors into socially approved behaviors. Thus, euphemisms can make harmful conduct respectable.[54] For example, "right sizing," a favored term for layoffs, "focuses attention toward the economic benefits and away from the human costs of putting people out of work."[55]

CEOs in any high-profile setting should be aware of, and be able to justify, the major rhetorical aspects of the discourse they present. Thus, a CEO should be highly alert to the metaphors used, the structure of the discourse presented, and the embodied logic, assumptions, euphemisms, appeals to authority, appeals to emotion, and omissions. All are part of the art of persuasion.

Sloan's Opening Written Statement

Framing

The first few words uttered by a speaker or writer offer important clues to the framing. Sloan's opening paragraphs framed Wells Fargo to show it had made "progress" and was a better company under his leadership. Lines 1–4 (see appendix B) emphasize that Sloan appeared before the committee without the compulsion of a subpoena. The pronoun "I" signals that Sloan, the CEO, is the accountable person. His use of words with positive connotations ("appreciate," "discuss," and "opportunity") frames his appearance in a positive, voluntary, and (almost) eager light. The use of "discuss" envisages an interchange of (presumed) equals: Sloan and the Senate committee. The implication is that both are interested in a common dialogue. The word "progress" connotes movement in a desirable direction and an improvement.

Sloan frames the responsibility for the matters under consideration as residing with Wells Fargo, not specific human beings. He asserts that Wells Fargo "has made" this "progress." This ascription of agency to an amorphous entity de-emphasizes the roles and accountability of human beings and plays down their potential culpability. However, because a company is inanimate, it cannot experience "great disappointment" (line 5) – only actual people can. Thus, references to the entity, Wells Fargo, mask the culpability of specific identified humans for the scandalous conduct.

The opening four paragraphs frame Wells Fargo and Sloan favorably. Sloan acknowledges the "problems" because "our Community bank" did not recognize the "full scope and seriousness regarding the problems" (lines 6–7). He admits deficiencies in the company's state of knowledge and actions and also asserts that "all of you were right to criticize us" (lines 10–11). Crucially, he declares that this criticism was heard and (apparently) is being acted upon. Thus, this framing paragraph is one of admission and implicit shame. It acknowledges that insight and action by Wells Fargo is required to achieve redemption.

The overall intent of the introductory framing is twofold: to impress the audience with Sloan's noble commitment to ethical conduct and to assert his capacity for entering moral judgments. Through his language, Sloan purports to know what is right and wrong ("you were right to criticize us," lines 10–11); what is good and bad ("Wells Fargo is a better bank today," lines 18–19); and what is acceptable and not acceptable ("That was unacceptable," line 17). There is a hint of hubris in Sloan's claim that the bank is "better [under his leadership] today than it was a year ago" and that next year it "will be a better bank than it is today" (lines 19–20).

Sloan takes the moral high ground by accepting responsibility for recognizing the company's past mistakes and correcting them. He seems keen to legitimize his endeavors to engender an ethical culture and to portray himself as part of the solution and not part of the problem. However, any attempt to distance himself, even implicitly, from implication in the mistakes, dysfunctions, and failed responses of the past ignores that he was at various times (and to varying degrees) part of the senior management team collectively responsible for those "mistakes."[56]

Nonetheless, by the personal pronoun "I," Sloan is the one who "heard [the committee] … customers … and team members" (lines 11–12). He is the one who is "deeply sorry" (line 13) and who "apologize(s) for the damage done" (line 14). In contrast, the Wells Fargo failures that led to Sloan's appointment as CEO are attributed collectively. Thus, "*we*" failed because "*we* recognized [the seriousness] too late" (line 6); "*we* had not fully grappled with the damage" (line 8); and "*we* came … without a good plan" (line 10). His statement that "the bank's leaders [*we*] acted too slowly" (line 17) is incomplete. He should have admitted, "including myself."

Ideology

In framing the introduction, Sloan refers to "customers and team members" three times (lines 9; 11–12; 14) and to the "public's trust" (line 21). However, he does not mention shareholders. This privileging has ideological overtones. Sloan might have been embarrassed to offer any hint that he prioritized the interests of shareholders over other stakeholders. His sensitivity was possibly due to public concerns that shareholders had benefited from additional profits generated by the bank's scandalous behavior. Such exclusion is at odds with Sloan's prior statements about the scandal in which he mentioned shareholders *and* investors.[57] Sloan is silent too about the extent to which directors and senior managers (including himself) benefited through enhanced remuneration from the bank's unethical practices.

Sloan frames himself as a "penitent learner able and willing to improve."[58] Despite repeating the keyword "team members" 20 times, he distances himself from his management colleagues. They are portrayed as being late in recognizing issues, having no plan to solve problems, and being deficient and somewhat hapless individuals who respond slowly. Thus, Sloan devalues his colleagues and "silences" them.

Metaphor

Sloan's use of the subtle and nuanced underlying metaphor of the PENITENT LEARNER[59] is striking. Through this metaphor he portrays those who have failed Wells Fargo as now being determined to redeem themselves by earning back trust. The penance implied in this "awakening" would most likely appeal to those members of the Senate committee who were keen to endorse core American religious values. Thus, the metaphor seems highly likely to pass the "resonance test."[60] Ideologically too, there is a "vision of human possibility"[61] that would most likely have appealed to the senators.

The "not fully grappled" metaphor (line 8) seems likely to have had positive ethical impact because it conveys the difficulties Wells Fargo experienced in coping with a confronting situation. Nonetheless, "grappled" is a distracting euphemism because it diverts attention from the apparent obliviousness of senior management of Wells Fargo to the odious practices the company adopted over several years. The metaphor is also confounding. The uncertainty and clumsiness it implies sit oddly with the cool cocksureness that Sloan presents in his bold assertion that "we will get it right" (lines 159–60).

A STAGECOACH metaphor courses through Sloan's statement, evoked partly by the name Wells Fargo. This iconic metaphor is deployed as a part of a larger pervading metaphor of Wells Fargo being on a JOURNEY to restore trust.[62] The Wells Fargo stagecoach is proclaimed to be an "enduring symbol … of the company's heritage of service, stability, and innovation."[63] This symbolism draws upon linguistic and visual discourses of the American West that are embedded in American culture. For many years, the cover of Wells Fargo's annual report displayed images of a stagecoach – a metaphor that "symboliz[es] a bank that comes through for its customers."[64] The imagery is so potent that Wells Fargo used it in video advertisements in 2018 to help repair its damaged reputation.[65] The metaphor conjures thoughts of the (alleged) "Old West" traditions of dependability and commitment.[66] Through this metaphor, Sloan imagines Wells Fargo to be a bank that will deliver for its customers (just like a Wells Fargo stagecoach of the Old West). The metaphor WELLS FARGO IS A STAGECOACH envisages a journey through an often hostile and difficult territory. The implication is that the community can be confident that Wells Fargo will do so safely and will arrive at planned destinations on time.

Thus, Sloan exploits a metaphor that has long been associated with the company. His intent is to display the company's contrition to stakeholders and to legitimize its promise to do better in the future. He reinforces a commitment to "restore our reputation and our customers' trust and to make Wells Fargo the finest and most ethical company it can be" (lines 198–9). The idea that the company is on a path to "restor[ing] [its] reputation" is a personal pledge by Sloan. Perhaps, metaphorically, Sloan conceives himself as the stagecoach driver.

Sloan's metaphors are largely, but not entirely, principled and ethical. They appear to satisfy the resonance and history tests mentioned earlier. However, they fail the proportionality and quiet room tests.[67] Perhaps those reading, watching, and listening to the opening testimony are being manipulated just a bit.

Rhetoric

Sloan enlists a patriotic euphemism to describe Wells Fargo as "this important American institution" (line 15). This seems intended to elicit a sense of community and to offer a veiled warning to the Senate committee that it should tread carefully because the bank has considerable power and influence. Sloan's rhetoric reinforces the "cultural assumption"[68] he promoted on August 4, 2017, when he referred to Wells Fargo as "this treasured 165-year-old institution."[69] Seemingly by resort to this reference he was seeking to enroll the emotional allegiance of the senators in venerating Wells Fargo.

Commendably, Sloan describes the problems confronting Wells Fargo in language free of euphemism, as "the sales practices scandal" (lines 8–9). The word "scandal" acknowledges the seriousness of the misdeeds in which Wells Fargo was involved. By naming some of the company's sales practices a "scandal," Sloan uses language accurately and ethically. Nonetheless, Sloan's two uses of "mistakes" are euphemisms. He says "… we will compensate every customer who suffered because Wells Fargo made mistakes" (lines 35–6). The word "mistakes" clouds the location of agency. The "practices" Sloan refers to were caused by human beings (including senior executives) and the management control systems those executives designed and implemented. Thus, naming the entity Wells Fargo as the agent responsible for these "mistakes" ignores the agency of the specific people involved. "Mistakes" is deployed in its softer sense of "misunderstanding" rather than that of "blunder."

Sloan's eight uses of the word "problem(s)" are troubling. From an ethical perspective, such usage softens the severity of scandalous actions by some Wells Fargo staff. Again, Sloan ignores the agency of the Wells Fargo leaders who condoned such actions (implicitly or explicitly) and oversaw the dysfunctional management control systems involved.

Sloan describes the fundamental structural changes in Wells Fargo's management control system that prompted the move from a decentralized structure to a more centralized one (lines 97–107). However, his description is misleading since this very large company had been led centrally to a significant degree. Sloan alleges that the prior version of the company's management control system was too decentralized, leading to severe dysfunction. He should have acknowledged that formal decentralization in key areas, such as in sales practices, was subject to management override.

In a section titled "Making Things Right with Our Customers" Sloan begins: "The entire Wells Fargo team, all 270,000 of us, is committed to making things right for customers the bank let down. This is a big job, and we will get it right" (lines 158–60). These cliché-ridden sentences obscure underlying assumptions about the nature of the human world of organizations and the fallible people therein. The bravado of "we will get it right" invokes an implicit assumption of senior management infallibility. Such assumptions, or what are labeled "key organizing terms," should be examined for their "powerful ambiguities, ironies, and twists and turns [and their] slogans that simultaneously command emotional allegiance and are devoid of precise meaning."[70]

The assertion that the "entire Wells Fargo team, all 270,000 of us, is committed to making things right for customers the bank let down" uses TEAM as a powerful metaphor for the company as a whole. The cliché of "the team" is enhanced rhetorically in the larger term "Wells Fargo team" to evoke the stagecoach/American frontier image. Sloan also asserts that the "entire Wells Fargo team," literally every human working for the company ("all 270,000 of us"), are thus committed. This suppresses the reality of Wells Fargo's social and human complexity. It is based on the superficial assumption about leadership and followership that everyone in a large organization is committed to a specific goal.

What is implied by the word "committed" is unclear too. This word is a slogan that appears intended to subtly enlist the emotional allegiance of the Senate committee. Similarly, the goal of "making things right for customers the bank let down" is a slogan "that simultaneously command[s] emotional allegiance [but is] devoid of precise meaning."[71] The euphemism "customers the bank let down" very mildly acknowledges that "the bank" (not its leaders and its dysfunctional management control systems, but some abstraction) committed acts that (mildly) "let down" people.

Concluding Comments

The blatant and widely publicized unethical acts of Wells Fargo over many years, and the management systems and culture that encouraged such unethical actions, were all a prelude to Sloan's appearance before the Senate committee. The setting was an opportunity to establish a tone at the top at Wells Fargo that would publicly reinforce a re-discovered culture of ethical propriety. In addressing this opportunity, Sloan relied strongly on the symbolism of the Wells Fargo stagecoach metaphor.

Some aspects of Sloan's written language demonstrate positive ethical features and outcomes. The contrition implied in the pervasive redemptive metaphor of a PENITENT LEARNER seems intended to invoke an ethical restoration in the minds of observers because "learners [presumably including organizations that learn, such as Wells Fargo] are likely to be accorded less blame than powerful pedagogues for errors and mis-judgements."[72]

On the negative side, use of the STAGECOACH metaphor seems a blatant attempt to benefit from that metaphor's widespread embedded cultural entailments of commitment and dependability. Used in this way, the metaphor is highly ironic, inappropriate, and possibly manipulative. The sales practices scandal and other scandals clearly show Wells Fargo was not a company that customers could depend on to do the right thing consistently and get them to their intended (financial) destination.

The ethical effect of the euphemisms Sloan used is mixed. The word "scandal" is an accurate and ethically appropriate word to describe what has occurred. However, the euphemisms "mistakes" and "let down" soften the odiousness and the severity of what has occurred.

An ethically positive "vision of human possibility" courses through the statement. Nonetheless, its framing disguises human agency for the bank's scandalous practices by excluding Sloan and the senior management team from any personal implication in the "mistakes." Thus, Sloan's written statement omits crucial information and "screen[s] out problems."[73] Such "screening out" was predicated on unsustainable and superficial assumptions about leader/follower relations and was part of an ethically unsatisfactory distancing of senior management, particularly Sloan, from responsibility for the scandals. The fact that senior management had the authority to monitor and override decentralized decision-making processes was ignored.

On balance, the negative features of the language outweigh the positive features. Sloan's written language attempted to re-invent Wells Fargo as trustworthy and ethical in a high-profile rhetorical event that should have been, overtly and covertly, ethically pristine. Although Sloan's written language made a case that there had been an ethically virtuous epiphany in managerial mindset, it was unconvincing. Sloan's language failed to redeem Wells Fargo for its poor ethicality. Ultimately, Sloan's claims that Wells Fargo would be better in the coming year and would "get it right" were exposed as fake by subsequent events.

chapter five

Deception

CEO language can signal the possibility of a tone at the top that tacitly condones deceptive conduct or the possibility of active involvement by a CEO and senior executives in deceptive practices. A large body of research has reported signs of untruthful behavior in particular words that people (including CEOs) choose.[1] For example (and as we elaborate later), deceivers are prone to divert suspicion from their wrongdoing by reducing direct references to themselves, by increasing the positive tone of their language, and by using more words of extreme positive emotion. An especially rich source of signals of deception is the informal or impromptu oral communications of CEOs, such as doorstop interviews with journalists. In such settings, responses to questions are usually not planned strategically or prepared in advance. This source is especially fruitful when a CEO is provoked or under stress.

Several language analysis techniques can help detect deception in written and oral communications and differentiate truthful statements from fabricated ones.[2] Although no single cue can identify deception reliably, analysis of language can raise suspicions and identify particular communications that warrant further investigation.

Most CEO communications are unaudited and susceptible to manipulation. There are no regulatory guidelines, for example, mandating what should or should not be included by CEOs in their letters to shareholders. CEOs under pressure to attain financial targets (such as earnings per share) have ample scope and incentive to use their oral and written communications to disguise manipulations of accounting and other performance measures.

In this chapter we explore the language used by Ramalinga Raju, CEO and chair of the failed major Indian multinational company, Satyam. This case demonstrates the potential usefulness of several language-based methods for detecting deceptive conduct. The source documents involved are

Raju's letters to shareholders in the annual reports of Satyam from 2002–3 to 2007–8 and Raju's letter of January 7, 2009, in which he confessed to engaging in fraudulent behavior.[3] We highlight how Raju's word choice changed noticeably in his five annual report letters prior to the collapse of Satyam. The changes occurred as the scale and impact of Raju's deceptive conduct increased and the pressure on him mounted.

Selection of an individual word or phrase can signal deceptive behavior. The global accounting firm Ernst and Young, in collaboration with the US Federal Bureau of Investigation, has developed fraud evaluation software that monitors the words used in emails by corporate employees.[4] Examples of the phrases monitored are "cover up," "write off," and "nobody will find out." The software tracks the use of rationalization phrases such as "not hurting anyone," "fix it later," and "told to do it." It also searches for signs of hidden activities, such the terms "call my mobile" or "come by my office."[5] However, users of text analysis tools such as this must be alert to the context of the monitored language. For example, the words "cover up" would be innocuous if this referred to applying sunscreen lotion.

Individuals engaging in deceitful communication have the complicated task of keeping track of their lies to maintain credibility and to do so while simultaneously portraying sincerity. Additionally, they have to deal with higher cognitive complexity because they must be alert to the relationships between an increasing number of elements in their deception. Consequently, their emotional reactions change.[6] The threat of being found out induces a tenseness in them that often is accompanied by physical and emotional discomfort.[7]

Liars often must increase their thought processes to ensure consistency in the story they are telling and to avoid contradicting themselves. Yet, simultaneously, they need to provide a plausible story to support their deceptive claims.[8] Thus, they tend to exercise greater caution in what they say and write. Of particular pertinence to the case of Raju and Satyam, discussed in this chapter, is the contention that as the consequences of being found out became more severe for Raju, the "tenseness and cognitive load"[9] he experienced became more severe too.

Deceivers have to control their body language, facial expressions, and the structuring of their story.[10] It is cognitively more demanding to construct an account based on falsehood and fabrication than it is to tell the truth. A deceiver is less prone to use "exclusive" words, such as "except," "but," and "without." Additionally, there is likely to be a negative correlation between cognitive complexity and the use of motion verbs such as "go," "walk," and "run."[11] This is because truthful individuals have experienced what they are communicating. Thus, their statements usually include more details of what they perceive as reality. In contrast, deceptive individuals construct a falsified account and are prone to use fewer "exclusive" words.

"Explainer" words (such as "because," "since," and "in order to") are highly correlated with anxiousness and are often associated with guilt.[12] If a liar is feeling anxious and/or guilty, the language he or she chooses will be evidenced by more explainer words.[13]

Three language-based cues that have been identified as likely to signal deceptive conduct are (1) personal pronoun use, (2) frequency of words of high positivity and extreme emotion, and (3) lexical density and language diversity.[14] These cues are discussed below.

Personal pronouns. Extensive use of first-person *singular* self-referential pronouns (I, me, my, mine, myself) creates a sense of intimacy and familiarity with recipients. Such use helps allay doubts,[15] declares an individual's ownership of a statement, and is tantamount to a projection of honesty.[16] A study using an unmatched sample of scam and non-scam emails found that first-person *singular* pronouns occurred 30.42 times per 1,000 words in scam emails, but only 4.41 times per 1,000 words in non-scam emails.[17] In that study, the proportion of first-person *singular* pronouns to first-person *plural* pronouns (we, us, our, ours, ourselves) was 63.1% in the scam emails, but only 17.5% in the non-scam emails.

Decreased use of self-reference first-person *singular* pronouns and increased use of collective first-person *plural* pronouns can be a blame-shifting or disassociation strategy that is intended to distance individuals from the deceptions in their statements. The effect is to shift responsibility to others and to avoid a declaration of full ownership of the statements made.[18] Use of first-person plural pronouns such as "we" suggests that one is not fully committed to what one is expressing and is omitting something. Indeed, because people are less likely "to blame themselves ... they speak about their accomplice[s] ["we"] in addition to themselves."[19] In 2000, a transition from the use of "I" to "we" occurred in the open letter to shareholders signed by John Roth, CEO of Nortel Networks, and published in major Canadian newspapers. By dint of this transition, Roth attempted to distance himself from impending bad news and to position himself so that he would not be held personally accountable.[20]

Words of high positivity and extreme emotion. The degree of guilt deceptive individuals feel for the effects of their behavior is reflected in the tone of the words they choose.[21] A study of the language in a conference call between the executives of Lehman Brothers and financial analysts found that Lehman's former CFO, Callan, used excessively positive language to distract attention from the firm's deteriorating financial position.[22] Callan used positive words such as "great" (14 times), "strong" (24 times), and "incredibly" (8 times). In contrast, she used negative words such as "challenging" six times and "tough" once.[23]

Lists of extreme positive and extreme negative words have been developed to help assess the emotion in analysts' conference calls.[24] A frequent finding has been that there is a positive correlation between the likelihood of deception and the incidence of words of extreme positive emotion. Deceptive managers are claimed to over-exaggerate positive news to obscure negative news.[25]

When people are telling a lie they often experience emotional reactions[26] that are reflected in their written and oral communications. Deceptive CEOs are likely to use more words of extreme positive emotion and fewer words of extreme negative emotion during quarterly earnings conference calls.[27] An explanation for this is that the deceiving CEO inwardly feels very emotional and guilty, and fears being exposed to public humiliation. In exhibit 5.1, we reproduce a frequently applied listing of words of extreme negative emotion and extreme positive emotion. Then, in respect of Satyam's CEO Ramalinga Raju, we illustrate how his underlying feeling of guilt and desire to protect his blossoming reputation appear to have influenced his use of extreme negative words and extreme positive words.

Lexical density and diversity. Lexical density is another feature of deception in language.[28] Lexical density measures "the percentage of content words (nouns, verbs, adjectives, and adverbs) to all the words in a given text (content words plus grammatical words)."[29] A common measure of lexical density is Wendell Johnson's (1946) Type-Token Ratio (TTR). This ratio is calculated by dividing the number of distinct words in a text (known as "types") by the total number of words (known as "tokens"). For example, the sentence, "One small step for man, one giant leap for mankind" has a TTR of 0.80 – eight non-repetitive words divided by ten in total.[30] A high TTR indicates avoidance of overstatement.[31]

The lexical diversity of people telling lies (as measured by the TTR) is thought to be lower than if they were not telling lies. In the context of *oral* communication, "high credibility sources" (presumably including CEOs) are aware that "a speaker using unfamiliar words will be better liked and more respected than one using common words."[32] Thus, people telling lies will respond by using speech with a "preponderance of synonyms rather than repetition of the same words." Liars seem to believe that if there is "more vocabulary diversity than usually expected for oral communication [this] may produce favourable attitudes towards [them]."

Exhibit 5.1 Words of extreme negative emotion and extreme positive emotion

Extreme Negative Emotions
abominable, abortive, absurd, advers*, ambitious, annihilating, annihilative, atrocious, awful, badly, baffling, barbarous, bias, breach, brokenhearted, brutal*, calamitous, careless*, catchy, challenging, cockeyed, coerce, crafty, craz*, cruel*, crushed, cunning, curious, danger*, daunting, daze*, defect*, degrad*, demanding, demeaning, depress*, derisory, despair*, desperat*, despicable, destroy*, devastat*, devil*, difficult*, dire, direful, disastrous, disgraceful, dodgy, dread*, exasperating, exorbitant, extortionate, fail*, farcical, farfetched, fatal*, fateful, fault*, fearful*, fearsome, fierce, finished, fright*, frustrat*, funny, grave*, griev*, guileful, hard, harebrained, harm, harmed, harmful*, harming, harms, heartbreak*, heartbroke*, heartless*, heartrending, heartsick, hideous, hopeless*, horr*, humbling, humiliat*, hurt*, idiot, idiotic, ignominious, ignor*, implausible, impossible, improbable, inauspicious, inconceivable, inferior*, infuriating, inglorious, insane, insecur*, intimidat*, jerk, jerked, jerks, kayoed, knavish, knocked out, knotty, KOd out, KO'd out, laughable, lifethreatening, luckless*, ludicrous*, maddening, madder, maddest, maniac*, menace, mess, messy, miser*, misfortunate, mortifying, muddle, nast*, nonsensical, outrag*, overwhelm*, painf*, panic*, paranoi*, pathetic*, peculiar*, pessimis*, pickle, piti*, precarious, preconception, prejudic*, preposterous, pressur*, problem*, reek*, resent*, ridicul*, roughshod, ruin*, savage*, scandalous, scourge, serious, seriously, severe*, shake*, shaki*, shaky, shame*, shock*, silly, skeptic*, slimy, slippery, squeeze, steep, strange, stunned, stupefied, stupid*, suffer, suffered, sufferer*, suffering, suffers, sunk, terribl*, terrified, terrifies, terrify, terrifying, terror*, threat*, thwarting, ticked, tough*, tragic*, transgress, trauma*, tremendous, trick*, trigger-happy, ugl*, unbelievable, unconscionable, unconvincing, unimaginable, unimportant, unlucky, unmanageable, unspeakable, unsuccessful*, untoward, unworthy, usurious, vehement, vexing, vicious*, victim*, vile, violat*, violent*, vulnerab*, washed-up, wicked*, withering, wonky, worst, worthless*, wretched, very bad

Extreme Positive Emotions
amaz*, A-one, astonish*, awe-inspiring, awesome, awful, bang-up, best, bless*, brillian*, by all odds, careful*, challeng*, cherish*, confidence,

confident, confidently, convinc*, crack, cracking, dandy, deadly, definite, definitely, delectabl*, delicious*, deligh*, deucedly, devilishly, dynam*, eager*, emphatically, enormous, excel*, excit*, exult, fab, fabulous*, fantastic*, first-rate, flawless*, genuinely, glori*, gorgeous*, grand, grande*, gratef*, great, groovy, hero*, huge, illustrious, immense, in spades, in truth, incredibl*, insanely, inviolable, keen*, luck, lucked, lucid*, lucks, lucky, luscious, madly, magnific*, marvellous, marvelous, neat*, nifty, outstanding, peachy, perfect*, phenomenal, potent, privileg*, rattling, redoubtable, rejoice, scrumptious*, secur*, sincer*, slap-up, smashing, solid, splend*, strong*, substantial, succeed*, success*, super, superb, superior*, suprem*, swell, terrific*, thankf*, tiptop, topnotch, treasur*, tremendous, triumph*, truly, truth*, unassailable, unbelievable, unquestionably, vast, wonderf*, wondrous, wow*, yay, yays, very good

* = and words with this stem.
Source: Larcker & Zakolyukina (2010).

The DICTION content analysis software program (described in appendix A) has been used widely to analyze the semantic tone and lexical diversity of CEO text.[33] DICTION scores for one of its master variables, CERTAINTY, can be especially insightful in view of evidence that low certainty is associated with a high probability of deception.[34] Thus, a high probability of deceptive conduct is likely to be associated with low out-of-normal range DICTION scores for CERTAINTY.

The Deception of Ramalinga Raju, CEO of Satyam

We begin our analysis by outlining the circumstances that led to Ramalinga Raju's deceptive behavior at Satyam. We draw attention to the mounting cognitive load Raju was likely to have experienced in coping with his deception. We argue that this pressure on him was manifest in his use of pronouns, positive words, and words of high emotion and in the lexical diversity in his communications.

The morning of January 7, 2009, heralded the biggest corporate scandal India had ever experienced. On that day, Ramalinga Raju (hereafter Raju) resigned as CEO and chair of Satyam, one of India's largest companies. Satyam was a software services company with annual revenues (then) of approximately US$2 billion and operations in 66 countries. Satyam first listed on the Bombay and Hyderabad stock exchanges in 1992, and on the New York Stock Exchange in 2001. The company grew rapidly by providing outsourcing and consultancy services to 185 *Fortune* 500 companies, including General Electric, Nestlé, and British Petroleum.[35] Satyam was a "household name across India."[36]

Raju's resignation was unique because it was accompanied by a confession letter.[37] This was dated January 7, 2009, and was addressed to the board of directors of Satyam. In it, Raju confessed that he had inflated Satyam's earnings and assets since 2001.

The letter begins with Raju expressing "deep regret" and mentioning the "tremendous burden that I am carrying on my conscience." He asks the board to note, among other things, that

- the balance sheet on September 30, 2008, "inflated (non-existent) cash and bank balances of Rs [Rupees] 5,040" crore; included "accrued interest of Rs 376 crore, which is non-existent"; included "an understated liability of Rs 1,230 crore on account of funds arranged by me"; and "overstated debtors' position of Rs 490 crore (as against Rs 2,651 reflected in the books)";[38]
- in the September quarter of 2008, the reported operating margin of Rs 649 crore (24 percent of revenue) should have been an operating margin of Rs 61 crore (3 percent of revenue).

Thus, in effect, Raju confessed that approximately US$1.06 billion of Satyam's bank balance of US$1.14 billion (reported in the company's financial statements at September 30, 2008) did not exist.[39] He also confessed that accrued interest of US$79 million was fictional, liabilities were understated by US$261 million, debts were overstated by US$103 million, and revenue for the (then current) quarter was 20 percent lower than reported.

Raju's confession included the telling observation that the amounts concerned grew over the years to "unmanageable proportions as the size of the company operations grew significantly." He explains that "as the promoters held a small percentage of equity, the concern was that poor performance would result in the takeover, thereby exposing the gap." He likens the situation he confronted to "riding a tiger, not knowing how to get off without being eaten."

Raju claimed that he had not taken "even one rupee/dollar from the company" or otherwise "benefited in financial terms on account of the inflated results." He makes three recommendations regarding the way ahead for Satyam, and then states: "I sincerely apologise to all Satyamites and stakeholders … for the current situation." Raju resigns as chairman and finishes by stating: "I am now prepared to subject myself to the laws of the land and face the consequences thereof."

The deception Raju confessed to was undetected and unreported by Satyam's auditors PricewaterhouseCoopers.[40] The fraud was perpetrated by Raju and some accomplices. They had forged confirmation letters from several banks to indicate that Satyam held money in fixed deposits. They doubled sales receipts of approximately 600 major clients. Satyam's ex-chief financial officer Vadlamani Srinivas confessed he "abetted [Raju] in the planning … of the accounting deceptions involved."[41] Raju's confession raised serious questions about the integrity of Indian entrepreneurs and business regulators, the professional competence of Satyam's auditors, and the appropriateness of corporate governance procedures in India.

As CEO and chair of Satyam, Raju operated in a complex Indian business environment that was torn between the pressures of globalization and traditional cultural values. India's lack of a broad culture of dissent rendered many shareholders and independent directors reluctant to question founders of a company (such as Raju). This was cited as a possible reason for the failure of corporate governance and regulatory oversight of Satyam.[42] Promoters of Indian companies (such as Raju) tended to control all important decision making, sat on the board of directors, occupied top managerial positions, and exercised full control over management.[43]

Ramalinga Raju was born in humble circumstances in Andhra Pradesh in 1954. He completed a Bachelor of Commerce at Andhra Loyola College and an MBA at the University of Ohio. In the 1980s, he was recognized as an outstanding business executive in India's construction and textiles industries. In 1987, he moved to Satyam and soon became one of the richest Indians and an influential business leader.[44] Raju's Indian university teachers describe him "as obedient, well-mannered, soft-spoken, extremely helpful and with an obliging nature."[45] Satyam employees describe him as "humble, generous, introverted, but with a secretive nature." His business associates claim he was a "control freak" who craved full control (especially over finance) and that he often worked "tirelessly from the crack of dawn till late at night." Importantly, in the present context, Raju was described as "shrewd and manipulative with the knack of cultivating the right people" and as a "secretive person, not sharing much information even with his family and friends."

Raju won the Ernst and Young Entrepreneur of the Year Award in 2007. His speech accepting that award reveals some telling aspects of his personal motives, inclinations, and intentions. He said,

If you are an entrepreneur, *there will always be expectations that you need to meet* – and *there's no running away from that*. So long as you are transparent and the shareholders have faith in your transparency and the decisions you take, it will be all right for you. However, *you need to constantly take course-correcting measures* as you go quarter on quarter. (italics added)[46]

Raju plausibly effected the "course-correcting measures" he mentions by using the text of his letters to shareholders to "not run away" from the "expectations" he believed that he needed to meet.

The extent and intensity of the personal recognition and stellar reputation that Raju had achieved in the decade prior to his confession in 2009 placed him under great pressure to present himself and Satyam in a highly favorable light. This is an important consideration in understanding what motivated the changes in his written narratives as CEO and chair in the period 2002–3 to 2007–8. The growing scale and probable effects of his deceptions seem likely to have influenced him to change the way his narrative presented Satyam to the public.

The first warning signs that everything was not aboveboard at Satyam came in September 2002[47] when "Raju's shenanigans caught the attention of the Indian income tax department … [and] … the department of company affairs, which felt that there was something wrong somewhere [with] Satyam's accounting practices."[48] Raju and his family members were alleged to have evaded income tax. A deputy director of investigations in the Indian tax office, Ms. S. Padmaja, noticed a sudden increase in the filing of H-15[49] forms by members of Raju's family. These forms were completed to avoid the need to submit income tax returns and thereby preclude disclosure of the money Raju had siphoned out of Satyam, deposited in family bank accounts, and applied to share trading activities.[50] Ms. Padmaja filed a report on this matter and pursued further investigations. However, she was transferred suddenly to another city, despite her investigations still being in progress.[51]

At about the same time, Satyam was accused of non-compliance with US Generally Accepted Accounting Principles and of violating the *Indian Companies Act 1956*. The prospect of ultimate exposure must have loomed large in Raju's mind. Nonetheless, Satyam and Raju were not subject to any other prominent suspicion-raising controversy until December 16, 2008, when the Satyam board authorized the acquisition, for US$1.6 billion, of two real-estate properties (Maytas Properties and Maytas Infrastructures). Raju and his family held substantial stakes in these properties. The potential conflict of interest surrounding this deal stirred an outrage in financial markets and Satyam's share price plunged 30 percent overnight.[52] Investors described the proposed acquisition as a case of the promoters "siphoning money out of Satyam."[53]

On January 6, 2009, four days before investment bank DSP Merrill Lynch was scheduled to make recommendations to the Satyam board, DSP Merrill Lynch canceled this commitment, citing its awareness of "material accounting irregularities [at Satyam]."[54] The startling revelations in Raju's confession letter were published the following day. In contrast with his public projections over the prior decade (that Satyam had been performing extremely well and was expanding its customer base globally) a different reality was exposed – that the company's revenues, operating profits, and net assets had been grossly and consistently overstated at Raju's instigation.

Raju confessed that the proposed acquisitions were his "last attempt" to salvage his ongoing deception of "[filling] the fictitious assets with real ones." This statement implies there had been previous and persistent attempts to do so. Accordingly, it seems reasonable to believe that Raju's choice of language in his annual report letters would have attempted to conceal his deceit.[55] Did the words used by Raju signal deceptive conduct? Below, we analyze Raju's letters as CEO and chair of Satyam in five annual reports (for financial years 2002–3 to 2007–8) and his confession letter. Are there signals of deception in the use of personal pronouns; in the frequency of words of positivity, negativity, and of extreme emotion; and in the lexical diversity of his text?[56]

Personal pronouns. The extent to which there was a collective (rather than individual) apportionment of responsibility in Raju's letters can be gleaned by monitoring the frequency of first-person *singular* pronouns (I, me, mine, my, myself) and first-person *plural* pronouns (we, us, our, ours, ourselves). An increase in deception is likely to be represented by a reduction in first-person *singular* pronouns and an increase in first-person *plural* pronouns.[57] Drawing from this, it is reasonable to contend that as the scale of Raju's fraud developed over time, his use of first-person *plural* pronouns would have increased too. Indeed, this was found. In Raju's letter for fiscal year 2002–3, four of the nine first-person pronouns (44 percent) were plural. In comparison, in 2006–7, 82 of 84 first-person pronouns (98 percent) were plural.

Words of positivity, negativity, and extreme emotion. Raju's letters were increasingly positive in tone as the scale of his deception grew. The tone of a text is calculated as the difference between the positive and negative word count, divided by the sum of the positive and negative word counts:[58]

$$Tone = \frac{(\text{Positive word count} - \text{Negative word count})}{(\text{Positive word count} + \text{Negative word count})}$$

The positive and negative words used to calculate this measure are shown in exhibit 5.2.

Exhibit 5.2 Positive and negative words

POSITIVITY Word List
Positive positives success successes successful succeed succeeds succeeding succeeded accomplish accomplishes accomplishing accomplished accomplishment accomplishments strong strength strengths certain certainty definite solid excellent good achieve achieves achieved achieving achievement achievements progress progressing deliver delivers delivered delivering leader leading pleased reward rewards rewarding rewarded opportunity opportunities enjoy enjoys enjoying enjoyed encouraged encouraging up increase increases increasing increased rise rises rising rose risen improve improves improving improved improvement improvements strengthen strengthens strengthening strengthened stronger strongest better best more most above record high higher highest greater greatest larger largest grow grows growing grew grown growth expand expands expanding expanded expansion exceed exceeds exceeded exceeding beat beats beating

NEGATIVITY Word List
Negative negatives fail fails failing failure weak weakness weaknesses difficult difficulty hurdle hurdles obstacle obstacles slump slumps slumping slumped uncertain uncertainty unsettled unfavorable downturn depressed disappoint disappoints disappointing disappointed disappointment risk risks risky threat threats penalty penalties down decrease decreases decreasing decreased decline declines declining declined fall falls falling fell fallen drop drops dropping dropped deteriorate deteriorates deteriorating deteriorated worsen worsens worsening weaken weakens weakening weakened worse worst low lower lowest less least smaller smallest shrink shrinks shrinking shrunk below under challenge challenges challenging challenged

Source: Henry (2008, p. 387).

The theoretical maximum value of *tone* is +1 (perfectly positive). The theoretical minimum is −1 (perfectly negative). Using this measure of tone, a study of 1366 annual earnings press releases in the telecommunications and computer industries between 1998 and 2002 found a mean value for tone of 0.568. Several observers have claimed there is a bias toward positive language in annual reports[59] and that a tone measure of between 0.5 and 0.6 should be expected.

Persons engaging in deception are likely to allay scrutiny of their affairs by choosing words with a highly positive tone. The use of negative words in the chair's statements in annual reports has been associated with subsequent company failure.[60] There seem good grounds to believe that the tone of Raju's letters would consistently be highly positive – and that this would be increasingly so as the scale of his deception grew. This was found to be the case.

Raju's CEO letters projected a highly positive tone throughout. The observed score for tone in each letter ranged from 0.586 to 1.00 – all higher than the mean score of 0.568 observed in the study of annual earnings press releases mentioned previously.[61] The frequency of Raju's extreme positive words increased from 2002–3 onwards. The ratio of extreme positive words to extreme negative words was 44 percent in 2002–3, but this jumped strongly to 82 percent in 2003–4. This result is consistent with conjecture that probing by the Indian tax officials and company regulators in 2002–3 would have made Raju skittish. Thus, it is not surprising that the tone of Raju's letters became noticeably more positive. Indeed, the maximum possible score for positivity (1.00) was achieved in 2006–7.

These findings are consistent with Raju deliberately putting an increasingly positive spin on Satyam's results and prospects as the scale of his deception grew. He was keen to allay concerns about the company's true financial performance and his ethical conduct. Thus, it is not surprising that Raju's letters revealed a high ratio of extreme positive words to extreme negative words in the three financial years immediately prior to his confession. In 2007–8, for example, Raju used 17 words of extreme positive emotion to one word of extreme negative emotion. Such usage suggests Raju attempted to put a positive spin on the matters reported. This is consistent with the argument that his emotional state was affected by the ongoing deception and that this, in turn, influenced him to use more words of extreme positive emotion. However, any assessment of these results should be mindful that senior executives such as Raju would be expected "to use emotionally vibrant terms [because they are] cheerleaders for their company."[62]

A study of Raju's CEO letters to shareholders[63] using DICTION text analysis software reported that scores for the master variable, CERTAINTY, prior to the confession letter were all in the expected normal range. However, the level of confidence indicated by the CERTAINTY variable seemed to follow a three-step function. For 2002–3 and 2003–4, the score for CERTAINTY was 52.25. As pressure built up on Raju because of his deceptive conduct (that is, from 2003–4), the score fell to 49.5 and plateaued there for four years. Then, in the confession letter of 2009, it collapsed significantly to 42.87 and became considerably out of normal range. This pattern is consistent with the view that falling levels of certainty reflect the accumulating impact of deceptive written communications. What is seemingly counterintuitive is the low score for CERTAINTY in Raju's very public confession letter. However, this can be explained by subsequent revelations that Raju's confession letter was less than honest because it disguised further irregularities in Satyam's affairs.[64]

Additional insight to lexical diversity can be obtained by delving into the elements that comprise the CERTAINTY master variable. CERTAINTY is calculated by DICTION as comprising measures for the following component variables:

(TENACITY + LEVELING + COLLECTIVES + INSISTENCE) − (NUMERICAL TERMS + AMBIVALENCE + SELF REFERENCE + VARIETY).[65]

Closer examination of the level, pattern, and in-range/out-of-range characteristics of these component variables is instructive. The scores for one of these component variables, NUMERICAL TERMS, are revealing. They suggest an apparent reluctance by Raju to use numerical terms (at least as "numerical" is defined by DICTION) in his high-profile CEO letters.[66] This is consistent with Raju not wanting to alert readers to his deceptive conduct. If he had made specific, quantified claims, they probably would have attracted unwanted scrutiny. Thus, Raju under-used numerical expressions. Such a view is consistent with evidence that the exclusion of quantitative information in company narratives is a way of managing external perceptions.[67]

Concluding Comments

The language in Raju's annual report letters reveals strong use of first-person *plural* pronouns, a dominant positive tone, and a preponderance of words of extreme positive emotion. However, Raju's confession letter reverted to high use of first-person *singular* pronouns, and an almost even use of extreme positive and negative words.

The choice of words in the CEO letters signed by Raju suggests he was aware of the likely harmful effects of public disclosure of Satyam's real financial position and that he adjusted his language accordingly. Raju attempted to shift the blame for Satyam's underlying (but undisclosed) problems by transitioning from the use of a singular "I, me, my, myself" (Raju) to a collective "we, us, our, ourselves" (the directors and shareholders of Satyam). The tone of the letters (as evidenced by positive/negative language choice) suggests that Raju engaged in impression management by applying a positive spin. This helped him to preserve his reputation in the business community and maintain the belief of shareholders, business commentators, and market regulators that he was leading Satyam astutely.

The emerging picture is that Raju found himself under increasing pressure to conceal the deceptions he had orchestrated. Fear of the opprobrium that would befall him from public exposure affected his written communication choices.[68] Raju chose words that helped him to disassociate from responsibility for the performance of Satyam and allowed him to share blame with others.

Parties to financial reporting and corporate governance processes should consider using the analytical methods elaborated here as part of their overall risk monitoring. These methods can be helpful in revealing signs of possible corporate distress and improper or deceptive behavior by CEOs and senior managers.

However, there is a caveat. If definite cues of deception are discovered and publicly disclosed, CEOs could adapt their communication practices to preclude offering those diagnostic cues. Thereby, they could avoid suspicion. This raises the possibility that the techniques suggested here might have a short effective life. Consequently, changes in linguistic behavior in response to such new public knowledge should be monitored diagnostically as well.

chapter six

Safety Culture

In this chapter we explore the tone at the top as evidenced in top leadership language, and the safety culture at British Petroleum [BP] prior to the *Deepwater Horizon* explosion in the Gulf of Mexico in 2010. We do so because of the considerable scope CEOs have to use language to construct the safety culture of large companies such as BP that are involved in risky operations.

At 9:45 pm on April 20, 2010, a large explosion rocked BP's *Deepwater Horizon* drilling platform 41 miles off the coast of Louisiana. Eleven workers were killed and many others were injured.[1] Oil hemorrhaged from the ruptured wellhead. The (then) US President Obama described this as "the worst environmental disaster America has ever faced."[2] BP's CEO at the time was Tony Hayward. *Deepwater Horizon* was owned by Transocean. Some other companies, such as Halliburton, were responsible for various functions related to the drilling operation. Nonetheless, BP (as operator of the platform and dominant player) was largely accountable for the disaster.[3]

Unlike our focus on *written* language in prior chapters, here we explore how tone at the top is influenced by the prepared *spoken* language (the speeches) of three CEOs of BP – Browne, Hayward, and Dudley. Analysis of the "organizational talk"[4] of CEOs of major corporations (as in their public speeches) provides a window on the culture [of an organization] and its approach to safety."[5] We draw principally on an interpretative close reading of the speech by CEO Tony Hayward to BP's annual general meeting (AGM) of shareholders on April 15, 2010, five days *before* the *Deepwater Horizon* disaster. In this speech, Hayward made the remarkable claim that safety was his "number one priority." For us, the speech highlighted the tension between BP's quest for economic efficiency and cost control on one hand, and its (presumed) desire for a strong safety culture on the other.

We also briefly analyze the transcripts of 18 other speeches Hayward delivered before the *Deepwater Horizon* explosion. These are insightful since "the speaker's life, insofar as it is public, forms a long prelude to his speech."[6] Exhibit 6.1 summarizes the date, title, venue, and number of words in each of these 18 speeches. We also briefly compare the text of Hayward's speeches as CEO of BP *before* the 2010 AGM, and the text of 125 speeches presented by his predecessor as CEO (from 1997 to 2007), Lord Browne of Madingley. Both sets of speeches yield insights to BP's ambient safety culture, tone at the top, and to each CEO's leadership-through-language.

Exhibit 6.1 Hayward's corpus of 18 speeches prior to 2010

	Date	Title	Venue	Words
1	June 4, 2007	Delivering Technologies via Carbon Markets	GLOBE Legislators Forum, Berlin	2,992
2	June 11, 2007	Securing the Future – An Oil Company Perspective	EAGE Annual Conference, London	2,203
3	June 17, 2007	Investing in Russia: A BP Perspective	Investing in Prosperity Conference, Moscow	2,311
4	Nov. 8, 2007	Energy, Security, and America	Houston	2,000
5	Apr. 17, 2008	Speech, 2008 Annual General Meeting	Docklands, London	2,224
6	June 9, 2008	How to Expand Energy Supply in the 21st Century	13th Asia Oil & Gas Conference, Kuala Lumpur	3,141
7	June 30, 2008	Speech, World Petroleum Council	World Petroleum Council, Madrid	1,847
8	July 3, 2008	Speech, London 2012 Olympic Games Sponsorship Event	British Museum, London	626
9	Nov. 25, 2008	Delivering Energy for Sustainable Growth	Tsinghua University, Beijing	3,006
10	Dec. 17, 2008	Remarks, Prince of Wales's Third Annual Accounting for Sustainability Forum	London	1,291
11	Feb. 10, 2009	28th CERA Executive Conference, Opening Speech	Houston	2,401

12	Apr. 16, 2009	Speech, 2009 AGM	ExCel centre, London	2,205
13	May 14, 2009	Speech, Accepting the Institute's First Energy Innovator Award	Institute of The Americas Conference, California	1,746
14	Oct. 8, 2009	The Role of Gas in the Future of Energy	World Gas Conference, Buenos Aires	2,000
15	Oct. 20, 2009	Meeting the Energy Challenge	Oil and Money Conference, London	2,330
16	Oct. 29, 2009	The Harsh Realities of Energy	MIT, Boston	3,275
17	Dec. 4, 2009	Energy Pathways, Setting a Course to a Sustainable Energy Future	World Oil and Gas Assembly, Bangalore	2,635
18	Mar. 23, 2009	Energy Security through Diversity	Peterson Institute	2,608
Total Words				40,841
Average Words per Speech				2,269

Source: www.bp.com.

In examining Hayward's 18 speeches prior to the 2010 AGM, we focus initially on the keyword "safety." This keyword has significant rhetorical potency[7] because it helps to construct an organization's safety culture and indicate whether safety is a desired organizational state. Consistent with such a view, it is a "good sign" if "references to safety" are among the "basic assumptions of an organization."[8]

We investigate whether the language in the speeches of Hayward and Browne reflected a tone at the top that was consistent with an enduring safety culture at BP. We also explore the extent to which, and how, CEO-speak influenced safety culture prior to the explosion. Did the language in the speeches contribute to an ideology of economic efficiency and cost control? Was the language *in*consistent with an enduring safety culture?

BP's Safety Culture

On June 17, 2010, the US Congressional Committee on Energy and Commerce investigated the *Deepwater Horizon* tragedy. Member of Congress Bart Stupak, in his opening statement to the committee, raised concerns about the ambient corporate culture at BP. He specifically implicated Tony Hayward (BP's CEO) together with Lamar McKay (chairman of BP America), Doug Suttles (chief operating officer), and exploration rig managers, claiming that the culture of BP reflected "a willingness to cut costs and take greater risks."[9]

Stupak's concern appears justified. BP had a long history of calamitous accidents before Hayward became CEO in 2007. These included a substantial oil pipeline rupture at Prudhoe Bay in Alaska in March 2006. There was also an explosion and fire at the Texas City refinery in Texas in March 2005. This resulted in 15 deaths and 170 serious injuries. BP's self-convened safety review of this latter tragedy was published in the *Report of the BP US Refineries Independent Safety Review Panel*, in January 2007. This is widely referred to as the *Baker Report*.[10]

The *Baker Report* was highly critical of BP's leadership in operational safety matters, concluding that before March 2005 there was "little to indicate … BP corporate management had effectively demonstrated its commitment to process safety."[11] The *Baker Report* admonished BP's leaders for not providing "effective process safety leadership" or establishing "process safety as a core value across all [BP's] five US refineries."[12] The board of directors of BP and its CEO and corporate management were criticized for failing to "set the process safety 'tone at the top' and establish appropriate expectations regarding process safety performance."[13]

Carolyn W. Merritt, the US Chemical Safety Board's chair and CEO, was similarly harsh in the assessment she presented to the US House of Representatives Committee on Energy and Commerce on May 16, 2007. She drew attention to the "striking similarities" in "most if not all of the root causes" of BP's Prudhoe Bay pipeline rupture in 2006 and the 2005 explosion at the BP Texas City refinery. Among the matters she highlighted were budget and production pressures that ultimately harmed safety, glaring deficiencies in how BP managed the safety of process change, untaken actions to remediate safety problems, and flawed communication of safety lessons.[14]

Thus, there are plausible grounds to believe that in the decade leading to the *Deepwater Horizon* explosion, the language of BP's top management did not reflect a strong, separately identifiable safety culture. Rather, interest in safety was linked to a broader organizational culture that stressed operational efficiency, management control, cost efficiency, and profit. Here we explore whether the speeches of BP CEOs Hayward and Browne suggest that BP paid lip service to safety.

Although safety has many "contested meanings,"[15] one important feature is that "safety culture should not be something separate from, or an addition to, an organizational culture."[16] Rather, safety should be an integral constituent of organizational culture.

Drawing from the safety science literature,[17] we define safety culture as

> … the ongoing construction of underlying assumptions, beliefs, values and attitudes shared by members of an organization in moving to an environment characterized by a quest for an absence of harm.[18]

In a large, global enterprise such as BP, numerous groups of people are engaged in widely varying forms of work that have divergent safety risks. Thus, the social construction of a unitary, organization-wide safety culture is problematic.

We investigate whether the top leadership language of BP influenced "individual perceptions of reality and sense making" regarding safety.[19] We carefully analyze Hayward's use of metaphor. This is because metaphors can frame what seems to be the "natural" or "obvious" way of talking, speaking, and writing about a topic, including identifying problems and solutions.[20] Metaphors have a strong capacity to contribute to the (social) construction of a safety culture.

BP before the *Deepwater Horizon* Disaster

Context is very important in interpreting text.[21] Although most people would expect that a large, mature, complex company engaged in high-risk operations such as BP would ensure it had a strong safety culture, this seemingly was not the case. As explained earlier, BP had sustained several major safety crises in the decade preceding the *Deepwater Horizon* explosion and many lesser reportable safety breaches too.

A few months after the *Deepwater Horizon* explosion, Hayward's replacement as CEO, Bob Dudley, confessed publicly that BP did not have an adequate safety culture prior to the explosion and that things had to be "shake[n] up."[22] BP's safety history gave Dudley good grounds for such a stance. The *Baker Report*'s assessment of the causes of the 2005 explosion of BP's Texas City plant was damning.[23] That report expressed strong concern about BP's lack of leadership in setting "the process safety 'tone at the top.'" Farley, a lawyer assisting the Baker panel, recommended that one of the "core elements for a successful safety culture" was the adoption of "the right tone at the top." He made it clear that safety is a core value and involves sending a highly visible message, beginning with the board and continuing down the line. Upper management must then "walk that talk."[24] BP's board of directors and top management (and most people associated with BP) are likely to have been aware in 2007 of the *Baker Report*'s severe and detailed rebuke of BP for its deficient safety culture.

The report of the US Chemical Safety and Hazard Investigation Board (CSB) on the Texas City refinery explosion in 2005 admonished BP for its safety culture and attributed responsibility to "organizational causes embedded in the refinery's culture," as follows:

- BP Texas City lacked a reporting and learning culture. Reporting bad news was not encouraged and often Texas City managers did not effectively investigate incidents or take appropriate corrective action.
- BP Group lacked focus on controlling major hazard risk. BP management paid attention to, measured, and rewarded personal safety rather than process safety.
- BP Group and Texas City managers provided ineffective leadership and oversight. BP management did not implement adequate safety oversight. [25]

The lessons from the Texas City explosion and many other safety crises at BP had not permeated the company by 2010. According to Steffy, a Houston-based journalist,

> [d]espite Hayward's vow to make safety a priority, and despite all the procla-
> mations of the "new BP" ... its management structure was still convoluted,
> accountability was hard to find, decisions were made by committee, and cost
> cutting and financial performance continued to overshadow operations.[26]

Steffy's assessment is supported by the opening statement of William K. Reilly, co-chair of the US National Commission on the *Deepwater Horizon* Oil Spill and Offshore Drilling, to that Commission on November 9, 2010. He stated, "We know a safety culture must be led from the top and permeate a company. ... BP has been notoriously challenged on matters of process safety."[27]

CEO Language and the Construction of a Safety Culture

CEO-speak has strong potential to help construct "the right tone at the top" and to enshrine safety as a core organizational value. The language of CEOs of large, complex organizations involved in risky endeavors can strongly influence safety by propagating and enabling "shared beliefs and values" relating to safety.[28] Such a view is consistent with thinking that although "culture is created by shared experience … it is the leader who initiates this process by imposing his or her beliefs, values, and assumptions."[29] CEO-speak is a primary means of such imposition.

Many CEOs talk and write about safety and the various structures, systems, and policies involved. They purport to elicit and reward safe behavior. Sometimes their speeches and other communications reflect a *normative* view of safety culture.[30] Sometimes they are *pragmatic* too, by talking and writing about specific practices that are designed to enable safety.[31] The earnestness and clarity of such talking and writing can indicate whether safety is an "overriding commitment."[32] Also important is the "vocabulary of safety leading";[33] that is, the set of related words guiding a CEO's organizational communications regarding known and unknown risks and dangers.

Through their written and oral discourse, CEOs can foster a corporate climate in which a safety culture is actively developed. They can encourage staff to aspire to achieve an absence-of-harm environment. The tone at the top rendered by CEO-speak can reinforce a safety consciousness. Furthermore, an organization's commitment to safety and a safety culture[34] must be reinforced by, and not be at odds with, key aspects of the organization's management control processes and systems (such as compensation incentives).

CEO Speeches

A company's annual general meeting (AGM) is "an essential aspect of corporate governance."[35] The AGM provides an opportunity for a CEO to communicate directly with shareholders. However, shareholders are only one of many groups interested in the speech given by the CEO to the AGM. A wide range of other stakeholder groups (including employees, unions, environmental activists, competitors, the public at large, and various news media) are also attentive to the words of the CEO. Thus, the CEO's speech is an integral part of what makes an AGM "a primary vehicle for perpetuating … corporate culture."[36] The speech can help stakeholders construct meaning by identifying, labeling, and organizing events and ideas, including strategies and performance measures.[37] Whatever the CEO includes (or excludes) is noticed. The speech is not merely a ritual but "a powerful setting for accountability."[38]

Hayward's speech on April 15, 2010, to BP's AGM in London comprised 2,323 words. This was his third such speech as CEO to an AGM of BP. Analysis of Hayward's speech helps to understand his leadership-through-language with respect to safety. Did the language he used contribute positively or negatively to the ongoing construction of BP's safety culture? Did the speech refer directly or indirectly to safety? Given the company's purported renewed concern for safety at the time of the speech, it would be reasonable to expect to find strong explicit mentions (and subtle *implicit* instances) of espoused values and attitudes regarding safety, together with a formal statement of BP's philosophy regarding safety.

The word "safety" was used only 17 times in the corpus of Hayward's 18 speeches (comprising 40,841 words) *prior* to his 2010 AGM speech (see exhibit 6.1). This frequency is low considering BP's poor safety history and it supports conjecture that senior executives were not engaged actively in normative discourse to promote a strong safety culture. Hayward mentions "safe(ty)" in referring to a corporate project (speech 3); safe(ty) (of) oil supplies (speeches 4 and 18); and the title of a BP report (speech 10). The word "culture" appears only four times but none of these uses is linked to safety.

Such results are not surprising given that Hayward's predecessor as CEO, Lord Browne, used the word "safety" only 56 times, and the word "safe" only 15 times, in the 332,847 words comprising his 125 public speeches as CEO from May 19, 1997, to April 26, 2007.[39] In contrast, Browne used the word "cost" 224 times – about three times more than "safe(ty)." He used the word "culture" 39 times, but in ways that were not associated with safety or with words related to safety.

A similar pattern has been found for Boeing. This company's safety culture was scrutinized after the crash of two Boeing MAX 737 aircraft in October 2017 and March 2018, causing 346 deaths. A word search of Boeing's annual reports for a five-year period prior to 2018 and for its principal competitor, Airbus, is instructive. Boeing used words with the stem "safe" 76 times while Airbus used these words 397 times. In their respective annual reports for 2018, "Boeing used two profit words for every safety word, while Airbus [used] one profit word for every safety word."[40] This is not surprising in view of criticism that (then) Boeing CEO Dennis Muilenburg was "part of a culture of excessive bean counting ... [and supported a] ... cost–cutting ethos."[41]

CEO Hayward's 2010 AGM speech

We now present fourteen observations of Hayward's speech to BP's AGM in 2010. The entire speech, with line numbering added, is reproduced in appendix C.

Lines 63–8: Our priorities which lie at the heart of all our operations remain safety, people and performance ... Our focus on safe and reliable operations is now strongly embedded in all our businesses; we are continuing to build on the core capabilities of our people; and we have started to see the benefits of improved operational performance flowing through to the bottom line.

Observation 1. Hayward's claim that safety, people, and performance are "at the heart of all our operations" emphasizes the centrality of safety, people, and performance. However, the metaphor of the heart as a source of organic life-sustenance seems incomplete because Hayward fails to mention the brain, the source of cognitive leadership. Although mentioning "safety" before "people" and "performance" seems a positive indicator of the rhetorical construction of a safety culture,[42] it is not clear who the "people" are to whom Hayward refers. Are they all possible stakeholders in BP, including those whose lives were disrupted by the company's activities? Or is his view restricted to shareholders and (perhaps) employees?

The modifier "remain" implies that such importance was always the case and continues to be so. However, the use of "now" in "Our focus on safe and reliable operations is *now* strongly embedded in all our businesses" implies that such a focus was not "strongly embedded" previously. Thus, there is an inconsistency between the words *remain* and *now*. How can anyone lead a major global oil company without attending constantly to an embedding of "safe and reliable operations"? Further, by listing "safety," "people," and "performance" separately, Hayward apparently regards safety as something that can be compartmentalized. He does not seem to regard safety as an "integral constituent"[43] of BP's culture.

Observation 2. Hayward claims that BP's "focus [is] on safe and reliable operations." However, he mentions several "focuses," thereby diluting the rhetorical effectiveness of the word "focus." We are told BP is "*focusing* on deepening our capability by putting the right people with the right skills in the right place" (lines 85–6). In line 112, the claimed "*focus*" on "efficiency" is a "steadfast" one, suggesting that "efficiency" is a primary focus. Can such a focus on "efficiency" be reconciled with the "safe and reliable operations" mentioned earlier? Can a company have multiple focuses, not a unitary focus? If so, a complex company such as BP must necessarily establish operational and management control systems to effect multiple focuses in meaningful ways. There is no mention of such systems. In telling his audience what is being focused on, Hayward glides over the problematic nature of the "focusing" involved.

Lines 70–4: Safety remains our number one priority and I'm pleased to report we can see clear progress. There has been a significant reduction in the frequency of recordable injuries and the number of major incidents related to integrity failures has also fallen. At the same time we're reducing containment losses in our operations.

Observation 3. Even though it is alleged "safety remains our number one priority", the criteria for "we can see clear progress" are not elaborated well. Indeed, a comparison of the facts provided regarding safety, and those stated later in respect of financial performance, is telling. Only one of the 24 performance measures Hayward mentions in his speech (see exhibit 6.2) refers to safety ("recordable injuries," line 72).[44] Hayward could have touched on many safety matters; for example, is a culture of operational safety exemplified by regular safety meetings and by rewarding safety improvement suggestions? How is safety performance embedded in

---

Exhibit 6.2 Performance measures in Hayward's speech to BP's AGM on April 15, 2010

Performance Measure	Line Number(s) in Speech (Appendix C)
cost(s)	40, 55, 100, 104, 108, 129
investment/invest	44–5
cash flow	53
recordable injuries	72
number of major incidents related to integrity failures	72–3
containment losses	73–4
matching people, skills, places	86
competitive gap	94
efficiency	100, 102, 112, 184, 185, 198, 206
refining margins	110
reserves replacement	123, 124, 169
production growth	124–5, 154–5, 157
headcount	132
new (oil) resources, projects	152, 159
larger, advantaged refineries	175
supply optimization capability	176–7
earnings (return on capital) versus peers	182
value chain/supply chain performance	106, 185
upstream project execution	186
safe and reliable operations	193
clearer accountabilities	195
standard designs and equipment	196–7
new culture	202
costs, capital efficiency and margin quality	206–7

employee compensation systems? What influence did the *Baker Report* have on safety? Does the "significant reduction" mentioned mean significant in a statistical sense? What does the expression "integrity failures" mean?

How can safety be "our number one priority" when "safety" is mentioned only twice in the speech's 2323 words? This implies a simple view of a complex concept. Hayward focuses instead on the financial numbers and the importance of driving down costs. The emphasis on non-safety performance measures is evident in the summary in exhibit 6.2 of the various financial and other (non-safety) performance measures he mentions. The privileging of financial performance over safety is reflected by the preponderance of accounting-based non-safety-related performance measures and by failure to acknowledge the complexity of safety culture as an evolving and ongoing organizational challenge.

If safety (rather than cost cutting) is an overarching objective at BP, some tangible justification should be offered regarding how safety is improved, or at least maintained. Any explanation should go beyond merely alluding to myopic after-the-event metrics such as reportable incidents. Hayward's emphasis on financial and economic performance measures directs attention to shared beliefs and values *other than* safety. Thus, a normative view of safety culture[45] is served poorly.

Observation 4. The metaphor DRIVE appears six times. "Driving" and "driven" are used once each. These uses reflect Hayward's approach to leadership. His claim at line 100–1 that "The drive to increase efficiency and reduce costs remains a key focus for everyone at BP" is hyperbole. Everyone? The root metaphor "drive" suggests that Hayward's leadership is characterized by a relentless push to increase efficiency and reduce costs. Such behavior seems inconsistent with the ongoing construction of a safety culture.

A firm such as BP is highly unlikely to be able to drive down costs *and* improve safety simultaneously.[46] How does Hayward know that *everyone* in BP has a common focus on greater safety at reduced cost? This presumes a type of unitary organizational culture that is unrealistic in a large company that undertakes work with high risk.

Observation 5. Hayward does not use safety-related words such as "risk," "hazard," "maintenance," "repair," "prevent," or "accident" as part of a "vocabulary of safety leading."[47] There are parallels here with the "faster, better, cheaper" ideological credo of the National Aeronautics and Space Administration in the early 1990s. This credo was implicated as a cause of the disintegration of the *Columbia* space shuttle on re-entry to the Earth's atmosphere in 2003 and the deaths of its seven crew.[48]

> **Lines 103–9**: [W]e are leading our peer group in driving down [upstream] production costs, with BP's unit costs in 2009 12 percent lower than in 2008. We will maintain this momentum through activity choice and in the way we manage the supply chain. ... our efficiency initiatives have reduced [downstream] cash costs by more than 15 percent in 2009 and our goal over the next 2 to 3 years is to return costs to 2004 levels. For the group as a whole we reduced our cash costs last year by more than $4 billion.

Observation 6. The stress on "driving down production costs" and the claim that BP will "maintain this momentum through ... manag[ing] the supply chain" are mechanistic prescriptions. "Momentum," when allied with the many uses of "drive," reinforces the master JOURNEY metaphor. The emphasis on cost management and economic efficiency is confounding because it constrains the capacity of the tone at the top to help construct a safety culture.

The 12 percent reduction in BP's unit production costs in one year is astounding. Yet this is left as an unproblematic statistic. Although the word "cost" and its underlying concepts are far from straightforward, there is no hint of complexity. The sheer magnitude of the cost reduction should have been commented on. How did different production units contribute to reduce costs? The upshot is that cost is rendered rhetorically and ideologically unproblematic. So too is the potential for such a sudden, huge reduction to disrupt any potential safety culture.

> **Lines 110–13**: In 2009, lower oil and gas prices and weak refining margins created a challenging environment for the whole sector. But the operational momentum in our business and our steadfast focus on efficiency has clearly improved our performance relative to our peers.

Observation 7. The expression "operational momentum" suggests a large, unstoppable physical object. Hayward and his colleagues in the "refreshed" top management team (lines 83–4) seem to be claiming credit for engineering an entity that can progress largely unimpeded at a time when all major oil companies faced "a challenging environment" due to factors largely beyond their control ("lower oil and gas prices and weak refining margins"). Nonetheless, it is difficult to accept that the operational virtuosity displayed by BP (and fashioned by Hayward and colleagues since 2007) "has clearly improved our performance relative to our peers" (such as Shell and Texaco). Are BP's peers less astute and possibly relatively inept, as implied? Perhaps "our peers" did not drive down costs like BP or match people and skills in the way that BP alleges? Perhaps "our peers" are more safety conscious and better employers? Here "competitive talk" and the performance of peers is invoked to "generate consent" and "discourage potentially creative stakeholder conflict."[49] The implication is that the "focus on efficiency" is acceptable and virtuous because of pressures imposed by markets and competitors.

> **Lines 178–80**: [W]hile our portfolio ranks amongst the best in the industry, our financial performance has yet to fully reflect this. There is now a real opportunity to make this portfolio work harder for us and we intend to do just that.

Observation 8. The expression "make this portfolio work harder for us" seems to be a euphemism for "push operations and safety to the limit in the quest for profits." Who are the (unmentioned) people in "this portfolio"? Hayward seems to be thinking only of shareholders because the identity of "us" is apparent in lines 8–9. There he states candidly that he wants BP to "make our asset base work harder for our shareholders."[50] Any CEO with such a narrow focus runs the risk of ignoring that the economic welfare of shareholders in a company engaged in risky operations depends on constructing and enabling a robust safety culture.

The PORTFOLIO metaphor here views BP through a finance lens. This obscures the complexity and humanity of BP and suggests that BP's leaders prioritize the demands of financial capital markets. However, such a metaphorical perspective is inconsistent with the "embedding" of a safety culture at BP. The notion of "mak[ing] this portfolio work harder" and Hayward's expressed intent "to do just that" are single-focused and egregious. Although the rhetorical flourish involved *is* consistent with top-down management, it is *not* consistent with the ongoing construction of a safety culture.

> **Lines 181–6**: So how do we define the opportunity? There are many ways … from company-wide issues such as the gap in earnings versus our peers, to return on capital employed versus the competition; and from segment-level issues such as improving refining efficiency and closing the gap in fuels value chain performance in the US to improving efficiency in our drilling and in the execution of projects in the upstream.

Observation 9. Hayward adopts an inquisitorial, professorial pose for rhetorical effect. The expression "many ways to view it" signals the multiple perspectives that Hayward and colleagues have adopted. These involve accounting performance measures and/or measures that are not exclusively accounting-based, such as "improving refining efficiency." The focus is clearly on technical, economic, and financial measures.

The ways that Hayward "define[s] the opportunity" signal an awareness that success, or "opportunity," can be measured in many ways. This is a good thing when talking about the performance of BP. Hayward's stance contrasts with that of Enron's CEO Jeffrey Skilling and President Kenneth Lay. In 2001, they asserted that Enron was "laser-focused" on the singular and inapt accounting measure "earnings per share."[51] However, Hayward's performance targets for BP are not linked with his bold claim at line 70 that "Safety remains our number one priority."

> **Lines 187–8:** Whichever way you look at it, there are significant opportunities for improvement and in every case firm plans are in place to close those gaps.

Observation 10. Hayward is again resolute and is exercising top-down leadership. Are the plans negotiated with operating management? Are they inflexible? What are these "firm plans?" The audience should not be satisfied with this vagueness. Hayward's statement that "there are significant opportunities for improvement" acknowledges the multiplicity of ways to set targets and measure performance. However, "improvement" is to be gauged in terms limited to traditional accounting, finance, and market performance measures. There is no mention of safety-related measures.

> **Lines 189–91:** Our goal over the next few years is to realize the latent potential of our asset base by improving the efficiency and effectiveness of everything we do.

Observation 11. The assertion "by improving ... everything we do" is grandiose and not realistic. There are strong traces of a public relations persona – one that intends to induce a generally "feel-good" mood in the audience rather than provide a fulsome accountability narrative. Listeners (and subsequent readers) would most likely be disinclined to try to discern the entailments of the complex metaphor used ("latent potential of our asset base"). The implicit rhetoric and attendant ideology are singularly limited and unrealistic because all that is alleged to be needed to improve BP's world is a focus on economic "efficiency and effectiveness."

> **Lines 201–2:** All of this will be underpinned by our continuing investment in technology and by the new culture we are establishing at BP.

Observation 12. The casual reference to "establishing" a "new culture" at BP is the first mention of culture. Yet, creating a new culture is a major challenge that requires substantial effort. Is the idea of instituting a new culture consistent with such a casual mention? If the CEO refers to this new culture only in passing, what is the prospect employees will take it seriously? Hayward says no more about what this "new culture" is supposed to be. He does not mention how it differs from what preceded it. Is everyone just *supposed* to know?

> **Lines 208–11**: Of course the future looks challenging. It always does. But we have emerged from 2009 in great shape and with renewed confidence and determination. We can see the prize and we believe we are well positioned to capture it.

Observation 13. Hayward frames his conclusion using "the future" as a metaphor. The "of course" naturalizes the challenging nature of "the future" rhetorically and is reinforced by "It always does." These words carry the implicit message that Hayward and colleagues have always faced the trials posed by an unruly and unpredictable "broader environment" (line 11). This discursive strategy positions Hayward and his senior management colleagues in a forgiving space in which they have no control over this "challenging future." The use of "prize" is curious too. How is "prize" defined? Does it include a safer BP that arises from an accommodating proactive tone at the top? Who are the "we" who can (metaphorically) "see" such an ill-defined "prize"? How will "we" recognize it? Is a broad range of stakeholders (including "the public") envisaged within the "we"? Unlikely.

> **Lines 212–14**: I want to thank the employees of BP for their commitment – and I want to thank each of you as shareholders for your loyalty and support. I hope you will continue to support us on the journey that lies ahead. Thank you.

Observation 14. This is the only time that Hayward mentions "employees." Presumably, "employees" are the "our people" referred to at lines 66–7 and 82. If they are so good at outperforming their peers, they deserve more mention. Indeed, how does Hayward know about employee "commitment"? What is the likely level of commitment of the 7,500 employees who comprise the "headcount" reduction mentioned in line 132? Throughout the speech, when Hayward mentions people, he seems to be alluding to senior managers, not the other employees of BP.

Concluding Comments

Hayward's speech to BP's AGM is disingenuous. It encourages belief that BP is going to do what few (if any) complex, large corporations involved in high-risk undertakings can do or have done: drive down costs *and* increase capital efficiency *while* maintaining a first priority of safe and reliable operations. Does Hayward really believe BP can do this? Or is he simply telling (ostensibly) gullible shareholders what he thinks they and observers of the company want to hear? His speech is corporate jingoism: a deliberately "upbeat account"[52] and a public rallying cry.

Hayward claims to be close to "mak[ing] our asset base work harder for shareholders" (lines 8–9). While he is expansive about how and why economic efficiency will be achieved, he does not mention any implications for safety or operational management. Nor does he mention how cutting costs by "driving [them] down" will affect safety, employee welfare, job security, and good environmental citizenship. An implicit taboo here needs deconstructing[53] – the taboo against acknowledging the effect cutting costs will have on safety.

Any drive to increase efficiency (described variously by Hayward as reducing costs, countering cost inflation, driving down production costs, reducing cash costs by 15 percent) would probably affect other parts of BP's complex operations. There would be disadvantageous flow-on effects to one or more interrelated matters of safety, employee morale, job security, and the condition of capital equipment. The idea that economic efficiency can be achieved without affecting or compromising safety in any way is bold. Hayward seems obsessed with economic efficiency and beating competitors. Despite his platitudes regarding safety, the BP he leads will be "driven" to cut costs on operations and safety wherever it can. The tone at the top is one of "join us on a journey to a financial Nirvana – we'll be lean, keen and operationally sound."

The master metaphor coursing through the speech is BP IS ON A JOURNEY TOWARD A GREAT FINANCIAL PRIZE.

This is a classic example of the metaphor of the wagon train "voyaging across the hostile, virtually limitless, American frontier" on a journey involving "organized, self-confident leaders and acquiescent non-leaders [who] move forward towards the greater public good."[54]

Despite inevitable challenges in the path of the BP wagon train, the heroic trail boss [Hayward] will get all who travel with BP to their destination. The BP wagon train has moved ahead successfully because BP has "refreshed" its trail bosses (line 83) and has reviewed its "whole approach to the organization" of it (lines 84–5).

The speech dwells on what the excellent team, organization, and system of the BP wagon train has achieved. It has "closed the competitive gap," "restored momentum," and "[grown] production" (lines 95–6). Despite this, BP's wagon train is obsessed with its "track record" and what other wagon trains (its peers) are doing. The trail boss (Hayward) says "we can see the prize ... the journey that lies ahead" (lines 210, 214). Here the ideology is evident: the prize is a reward to capital. It is not a reward to labor, the environment, or social equity. The prize is *not* exemplary safety performance or a work environment that represents an absence of harm.

There are very few references to safety in Hayward's 19 speeches and in Browne's 125 speeches. This indicates that the concept of safety existed in a curious linguistic lacuna in BP's upper management. Hayward and Browne used language to shape a culture at BP that gave short shrift to safety. Their public speeches did not promote a safety culture but encouraged great attention to financial and operating efficiency and associated management control systems.

As a reinforcing point, we draw attention to a speech to the Economic Club of Chicago on January 13, 2012, (almost two years after the *Deepwater Horizon* explosion) by the (then) CEO of BP, Bob Dudley. He stated, "The *Deepwater Horizon* accident and oil spill took eleven lives, injured dozens more, and disrupted the livelihoods of people in the Gulf Coast region."[55] This is all far too mild. The *Deepwater Horizon* disaster was *not* simply an "accident" according to numerous observers.[56] Limiting comment to "livelihoods" is disingenuous too because it crudely ignores major health and environmental effects. Dudley's claim that "Despite our best efforts, some oil did reach the shore."[57] Some? The spill exceeded 210 million US gallons (about 795 million liters).[58] He ignores the likely ongoing effects of the vast quantity of oil dispersed in the Gulf of Mexico. He made no mention of any culpability for the effects of "the company's evident failure to bring the problem rapidly under control."[59]

The public speeches of a succession of CEOs of BP (Browne, Hayward, and Dudley) are troubling. Their CEO-speak was influenced unduly by an ideology of extreme economic efficiency. They did not use language that would have helped them to put in place a safe environment offering an absence of harm.

In the addendum below, we draw on the *Deepwater Horizon* case to argue that auditors should more closely audit a CEO's language and report its effects on operational safety risks, company culture, and tone at the top.

Addendum: Safety Culture, Auditing, and "Fairly Presented" Financial Statements

In June 2010, a class action lawsuit citing BP's "history of safety lapses, cost cutting and workplace disasters" was lodged in the US District Court in Louisiana on behalf of BP shareholders. The suit alleged that BP "misled investors before the April 20, 2010, *Deepwater Horizon* oil spill" by claiming it "had the technology to safely conduct" operations in the Gulf of Mexico. The suit cited "BP's long history of spills, fires and explosions" and alleged that "BP violated the Securities Exchange Act of 1934 by issuing false and misleading statements about safety, technology, inspections and precautions at its offshore oil facilities."[60]

BP's association with a series of *regular* major safety-related incidents in the past decade reveal it to be an industry outlier in safety consciousness and safety performance. Thus, it is not surprising that major legal proceedings were commenced against BP on the grounds of operational safety negligence. Indeed, in 2008, two years before the *Deepwater Horizon* explosion, we queried BP's tone at the top and ambient operational safety culture.[61] We were not alone in our concerns. Many observers of BP (such as industry analysts, journalists, academics, and representatives of labor unions) had been conscious of the company's cost-cutting mentality. This was described variously as "pugilistic" and "relentless" and as having "spawned a culture of disaster."[62]

Closer dialogue is needed between operational auditors, who are responsible for assessing a company's safety systems, and financial auditors. Given BP's poor safety record, the company's financial statements for accounting periods before April 20, 2010, should have established an account titled "provision for disasters" and adjusted this account at least annually. Doing so would be consistent with the tenor of the fairness of presentation objectives of International Financial Reporting Standards (IFRS). Providing for a major operational disaster would be consistent too with calls made in international professional, economic, and political arenas after the global financial crisis of 2008–9 for better appreciation (and disclosure) of business risk, broadly conceived.[63]

Our proposal for a "provision for disaster" is consistent with International Standard on Auditing 315 (ISA): Identifying and Assessing the Risks of Material Misstatement through Understanding the Entity and Its Environment (effective December 2009).[64] This standard defines "business risk" as "a risk resulting from significant conditions, events, circumstances, actions or inactions that could adversely affect an entity's ability to achieve its objectives and execute its strategies" (para 4a). ISA 315 calls on auditors to "discuss with management whether business risks relevant to financial reporting objectives have been identified and how they have been addressed" (para 17). Our call for a provision for disaster in BP's accounts is consistent with the thinking on which ISA 315 is predicated.

A close examination of BP's tone at the top and culture reveals a high likelihood that a major safety-related disaster would befall BP every few years. The company's operating history indicated it was prone to such disasters – and not just those caused by acts of nature. The class action lawsuit (para 180) points to BP's proneness to disasters. This was indicated in "internal communication by project managers to senior staff in BP … [that there was] … a serious risk of catastrophic disaster." Leveson, an industrial safety expert, has characterized BP as "an accident waiting to happen."[65] Steffy, a journalist, claimed that the company had a "fractured management system … [and] a culture that talks about safety, yet emphasizes profit."[66] Despite the apparent persistence of such behavior in BP, no acknowledgment of BP's susceptibility to disaster was included in the company's financial reports or identified by conventional auditing procedures.

BP's audited financial statements for 2008 and 2009 made no provision for the wide variety of environmental and legal costs the company could incur from a major future operational disaster. In our view, the absence of such a provision rendered BP's audited financial statements noncompliant with the broad fairness of presentation objectives of IFRS. The *Deepwater Horizon* explosion (or a similar operational disaster) was a reasonably foreseeable event given the portfolio of operational risks borne by BP, the company's tone at the top, and its poor safety culture. In the interests of fairness of presentation, there should have been a "provision for disaster" in the accounts.

Which of BP's specific ongoing exploration, drilling, and refining operations would be the site of a future disaster was almost impossible to predict. Nonetheless, there is a strong case that a liability existed and had been growing for many years. The deep water drilling in which BP was engaged is inherently hazardous. Consequently, the financial position and results of operations reported in the company's group accounts for 2009 were potentially misstated, probably materially so.

Any company that makes a provision for a disaster in its accounts would most likely face considerable backlash and reputational opprobrium. However, this would be beneficial in motivating improvements in operational safety culture. Ultimately, it would help to drive down the amount of the provision for disaster over time. At the very least, companies should be required to provide frank narrative assessments of the effects of likely unfa-vorable operational accidents and natural disasters. Auditors should regard tone at the top and corporate culture as meaningful audit concepts, con-sistent with the emphasis on understanding audit risk comprehensively, required by ISA 315.

A better and broader conception of audit risk will help identify cor-porate cultures that are overly partial to risk and help generate financial statements that are more reliable. Auditors should develop a deeper under-standing of the risks posed by any company's less-than-satisfactory safety culture.

chapter seven

Twitter

In this and the following three chapters, we focus on the *medium* CEOs use for their communications. We begin by directing attention to the social media platform, Twitter. This is a relatively new and potent technology for corporate communication. A stream of tweets from a CEO's personal Twitter account is often part of a wide range of communication media that a CEO uses to exercise leadership through language. Those tweets can build and maintain the CEO's personal image or brand and establish the actual and perceived organizational culture of the company the CEO leads.

This chapter outlines some of the benefits and pitfalls of a CEO's use of a personal Twitter account. As we elaborate below, in terms of benefits, tweeting can facilitate direct, "unfiltered" communication, provide faster and immediate lines of communication, and allow effective access to larger and different (usually younger) audiences. As for pitfalls, a CEO's personal tweets can expose inauthentic leaders and be used in an undisciplined and often embarrassing way. We also draw attention to some practical considerations and cautions when analyzing a CEO's personal tweets.

Twitter enables users to post short messages (tweets) to followers who have a publicly available profile. In January 2019, approximately 500 million tweets were sent daily and 326 million people used Twitter monthly. About 80 percent of Twitter users were not American. Users were skewed in favor of people who were urban, educated, and who had high incomes.[1]

Part of the popular appeal of Twitter lies in the ability of users to elect to "follow" (that is, monitor) any other user with a public profile. Each tweet is sent to all who follow the tweeter. Thus, users can interact with celebrities or CEOs by responding to their tweets. Unlike many other communication mediums, Twitter goes "beyond factual information to provide a wide range of public opinion on a topic … jokes, rumour, commentary and opinion."[2]

On November 7, 2017, the allowable length of tweet messages was increased from 140 characters to 280 characters. Tweeters can also upload photos or short videos and include links to them. Each tweet has a time-stamp indicating the time and date a tweet was sent. Tweets have operating system tags that state the type of device used to send the tweet. This is usually "via iPhone" or "via Android."

On August 4, 2020, the three most-followed persons on Twitter were former US President Barack Obama (121 million followers), Canadian singer Justin Bieber (112 million), and American singer Katy Perry (108 million).[3] On that date, the publicly accessible Twitter account of Virgin Group Chairman Sir Richard Branson indicated he had 12.6 million followers. The most prominent purveyor of tweets is (former) US President Donald Trump.[4] On August 4, 2020, he had about 84.5 million followers and had sent about 54,200 tweets.[5] His use of Twitter has been described as "a new form of presidential talk"[6] that enables the "politics of debasement."[7] Trump's tweets are claimed to contribute to a "semiotics of authenticity"[8] that has been instrumental in his political success.

The CEO-speak in Twitter messages can be analyzed in depth and with considerable subtlety using the close reading techniques demonstrated earlier. However, we do not apply these techniques here. Rather, we focus on several fresh analytical perspectives that have been prompted by the unique characteristics of Twitter.

The rise of Twitter and various other forms of social media (such as Facebook, Snapchat, and Instagram) has prompted research in many areas of corporate endeavor (such as reputation formation[9] and disclosure[10]). This has led to claims that Twitter is "used more actively for business" than Facebook.[11] Many CEOs are now prodigious users of Twitter. They value it as a strategic tool for conveying information to stakeholders (such as customers, employees, and investors) and for influencing opinions.

While technology changes (such as those involving Twitter) have led to a morphing in the mode of communications CEOs use, there is an unending necessity for CEOs to "lead through language." So, although social media (such as Twitter) represent a new technology of communication, the underlying essence of a CEO's language endures and perhaps becomes more potent. CEO-speak in a stream of tweets from a CEO's personal Twitter account should be recognized as an important element in establishing the actual and perceived culture of a company and in building and maintaining the CEO's personal brand.

We illustrate the benefits and pitfalls of a CEO's use of Twitter by introducing examples from a corpus of tweets on the personal Twitter accounts of

Uber CEO Dara Khosrowshahi and Tesla CEO Elon Musk.[12] Many of these tweets have attracted "likes": that is, expressions of "positive sentiment."[13]

Benefits

Unfiltered Communication

Twitter is an unmediated, almost real-time, personal connection directly between a CEO and a network of followers. Twitter allows CEOs to directly communicate with an intended audience without any filtering or sanitizing of their message by journalists or other intermediaries inside or outside the company. Thus, many tweets emanate from the mind of the CEO "without revision or reflection."[14] They constitute "a positive means for CEOs to engage in frank dialogue."[15]

Twitter can widen the number of readers of CEO-speak because it provides an additional avenue for CEOs to share information, interact with message recipients, air opinions, and share sentiments about an event.[16] Tweets from the personal "Twitter handle" (address) of a CEO can present the thoughts of an "authentic" or a "real" CEO and not the thoughts of a CEO who has been "lawyered up and filtered down."[17] In composing a tweet, a CEO has an opportunity "to construct an authentic self, mediated through … words, punctuation, images, filters, [and] emojis."[18] Thus, a CEO's tweeting can obviate much of the spin-fatigue, skepticism, and suspicion the public frequently holds toward corporate communications.[19]

Tweets can alert readers to a CEO's apparent thoughts and attitudes.[20] In the case of Uber's CEO Khosrowshahi, his tweet on November 14, 2017, commenting on the outcome of the Australian Marriage Law Postal Survey, reveals his thoughts on same-sex marriage:[21]

> Congratulations #Australia on moving forward with marriage equality – we're proud to show our support!

A benefit of Twitter is that it provides an opportunity for a CEO to (at least partially) control the agenda, to "initiate and influence online conversations" and to shape a company's public image.[22] CEOs can be "influencers" through Twitter. They do not necessarily need to rely on others to do so. However, it is possible that repeated use of Twitter by a CEO, especially if unmediated by experienced corporate public relations minders, can reinforce a CEO's narcissistic dysfunction. Thus, analysis of a CEO's tweets can facilitate access to that CEO's "inner identity and even mental health"[23] and be a revealing "high-tech mirror" of an extreme narcissist.

Rise of the Social Executive

The use of social media has given rise to a class of what are dubbed "social executives" or "social CEOs." These are "top executives who connect with investors directly, personally, and in real time through social media."[24] The personal tweeting practices of social CEOs contribute to the "communicative constitution" of the organization they lead.[25] CEOs identified as avid or frequent users of Twitter have included Marissa Mayer (Yahoo), Jeffrey Immelt (GE), Tim Cook (Apple),[26] Ariana Huffington (Huffington Post Media), and Jack Dorsey (Twitter).[27] Many political leaders use Twitter too.[28]

Social executives also use Twitter to connect with non-investor stakeholders, including employees, customers, regulators, and politicians. They are said to offer value-added content such as "industry insights, leadership tips and advice, commentary on news and trends" and to project a seemingly "authentic voice" that features "behind-the-scenes photos and videos showing off their company, teams, passions, hobbies, etc."[29] The first 100 tweets of Dara Khosrowshahi as CEO of Uber included 33 photos in which he appeared. These were mainly posed photos with company staff in a wide range of locales including Miami, Iran, Germany, Japan, India, and Chile. One such photo, included as part of Khosrowshahi's tweet on October 26, 2017, shows him in open-neck white shirt and dress jacket. He is seated at a small round table and smiling. Fourteen smiling women stand behind him in a semi-circle. All of the women are dressed modestly. Ten are wearing head coverings. A vase of white flowers is on the small round table, accompanied by six smaller vases. The accompanying text said:

> Honored to meet inspiring Saudi women today. Excited and proud to hear how our technology can provide more economic opportunities for all.

Managing Reputation, Culture, and Management Control Systems

Tweets can help CEOs manage their company's reputation, attract investor attention, and respond directly to consumer concerns. They can be especially helpful to any CEO with a mandate to change organizational culture, and/or a keenness to change a management control system. Twitter can be beneficial in stamping a CEO as a thought leader who is authentic, approachable, and human[30] and as someone who can positively influence "public trust and satisfaction" and "organizational reputation."[31]

Many of the photos in CEO tweets are of top management executives. They have important image-building consequences. Their interpretation is subject to limits imposed by visual style, composition, and social and historical contexts. Interpretation of photographic portraits of CEOs can be assisted by developing a "business media eye." Those with such an eye are familiar "with a stock of props, poses and visual cues associated with the representation of business leaders [and] with stylistic conventions common to media portrayals of ... business leaders ... and other important persons."[32]

Ideally from a corporate perspective, photos of CEOs in tweets should project an authenticity that is crucial for organizations and their top executives. Photos can influence opinion about the authority and legitimacy of individual business leaders and the collective business leadership they provide. Understanding how a CEO portrait will be viewed by audiences is important.[33] For instance, a photograph of a CEO in a modern office with a view of a modern capital of the world may emphasize the institution's global power.

Immediacy

Most tweets have the virtue of immediacy. The text, together with any embedded photographs, hyperlinks, and retweets, is disseminated widely and almost instantly. Usually tweets are accessed and read on smartphones. The communication is fast. Nonetheless, the "half-life of a tweet is 24 minutes";[34] that is, half of the interactions with a tweet occur, on average, within the first 24 minutes of sending.

Accessing a Larger and Younger Audience

Retweets can also help a CEO spread a message to larger and more diverse audiences. Retweeting occurs when followers forward tweet messages to *their* followers.[35] In the case of Uber CEO Khosrowshahi, his most retweeted tweet was one from an Uber software engineer, Theresa Cay, retweeted on February 26, 2018. This was then retweeted by 141 other Twitter users. It attracted 474 "likes." This tweet includes a photo of Khosrowshahi that shows him chatting with Microsoft CEO Satya Nadella. Khosrowshahi is dressed very casually in a t-shirt under a relaxed khaki sweater.[36] He is seated cross-legged on a stage in a comfortable chair, obliquely facing Nadella. The latter is dressed slightly more formally in a jacket and open-necked shirt. The two men appear to be engaged in conversation, with Nadella speaking – as signaled by his extended open-palm left hand and arm, as if to make a point. The accompanying text reads:

> Lessons from our fireside chat hosted by @Uber CEO @dkhos w/ @Micro-soft CEO @satyanadella: 1) Be a Learn-It-All, not a Know-It-All 2) There's a fine line between confidence & hubris 3) Move forward by admitting & learn-ing from mistakes 4) Incorporate empathy in everything you do. (pic.twitter.com/51SrvfHbHP)

Forty-five percent of Americans aged 18 to 25 use Twitter.[37] This sup-ports the claim that Twitter is "viewed positively by younger audiences."[38] Khosrowshahi (born in 1969) uses language in tweets that seems tailored to younger-generation readers, especially those born after 1996 and catego-rized variously as Generation Z, iGeneration, or Centennials. For example, Khosrowshahi frequently uses of a form of adjectival slang that is com-monplace in social media. In the corpus of 243 of his tweets as Uber CEO (compiled up to the date of the company's initial public offering in May 2019) he uses "awesome" 12 times and "cool" 5 times. He tweets that Uber staff (whom he refers to as "drivers," "our team," "women of Uber," "our Palo Alto office") are "awesome" – as are Uber products, the company caf-eteria, "the day," and feedback. On October, 6, 2017, Khosrowshahi tweeted that he had "the coolest job on the planet." This tweet was embedded with a link to a YouTube clip extolling Uber's experiments with self-driving vehicles. In other tweets he says, "It is very cool to join the team."

Khosrowshahi comments that in a photo in one of his tweets he is "a CEO trying to look cool." We see Khosrowshahi posing with a handsome Bollywood star. The two men are looking forward, arm–in–arm, into the camera. Khosrowshahi is dressed in an open-neck white shirt and dress jacket and has a broad smile. The Bollywood star has an open-neck black shirt and has a slight smile. The tweet contains the following text (and a nice example of self-deprecating humor):

> This is the part where the fancy CEO tries to look cool by posing with Bol-lywood superstar @iamsrk, the King Khan himself. Note to self: gotta work on my haircut …

Khosrowshahi claims that "Thank you letters are the coolest part of the job" as CEO. His overuse of "cool" suggests a deliberate tactic on his part to promote credibility and legitimacy with younger readers.

Pitfalls

Beware Restless Twitter Fingers

While being driven to the airport on August 7, 2018, Tesla CEO Elon Musk sent the following tweet to his 22 million followers:

> Am considering taking Tesla private at $420. Funding secured.

This and some following tweets prompted the SEC to accuse Musk of violating US securities legislation. He is alleged to have tweeted

> a series of false and misleading statements … [indicating] … that, should he so choose, it was virtually certain that he could take Tesla private at a purchase price that reflected a substantial premium over Tesla stock's then-current share price, that funding for this multi-billion dollar transaction had been secured, and that the only contingency was a shareholder vote. In truth and in fact, Musk had not even discussed, much less confirmed, key deal terms, including price, with any potential funding source.[39]

Eventually, the SEC required, among other conditions, that Musk "obtain the pre-approval of an experienced securities lawyer employed by the company" before sending tweets on such matters.[40]

Nonetheless, Musk's Twitter fingers were restless. On July 30, 2019, he tweeted the following uncorroborated information:

> Spooling up production line rapidly. Hoping to manufacture ~1000 solar roofs/ week by end of this year. (@elonmusk)

This tweet seems likely to have tested the SEC's resolve.[41]

In Los Angeles in December 2019, Musk's indiscretion with his personal Twitter account was highlighted in legal proceedings against him (which he defended successfully) for defamation. Musk was alleged to have described Vernon Unsworth, a British diver who helped rescue a dozen boys and their soccer coach from a flooded cave in Thailand, as a "pedo[phile] guy." In court testimony, Musk expressed regret for his tweet and claimed it was "dashed off" at a time when he was overworked and was a response to an unprovoked attack on him.[42]

What Musk tweets does matter. In August 2020, he had about 37.6 million Twitter followers.[43] Many people respect him and are prone to follow his advice.

Thus, "if he doesn't take coronavirus seriously, others might not, either."[44] On March 6, 2020, Musk tweeted that "The coronavirus panic is dumb" and on March 8 that the "fatality rate [from the disease is] also greatly overstated." Despite Twitter announcing new rules on March 19 to curb tweets that spread misinformation about the coronavirus,[45] a day later Musk tweeted the false claim that "kids are essentially immune" to the virus. CEOs should take greater care not to send such "problematic" and "off-the-cuff" tweets.[46]

A Forum for Rant, Sneer, and Negativity

Twitter should not be reified. Indeed, not all who have used Twitter are enamored with it. Twitter has been slated for being "human ugliness splashed large" and for morphing into something that is "mainly an affront now, [featuring] attack, grubbiness, overload of rant and sneer and negativity, humble and not-so-humble boasting and time-wasting comments."[47] For some, Twitter has become "a confected outrage machine … [used by] … malcontents who have nothing better to do than complain."[48] Twitter has been lambasted for being "a platform tailor-made for emotional outbursts, unfounded assertions and glib posturing."[49]

Users of social media platforms such as Twitter are alleged to have "coarsened debate [by] being abusive in a way they would never be in face-to-face encounter."[50] Twitter has been criticized for being a "privileged, cloistered" "echo chamber" and for fostering "a thinness of respect, compassion, politeness [and for being laden with] sneer and sheen and self-righteousness and spin, from all sides."[51]

Beware *Faux* Cues to Authenticity

Whether CEOs construct a personality as an authentic leader via their tweets or whether they are denounced as a fake often depends on whether they use "the right emoji, punctuation, cultural reference, or selfie."[52] Such an assessment arises because of the "intense scrutiny … applied to minute presentational cues" by users of social media. Many of them claim to be "'artifice detectives, looking for clues and cues of authenticity."[53] Their attitude reflects social media as "an environment where authenticity is simultaneously promised, demanded, and disputed … [because of] heightened sensitivity to cues."[54]

Thus, users of Twitter need to be alert to the important role that their "nuanced deployment of cues" has in impression management.[55] This message seemed to have been lost on US presidential candidate Hillary

Clinton and her advisers in 2016. Clinton's use of Twitter was mocked for being "more planned,"[56] "disingenuous," "inauthentic," and "continually following a script."[57] Among the traces of inauthenticity in her tweets were "high-quality graphics," absence of "any typographic idiosyncrasies or errors," consistent use of "fully and correctly punctuated sentences," and a lack of "spontaneous emotional tenor."[58] Much of this criticism is applicable to tweets sent by some CEOs too.

CEO Twitter Stereotypes

Alertness to various stereotypes of CEO users of Twitter can be beneficial in understanding CEOs' personalities; their attitudes to risk, privacy, and transparency; and how they might respond to future events.

CEOs who use Twitter have been stereotyped variously as *generalists*, *expressionists*, *information mavens*, and *business mavens*.[59] *Generalists*, the largest group, "share a wide range of content … personal opinions and interests" and business information dealing with strategy, products, and customers. They are retweeted and "liked" the least of the four groups. *Expressionists* are prone to tweet about non-business matters and to share their opinions about events, politics, and their daily lives. *Information mavens* "do not generally tweet information specific to their company" but share links to a broad array of "information, news and other happenings." They have the lowest number of followers and the least retweets and followers. *Business mavens* "use Twitter extensively and primarily share business-related content." This includes "new product announcements … customer references, and information about management initiatives and strategy." They also use Twitter "to share content related to personal opinions and interests." Business mavens are retweeted and "liked" more than the CEOs in the other three groups.

Uber CEO Khosrowshahi seems best classified in the generalist group. His first 100 tweets at Uber share a wide range of content, including personal information, opinions, and interests. The latter include his endorsement of Uber's support for the LGBTQI community, his opposition to sex trafficking, his acknowledgment that Martin Luther King was an inspiration to him, the date of his daughter's birthday and his Christmas present to her, his wife's opinion of him, and his assessment that Justin Timberlake is a "spectacular performer." Khosrowshahi's tweets also include information on business strategy (including intent to commercialize self-driving technology), new and existing products (Uber Express POOL, Uber Health) and customers (including those in London and Brazil).

Cautions in Analyzing Twitter

When analyzing tweets, several cautions should be observed.[60] Tweets are short. They often feature abbreviations and other characters not typically used in normal communications. These include, for example, "#" for hashtags — that is, a word or a phrase used to identify tweets on a specific topic. The use of hashtags makes it easier to categorize messages and find information on the same topic. The scope for application of text analysis software (such as DICTION[61]) to explore tweets is constrained because such software generally depends on conventional spelling and grammatically correct syntax and sentence structure.

One approach to analyzing tweets is to regard them as data that can be mined to elicit information. Such a view has been justified on the grounds that

> Twitter conversations are … held in web pages and in databases (Twitter's databases and others), they live as long as the devices that record them live … the fact that you can find early tweets with a search engine mean[s] that a popular tweet edges toward immortality. Or, … toward perpetual unimportance … Twitter is an environment in which communities and interest groups flourish and naturally find each other.[62]

The personal Twitter record of many CEOs exists, apparently intact, since whenever they first used the platform. For example, Uber's Khosrowshahi began using a personal Twitter account long before he joined Uber. His first available tweet[63] is dated December 7, 2011, and was sent when he was CEO of Expedia.

Two caveats need to be entered regarding the use of tweets as data. First, some hyperlinks embedded in a tweet (e.g., to a YouTube file), or the tweet itself, may be inoperative and unavailable despite some of the inoperative information being significant. Second, each individual tweet is potentially the center of a widening nexus of related tweets by others. These related tweets may contain useful information regarding the original tweet.

For example, on May 23, 2018, Khosrowshahi tweeted:

> Proud to play our part. I'm thrilled to partner with @AXA to provide ground breaking protection for independent workers who use Uber in Europe, giving drivers & couriers the peace of mind they tell us they want while preserving the flexibility they value. http://t.uber.com/AXAProtection_EN …

This tweet referred to an Uber decision to provide insurance for its European drivers. The tweet included a link (repeated in Khosrowshahi's tweet on the following day) to a laudatory tweet by French president Emmanuel Macron. It also contained a head-and-shoulders shot of French president Macron, outside in an overcoat:

> Technology has already changed all of our lives. Today, Uber takes a step forward to make #TechForGood. Every independent worker using Uber's platform will now be provided with insurance protection. Congratulations Dara Khosrowshahi for this historical commitment! (@EmmanuelMacron, verified account, May 24, 2018, pic.twitter.com/rxbs671TnR)

The 52 replies to President Macron's tweet revealed mixed reactions from French and other observers of Uber. For example, one negative reply was

> The truth is that #uberFR is NOT paying ANYTHING in France for healthcare system, pensions scheme, schools, police, hospitals etc. uberFR does large-scale tax evasion, and your support to Uber, President @EmmanuelMacron, is an insult to the heavily taxed working people of #France (@frenchtaxi, replying to @EmmanuelMacron @dkhos, May 24, 2018)

Twitter Mining and Typographical Texture

Twitter can be mined to understand the sentiment in a tweet.[64] This can be achieved through word search and frequency counts of words with positive, neutral, or negative sentiment. However, the task of capturing sentiment is complicated by the use of "emoticons, abbreviations, repeated characters (extended words), abbreviations and other words."[65] Analysts need to be alert to emojis, acronyms, and abbreviations such as gr8 (great), u r (you are), lol (laugh out loud), OMG (oh my God) and elongated words, such as "cooool" and "hiiiii." Unexpected CAPITAL LETTERS are usually meant to indicate shouting. Punctuation using multiple exclamation points (such as "!!!!") is usually meant to indicate "take particular notice of this."

Nonetheless, close examination of CEOs' distinctive uses of spelling, punctuation, and grammar in tweets can provide valuable insights to their personality, emotional state, impulsivity, and state of mind.[66] This distinctiveness has been demonstrated by the idiosyncrasies in (former) US President Donald Trump's tweets. They feature "unexpected CAPITAL letters (plus snarky brackets!), overuse of dashes − and, above all, whiny and patronising exclamation marks!!"[67] Trump's misspellings, typographical errors, neologisms, unconventional punctuation, and staccato sentences give his tweets a distinctive typographical texture and provide valuable insight to his "personality and emotional state."[68]

The timestamp and the operating system tags on a tweet are authenticity cues too. The timestamp can help assess a tweet's "authorship, unfiltered independence from staff, and emotional authenticity."[69] Thus, tweets with a timestamp late at night, or those sent instinctively in response to some "breaking news," seem more likely to have been written by the leader personally without the involvement of a public relations team. Such tweets are likely to provide a closer reflection of a CEO's "emotions rather than premeditated communications strategy."[70] However, caution is needed "because Twitter relativizes the time to the viewer's time zone."[71] Operating system tags (iPhone or Android) can indicate authenticity too, especially if the type of phone system a CEO uses is known. In the case of Donald Trump, his typographical texture, timestamps, and operating system tags are claimed to reflect "an idiosyncratic manner of speech" an "unfiltered emotional state" and his "impulsive personality, nocturnal restlessness, [and] unrefined passion."[72]

Concluding Comments

CEO-speak is pervasive in modern society and influences how corporations and their leaders are viewed. Technology has always strongly influenced the form and substance of CEO-speak. The rise of social media platforms has extended the reach of CEO-speak and has affected its character. Just as former US President Trump's use of Twitter has altered presidential discourse, so too has CEOs' use of Twitter altered CEO discourse. Some CEOs who are avid tweeters are seemingly untethered by corporate communication minders and lawyers. Others are apparently more cautious. Still others seem to avoid Twitter studiously.

A CEO's tweets are often unmediated. They need to be compared critically with pre-existing forms of CEO-speak: for example, with formal speeches and letters that are fashioned and delivered under the CEO's name and subjected to stronger mediation. Although the rise of social media platforms such as Twitter has altered some aspects of CEO-speak in fundamental ways, the often unmediated discourse of social CEOs is embedded inextricably in the larger discourse of CEO-speak. Thus, a CEO's tweets are part of a wide range of communication media used to exercise leadership through language – including for propagandizing. This is a matter to which we now turn.

chapter eight

Tweets as Propaganda

In this chapter we show how the CEO of Uber, Dara Khosrowshahi, used his personal Twitter account to promote Uber's controversial business model. Specifically, he used language that suggested Uber was committed to a shared values ideology – something that ran counter to how the company was actually run, according to media reports (such as those cited below).

Uber is best known for its app, launched in San Francisco in 2011, that "connects people who want rides with nearby drivers … willing to provide this service … Uber takes a percentage of each fare."[1] In October 2019, technology writer Navneet Alang claimed that tech companies (such as Uber) "see themselves as, well, tech: a service or app that is the in-between layer between things."[2] He contended that such a view "glosses over how these companies work in practice [by] employing people at cut-rate wages without [employee] benefits or safety" and that regulators should stop letting Uber avoid its "responsibilities … [and]… obligations to the people they employ and the cities where they exist." One of those responsibilities is an obligation *not* to demand "a free pass on respecting basic [worker] rights and protections [that] other workers have been fighting to win for centuries."[3]

Alang made these comments when Khosrowshahi had been CEO of Uber for just over two years. He was appointed on August 30, 2017 to replace Travis Kalanick at a time when Uber had a notorious reputation for pursuing a predatory business model, engaging in odious behavior, and being contemptuous of regulation.[4]

Under Kalanick's leadership as CEO from 2011 to 2017, Uber developed a toxic, aggressive, "asshole" culture.[5] This stemmed from its "win at any costs," "superpumped" strategy that encouraged "principled confrontation" and a "hustle-orientation."[6] In 2014, such behavior was manifest when some Uber managers condoned the deliberate sabotage of a competitor's operations by ordering rides, then canceling them[7] and when Uber staff used *Greyball* software to thwart the municipal officials responsible for enforcing passenger vehicle regulations.[8] Also in 2014, the odiousness of Uber's behavior prompted the transportation commissioner of Portland, Oregon, to liken Uber's management to "a bunch of thugs."[9] In 2015 and 2016, Uber used *Ripley* software to disrupt government raids on its offices.[10] At company retreats, Kalanick was reported to have encouraged a culture of consensual "hook-up" [for casual sex].[11]

Uber's "win at all costs" mentality was evident too in 2014 when Emil Michael, a senior vice president, is reported to have suggested that Uber "dig up dirt" on the personal lives and backgrounds of media figures who reported negatively about the company.[12] In August 2017, an analyst on American television business news channel CNBC, Jim Cramer, described Uber as "a company that's colossally crazy."[13]

Thus, it is not surprising that Khosrowshahi was hired in 2017 as a "new sheriff in town," charged with cleaning up Uber and rehabilitating the company's reputation post-Kalanick. Khosrowshahi's role was envisaged to include "building world-class products, transforming cities, and adding value to the lives of drivers and riders around the world while continuously improving [Uber's] culture and making Uber the best place to work."[14] Khosrowshahi's challenge was to change the company's culture to one epitomized by the catchphrase "We do the right thing." He needed to show that Uber's management championed good corporate values and a sense of community. To do so, he needed to legitimize top management and the decisions they made, establish trust, and show that Uber acted with integrity.

Uber's reputation was still the subject of intense critique in late 2019, two years after Khosrowshahi's appointment. In September 2019, for example, US Senator Richard Blumenthal, in a letter directed to Khosrowshahi, said,

> I write in the wake of deeply disturbing reports about sexual assault and harassment that have occurred through your ride-sharing app and your responses to those incidents ... I am further alarmed by Uber's public statements about this issue, which indicate a *brazenly careless attitude* about your responsibility toward your customers. (italics added)[15]

Had Khosrowshahi failed the challenge? In forming a view on this matter, statements in Uber's IPO documents in May 2019 are relevant. In the IPO, Uber asserted, "Changing our conduct and culture begins with a strong tone at the top ... We hold our senior leaders accountable for maintaining tone at the top."[16] So, did the tone at the top of Uber improve under Khosrowshahi's leadership? Did the company's conduct and culture improve? Did Khosrowshahi's CEO-speak successfully fashion an attractive image of openness at Uber and help construct a self-image of an authentic CEO? These questions are addressed below.

Khorowshahi had good reason to want to repair Uber's tone at the top and reputation. Trust in the company had been impaired during Kalanick's tenure as CEO. In a *New York Times* review of Mike Isaac's book, *The Battle for Uber*, Leslie Berlin highlights Kalanick's depiction as

> an evil bro-genius, bent on world domination through ride-sharing. A charmer when he wanted to be … [he] understood that Uber could succeed only if it grew faster than any competitor, attracting large numbers of riders and drivers … He let nothing get in the way of that growth – not the livelihood of drivers, not the health and welfare of employees, not the counsel of his own advisers, not the laws and regulations of multiple states.[17]

Many aspects of the intense and persistent criticism of Uber under Kalanick's leadership continued during Khosrowshahi's term as CEO. For example, many drivers complained about their unfair treatment by Uber. They were particularly upset by misleading statements regarding their potential earnings and by endemic underpayment.[18] Community members criticized the inadequacy of Uber's background checks of drivers, the use of cell phones by drivers, and the lack of wheelchair access to Uber vehicles.

Some festering safety and related issues came to a head in one of Uber's most important markets, London, in November 2019, when Transport for London (TfL) removed Uber's license to operate[19] because of "widespread instances of unauthorised drivers using [Uber's] ride-hailing app."[20] TfL regulators were concerned that many Uber drivers did not have "correct insurance." TfL was not "confident [Uber] could keep its passengers safe."[21]

Uber has been criticized also for levying fare surcharges during emergencies (known as "surge pricing") and for increasing traffic congestion and reducing patronage of public transport. Uber executives have been lambasted for privacy law breaches, gender discrimination, sexual harassment, and sexual misconduct in the workplace.[22]

To its credit, the company released its first-ever safety report in late 2019. However, Khosrowshahi hedged when asked by the *Washington Post* in December 2019, "When someone gets raped in an Uber, what are Uber's obligations?"

> Khosrowshahi's answers have it both ways. Uber is working hard … to reduce the rate of assaults to as close to zero as possible. And it's the first company to bring this level of transparency to the problem.

Yet sexual misconduct is a "societal problem," he said. Uber doesn't think it needs to tell the police about incidents reported to it. (Law enforcement was involved in only 37 percent of Uber's known rape cases, the company reported.)[23]

Below, we contrast Uber's dubious business model with the "nice" propagandizing image Khosrowshahi projected using his personal Twitter account.

Uber's Business Model

At the time Khosrowshahi began his appointment as CEO (August 30, 2017), Uber had been subjected to an unrelenting stream of highly negative publicity. Many civil and labor relations lawsuits had been lodged against the company around the world. In response, Khosrowshahi sought to effect a radical transformation of the company's culture and tone at the top. He seemed determined to humanize Uber by offering a charming public face. He appeared in Uber advertisements, was interviewed in a wide range of media, and attended well-regarded, high-profile conferences. Khosrowshahi also instituted numerous internal reforms. For example, he set up new employee feedback systems. This initiative seemed prompted by a desire to promote a cohesive culture and a caring and tolerant tone at the top.

Uber's inapt behavior up to (and beyond) the time of Khosrowshahi's appointment can be explained plausibly by two factors. First, the company's DNA was that of a typical, brash Silicon Valley startup; second was the behavior of its CEO Kalanick. The latter was prone to gaffes and acting in a highly insensitive way in public.[24] The company's behavior has also been claimed to be an inevitable outcome of the company's business model that epitomized "the tensions between traditional corporate norms and the unsettled state of digital organizations."[25] Did Uber's "corporate misbehavior reflect a given executive team" or was it due to the "company's pioneer status as a new type of company and organization"?[26] Perhaps an organization such as Uber – a sort of "digital Big Bang disrupter" – attracts leaders who are prone to being disruptors themselves

Uber differs radically from the traditional form of company. The company's drivers are viewed most emphatically as NOT employees or investors, despite them owning the cars involved in Uber's ride-sharing service.[27] This is a critical aspect of Uber's business model. Legal wrangling over whether drivers are contractors or employees is continuing in many jurisdictions globally.[28] For example, in a case brought before the Australian Fair Work Commission in November 2019, an UberEats driver, Amita

Gupta, claimed that her access to the Uber app had been denied because she was 10 minutes late with a delivery. Ms. Gupta alleged she had been sacked, despite working for "as many as 96 hours per week." The Transport Workers Union challenged the contractor status of Ms. Gupta, sought an end to "worker exploitation via an app," and argued for a cessation of the "dystopian conditions" endured by "gig economy"[29] workers.[30]

In March 2020, France's ultimate court of appeal, the *Cour de Cassation*, ruled that an Uber employee did not qualify as a self-employed contractor. The court held that genuine self-employed contractors should be able to manage clients themselves, set prices, and choose how to execute a task.[31] None of these criteria prevailed at Uber. This decision rendered Uber liable to pay more taxes and employee benefits (such as holiday pay), thereby upending its business model.[32]

The exploitation that Uber drivers claim to have sustained stems from Uber's business model. The driver's "jobs" with Uber "have become a fall-back for workers who have a hard time breaking into more stable, traditional positions. Most gig workers are young, and a disproportionate number are from racialized or immigrant communities."[33] Gig economy employers such as Uber typically claim that

> since their business models are "new" and "innovative," traditional labour regulations shouldn't apply. Giving gig workers the same rights as other workers – like a minimum wage, paid holidays, sick leave, pensions and workers' compensation – would interfere with their dynamic growth.[34]

Uber differs from non-gig economy businesses because the "flexible work arrangements, and distance from management to the front lines of customer service (via an independent third party) means that traditional managerial tools [e.g., those that emphasize financial controls and structures] cannot apply"[35] or are defective. Thus, Uber claims that it had to invent "new organizational forms, structures, and processes … [and] rely much more on cultural values than strict procedural discipline."[36] So, rather than attempt to codify behavior, Uber focuses on attaining "group cohesion through shared values."[37] In seeking this cohesion, it was critical for Khosrowshahi to generate "a compelling narrative" for drivers.[38] His CEO-speak, including through his personal Twitter feed, was important in eliciting this sought-after "cohesion through shared values."

Another important characteristic of Uber's business model is its intent to be a "Big Bang Disruptor":[39] that is, a company that disrupts the economic sectors it enters and the regulatory regimes governing those sectors.[40] Uber's pattern of "disruptive regulation" involves challenging incumbents in the taxi industry and disregarding local government regulations. This aspect of Uber's approach and underlying business model has been summarized as follows:

> [I]t would land in a new city ... and operate illegally there until the government was forced to allow it to stay. Its aggressive approach [was to] move fast and break things, and leave someone else to pick up the pieces.[41]

What often resulted was a dual regulatory regime that featured a form of "challenger capture ... in which the challenger [Uber] has largely prevailed."[42] Uber's business model is alleged to involve intentionally breaking the law, challenging the law, or engaging in disobedient activity in many jurisdictions.[43]

> [I]n most cities the taxi industry was heavily regulated. ... This did not deter Uber. It launched operations in cities around the world, often in violation of existing laws. ... When the company received a cease-and-desist letter early in its operations in San Francisco, it simply ignored the city's demand. ... Uber and its competitors have grown quickly, leveraging consumer support to challenge [long-standing] restrictive taxi regulations and lobbies. ... Public reaction has reflected a mix of popular approval and vociferous backlash.[44]

A key component of Uber's business model is its use of social media, including Twitter. This is used to mobilize mass support (among ride customers and community) for its illegal behavior and to challenge extant regulations. Thereby, Twitter reinforces the central role of disruptive technology in the success of the company.[45]

CEO-Speak as Propaganda

Most CEOs routinely portray the organization they lead in the best light. To do so, they often using hyperbole, engage in cherry-picking, and misrepresent indicators of company performance. However, using CEO-speak as a propaganda mechanism is more insidious. Propaganda is "the management of collective attitudes by the manipulation of significant symbols ... [through] alteration ... intimidation ... [and] economic coercion ..."[46] Khosrowshahi's CEO-speak using Twitter appears to reflect propagandizing behavior because it mobilizes support for an underlying "disruptive" rogue business model.

The main preconditions to "the successful use of propaganda as a means of social control"[47] include the will to use it, the skills to produce it, and the ability to access the means of dissemination. These preconditions all existed at Uber. Below, we examine how propaganda, as conveyed through Khosrowshahi's use of Twitter, deflected from and masked Uber's odious business model.

Before we do so, we draw attention to the view that CEO-speak as propaganda need not always be bombastic, but can be subtle. Khosrowshahi's propaganda sought to normalize Uber in the eyes of various stakeholders – in direct contrast to some of the activities and policies Uber was endorsing by its underlying business model. The propaganda of Uber's communications is evident in the substantial gulf between its CEO-speak on one hand and the way the company operated "on the ground" on the other.

Propaganda and the CEO's Twitter Account

A CEO's use of a personal Twitter account has become an increasingly important means of CEO communication in recent decades, especially for companies in the vanguard of the gig economy. Indeed, Uber has been so prominent in the gig economy that the word to describe the changes it has pioneered have entered the lexicon as the neologism *uberization*.

A CEO's personal Twitter account lends itself to the dissemination of propaganda in tweets. This is because tweeting is ostensibly an unmediated, almost real-time form of communication directly from the CEO. The text, language, and words the CEO uses in tweets and any embedded photographs, links, and retweets are disseminated widely and virtually instantly.

Khosrowshahi's presence and persona as a hip, energetic, knowledgeable, and youngish CEO facilitated his propagandizing, especially among young people. This was reinforced by numerous published photos of him, online and in other media, with heads of state, various dignitaries, and Uber drivers. These photos seemed intent on bolstering his image and on legitimizing what we allege to be propaganda issued with his authority. Consider, for example, a "hip" photograph that was included in Khosrowshahi's tweet on April 11, 2018. This shows Khosrowshahi and another man in front of the US Congress. Both are standing beside identical red bicycles. They are dressed in casual business attire and are wearing helmets. Both appear to both be smiling slightly. The accompanying text says,

> We are taking our vision of bringing multiple transit options into the app a step further with Uber Rent powered by @Getaround, a partnership w/ @masabi_com and an Uber Bike by @JumpMobility launch in DC. Just getting started!

Khosrowshahi's first tweet on his personal Twitter account as Uber's CEO included a photo of his face, passport-style, attached to a medallion. He is dressed semi-casually in a dark sports jacket and open-necked shirt. He is smiling and balding. He looks pleasant and not intimidating. This image seems intended to distance Khosrowshahi from the previous highly criticized CEO, Kalanick. The first name on the badge, Dara, is positioned above the last name in bigger type. Presumably this indicates a desire for a *"call me Dara"* culture of informality. The text of the tweet is

> #mynewbadge. I checked it and it works! Does @karaswisher have one of these? (@dkhos, verified account, Aug. 30, 2017)

The hashtag #mynewbadge makes it clear that Khosrowshahi is referring to his company identification badge. He says, "I checked it and it works!" as if he is mildly surprised. This feeble self-deprecating humor seems intended to make Khosrowshahi more authentic by showing he doesn't expect special privileges. It seems intended to promote an image of him as being just an ordinary, regular staff member. There is no indication on the badge or elsewhere in the photo that this is the new CEO – there is no class distinction. Since all other Uber employees have similar badges, the new CEO projects himself as laid-back and informal. The metaphor at play seems to be LEADERSHIP IS INFORMAL AND EGALITARIAN.

The tweet ends with the new CEO asking: "Does @karaswisher have one of these?" Why Khosrowshahi's first tweet would "name-drop" Kara Swisher, reputedly "Silicon Valley's most feared and well-liked journalist,"[48] is puzzling. Perhaps he wanted to signal respect for this prominent journalist. Or, more likely, perhaps he wanted to "announce himself" to an influential member of the press so that he could leverage this in the future to cultivate improved relations with her and help to generate positive news stories about Uber and its business model.

Broad Themes in Khosrowshahi's First 100 Tweets

There are many ways to analyze a person's Twitter activity[49] and reveal traces of their propagandizing. Here we concentrate on the themes, metaphors, and tone in Khosrowshahi's tweets. We also explore the words, abbreviations, and other symbols he uses to ascertain whether the tone displayed is positive, neutral, or negative. Such analysis is important because

Themes in Khosrowshahi's First 100 Tweets as CEO of Uber (n = 221 themes)					
Personal/ Family	Uber Company	Leadership	Social/Public Policy	Political	Drivers
16	74	50	54	10	17
(7.2%)	(33.5%)	(22.6%)	(24.4%)	(4.5%)	(7.7%)

the words, emoticons, and other language features of tweets can positively affect the "attitude of recipients toward the CEO, which, in turn, creates positive feelings towards the organization."[50]

Khosrowshahi's first 100 tweets addressed six major themes,[51] shown above by their frequency of occurrence.

The frequency of these themes is interesting when considered in conjunction with Khosrowshahi's intent to change Uber's culture. All of the themes are important in understanding Khosrowshahi's strategic priorities, his approach to leading Uber, and his use of CEO-speak to win support for himself, the company, and its business model.

While each theme is worthy of close analysis, here we focus on just one theme, "drivers." Before doing so, it is important to recall the most controversial aspect of Uber's business model: its steadfast contention that drivers are independent contractors, not Uber employees.[52] This classification is fundamentally important because it relieves Uber of legal obligation to pay drivers minimum arbitrated wages and associated entitlements, such as overtime pay and holiday pay. By classifying drivers as contractors, the company is not exposed to substantially higher costs.[53]

In May 2019, following a decision by the US National Labor Relations Board (NLRB) that drivers could be regarded as contractors, journalists highlighted some substantial implications for Uber. Scheiber, writing in the *New York Times,* claimed that the NLRB had handed "an important victory to Uber" and had dealt "a blow to drivers' efforts to band together to demand higher pay and better working conditions."[54] Scheiber pointed out that

> Contractors lack the protection given to employees under federal law – and enforced by the labor board – for unionizing and other collective activity, such as protesting the policies of employers … the conclusion makes it extremely difficult for Uber drivers to form a union.[55]

Uber's IPO registration statement identified one of the company's major risks as a circumstance where "Drivers were classified as employees instead of independent contractors."[56] The IPO elaborated on the consequence of such classifications, the various legal challenges the company is facing globally on this matter,[57] and the consequences of reclassifying drivers as employees:

> [W]e would incur significant additional expenses for compensating Drivers, potentially including expenses associated with the application of wage and hour laws (including minimum wage, overtime, and meal and rest period require-ments), employee benefits, social security contributions, taxes, and penalties. Further, any such reclassification would require us to fundamentally change our business model, and consequently have an adverse effect on our business and financial condition.[58]

Because of the financial and existential vulnerability of Uber to a reclas-sification of drivers as employees, it was critical that Khosrowshahi not provoke disaffection among drivers or encourage them to seek the better conditions that employee status would provide them. He needed to forge good relations with drivers, be perceived as their friend and supporter, bolster their self-esteem, and not antagonize them. His 17 driver-themed tweets, discussed below (and reproduced in appendix D), evidence him doing this.

The importance of drivers to Uber is emphasized strongly in Khosrow-shahi's tweet on October 4, 2017.[59] He asserts,

> We can never forget that drivers represent the heart of our service #UberEATS #nicesurprise

Through this tweet, Khosrowshahi invokes a potent, complex linguistic metaphor: DRIVERS REPRESENT THE HEART OF OUR SERVICE. The "heart" is a metaphor for A CONTAINER FOR EMOTIONS. It can be divided into the following sub-metaphors. THE HEART IS ...

LOVE.
KINDNESS OR GENEROSITY.
SINCERITY.
AFFECTION.
WORRY OR INTEREST.
SADNESS.
PITY OR SYMPATHY.
DESIRE.
COURAGE.

A MATERIAL.
A LIVING ORGANISM.
THE CORE OR CENTRAL PART OF SOMETHING.[60]

Khosrowshahi probably intended his use of heart to signal the last of these sub-metaphors: DRIVERS ARE THE CORE OR CENTRAL PART OF UBER.

This metaphor is a paradox because it is inconsistent with Uber's intense worldwide battle to classify drivers as independent contractors and not employees. Given Uber's aggressive stance on this matter and its claimed scant regard for drivers' remuneration, lack of training, and myriad other issues of concern to drivers, Khosrowshahi's tweet is propaganda. It sits oddly with the underlying reality of Uber's business model.

The inference that "drivers represent the heart of our service" is inconsistent too with the fact that the driver theme appears as just 7.7 percent of identified themes in Khosrowshahi's first 100 tweets. Since drivers are allegedly the "heart" or the core of Uber, one would expect them to receive more attention in the CEO's tweets.[61]

Khosrowshahi appears in five photos with drivers in the 17 tweets that reflect the "driver" theme: tweets 6, 14, 23, 42, and 64 (see appendix D). In each photo, Khosrowshahi is prominent, casually dressed, and in the company of drivers. All drivers are smiling and apparently happy at Uber. Their body language is positive (thumbs ups, fist pumps). Thus, the HEART (the drivers) are portrayed as representing AFFECTION: presumably affection for Uber, its business model, and its CEO. The accompanying text describes drivers as "awesome." The reference to them as "our partners" seems intended to generate a sense of collective identity. This helps Khosrowshahi evince a concern for shared values and project an image as a listener who is interested in what drivers have to say and who is prepared to act on their feedback.

Khosrowshahi's tweets strongly promote the mutually cohering interests of Uber management and drivers by stressing the importance management accords the concerns of drivers. This is evident in use of the words "feedback" (3 times), "meetings" (1), "partners" (2) and "driver-partners" (1). It is evident too in claims (tweet 42, see appendix D) that conversations with "drivers from all over at our very first Driver Advisory Forum [led to] awesome feedback that will feed into our product roadmap and business strategy going into 2018." But this image of concern is bizarrely counterfactual and flies in the face of what seems to be a high level of disregard by Uber for complaints made by disaffected drivers.

Many drivers have replied to tweets by Khosrowshahi using foul, offensive, and accusatory language, as below:

> Easy to invest money when you steal it from #uber [image removed] drivers all over the world. I WANT MY $120.17 FROM 7 MONTHS AGO @dkhos. #uberthieves. SCREW YOU!!ASSHOLE (@LuminousAI, replying to @dkhos)

The use of BLOCK CAPITAL LETTERS in emails or social media, as in this example, is usually taken to indicate anger,[62] shouting, or strong emphasis. There is no use of block capital letters in any of Khosrowshahi's 17 driver tweets. Nor is there any use of elongated words for emphasis (e.g., Sooooo!). Spelling and grammatical errors can indicate impulsivity.[63] But a grammar and spell-check of his first 100 tweets reveals only two instances of duplicated words – "at at" and "the the" – and one instance of spelling India with a lower case "i." There are a few social media abbreviations such as "u r" (you are), "pls" (please), "w" (with), "Q&A" (Question and Answer), "cuz" (because), and "convo" (conversation).

Khosrowshahi's tweets lack spontaneity and informality. They appear to be formal and well-edited, use carefully chosen words, and to have been orchestrated in advance of sending. Thus, the reflexiveness and freshness afforded by Twitter is lost. Typical of the lack of spontaneity is the following formal, seemingly sanitized tweet sent on April 12, 2018:

> Uber has a responsibility to help keep people safe. It's core to everything we do – that's why we're doubling down on safety, making it easier to share your trip w/ loved ones, and piloting tech that could save time and lives in an emergency.

Lack of spontaneity in tweets invites belief they have been vetted by public relations staff – and, indeed, that the tweets are possibly written by staff. The text of tweet 89 is presented in a long, complex, word-perfect sentence. This does not seem characteristic of an instinctive, genuine response by Khosrowshahi.

> When you see pics of parades in Ho Chi Minh and Hanoi, convoys in Jakarta, drivers bringing their families, waving goodbye and signing each other's jackets, you realize how much a part in everyday lives we play. #Respect (@dkhos, verified account, Apr. 10, 2018)

Khosrowshahi's tweets evidence an unremitting and unambiguous language of positivity, solidarity, and support for drivers. There are barely any negative words. Rather, the tweets use preponderantly positive words, such as "respect," "proud," "safety," "support," "happy," "love," "awesome," "honest," and "great."

In his corpus of 243 tweets up to the date of Uber's IPO, Khosrowshahi uses "team" 44 times. The Uber "team" is said variously to be "taking Uber to new heights" and "helping us build in Europe and beyond." There are 39 uses of "great." Khosrowshahi states he had "great meetings in London … in this great city." His interactions with staff were almost always "great" – "Great Q & A with our Seattle team," "great office visit [with] a terrific team [in Miami]" and "Great convo with drivers." Indeed, it seems that every meeting Khosrowshahi ever comments on publicly was "great" (including meetings with senior executives of Toyota Motor Company, a town hall meeting in Santiago, and a meeting with the Uber team in Dubai).

Khosrowshahi uses "excited" 25 times. He even claims to be "incredibly excited" four times, and "super excited" twice. He is excited by welcoming new executives, working with new partners, "what comes next," how technology can provide economic opportunities, and by experimenting with the commercialization of technology. Other positive words include "proud" (19 times), "good" (10), "right" (10), and "hono(u)red" (6).

Khosrowshahi's use of pronouns helps to sustain a collective responsibility for what Uber does. There are only three instances of first-person *singular* pronouns (I, me, mine, my, myself) in the 17 driver-themed tweets. In contrast, there are 17 first-person *plural* pronouns (we, us, our, ours, ourselves). Tweet 8 (September 22, 2017) co-opts the first-person plural pronouns to conjure the ideas of group cohesion and collective responsibility. Khosrowshahi alerts drivers (implicitly at least) that they are implicated in the problems Uber is facing: "we r far from perfect." In tweet 22 (October 31, 2017), Khosrowshahi refers to "getting our message out in Brazil." It is not Uber's message, but *our* message, a collective responsibility.

Khosrowshahi's language projects the image of a contented CEO who is comfortable (and indeed enjoys) being in the company of drivers. The CEO identifies with drivers by claiming to "know the feeling of the dreams they have" and to have had "great" meetings with them. He expresses delight in taking a selfie with them. He lauds drivers for their "awareness" and for being "everyday heroes." Nonetheless, he fails to mention the many Uber drivers who have been accused (and some convicted) of murder, rape, and other serious crimes. Khosrowshahi's text makes an appeal to drivers to "please work w/us to make things right." He attempts to relate to drivers by recounting, in highly positive terms, "the new Driver app," and claiming he "had a blast taking it for a spin." This seems directed to enhance his legitimacy as CEO.

Concluding Comments

Khosrowshahi's use of his personal Twitter account seems to have been intended to bolster his legitimacy in the eyes of drivers. His tweets portray the drivers and management of Uber as one big happy family – an image of cohesion and of respect for drivers – contrary to a wide swathe of empirical evidence. His tweets seem directed to remediate the ghastly tone and unsavory reputation the company had developed under former CEO Kalanick. Khosrowshahi glosses over the reality of driver-company relations at Uber. Drivers are *not* universally happy as his tweets imply. Rather, the company has been subject to strong, determined legal and industrial action by drivers around the world. Many drivers allege they have been exploited and "screwed over" by Uber and that the company has behaved like an "asshole" in respect of them and their claims.

Khosrowshahi's tweets present a propagandized view of Uber. The intent seems to be to have readers and the broader community adopt a wholesome view of the pervading mood of drivers and the merits of their complaints. The tweets can be regarded as propaganda. They are directed to normalizing the company and its relationships. This is despite the possibility of such normalization being precluded by the company's inherently abnormal business model.

chapter nine

Accounting-Speak

We now turn to another medium used for CEO communication – a "dialect" of CEO-speak that we call *accounting-speak*. By accounting-speak we mean the use of accounting concepts, terms, and measurements in oral and written public narratives. Despite having an often underdeveloped understanding of accounting, many CEOs use accounting-speak to support their strategic agenda and rhetorical objectives. In this chapter, we show how successive CEOs of Canadian National Railway (CN) used accounting-speak to justify the decision in 1995 to privatize CN. By invoking accounting-speak, the CEOs sought to sustain a claim that the privatization had been largely responsible for transforming CN from a Crown corporation losing billions of dollars into a free-market "iconic brand" by 2018.[1]

Accounting numbers and the words that accompany them (such as "asset," "write-down," "depreciation," and "accruals") form an arcane, subtle, and often perplexing (even to accountants) subset of language.[2] Many observers of the art of accounting falsely regard it to be completely objective. Rather, accounting has a dubious and well-deserved reputation for malleability and for reporting "rubbery figures." Indeed, dodgy accounting practices have been implicated in many widely publicized corporate crashes. In the case of Enron, the last published (and auditor-approved) financial statements prior to the company's collapse in 2001 conformed with accounting rules known as generally accepted accounting principles (or GAAP). The financial statements presented what seemed to be a picture of glowing financial health, yet such depiction was far removed from Enron's parlous underlying condition.

Accounting rules allow ample discretion to adopt alternative measurement methods. When calculating profit accountants and financial analysts often refer euphemistically to the exercise of such discretion as "earnings management." This allowable discretion gives rise to a lexicon rich in metaphor and to expressions such as "big bath accounting," "cookie jar reserves," "feral accounting," and "income smoothing." Thus, accounting measurements should not be regarded as axiomatically objective and beyond question, even if they have the imprimatur of GAAP or an unqualified audit report. The calculative technologies of accountancy are not "neutral devices for mirroring the social world."[3]

Despite accounting's history of generating less-than-perfect measurements, many pundits benignly accept the accounting-speak of CEOs as if the accounting measures they cite are unproblematic and scientifically accurate reflections of an entity's wealth and performance. But measures derived from accounting data such as the three we focus on here (net profit, operating ratio, and free cash flow) should be viewed skeptically. There is no precise scientific rigor in these accounting measures.

We draw on events *prior to*, *during*, and *after* the privatization of CN in 1995 to show how successive CEOs of CN used a form of accounting-speak that involved net profit, operating ratio, and free cash flow to accomplish strategic ends. We discuss the use of accounting-speak in the following three phases:

- *Pre-privatization phase* (1992 to February 26, 1995). In this phase, CN's (then) CEO Paul Tellier used accounting-speak strategically to enlist support for the privatization. Tellier painted a dire picture of CN's financial performance, lauded seemingly successful privatizations elsewhere, and endorsed the merits of downsizing (a euphemism for reducing the number of staff).
- *During privatization phase* (February 27, 1995, to November 17, 1995). This was the period between the announcement by the Canadian government of its intention to privatize CN and the closing of the initial public offering (IPO) of stock in CN. In this period, accounting-speak was used to encourage investors to subscribe for shares in CN.
- *Post-privatization phase* (November 19, 1995, to the present). Accounting-speak was used to portray winners and losers of the privatization and to laud the vision and wisdom of the privatization's promoters.

CN has been an important social and economic institution in Canada since it was established in 1918 as a Crown corporation. In 1995, the privatization of CN was the largest in Canadian history, converting CN into a corporation owned by shareholders and listed on the stock exchange. After 1995, the company expanded considerably, especially in the USA. By 2020, CN operated a rail network that extended from the Gulf of Mexico, through the USA, to the Atlantic and Pacific coasts of Canada.[4] The company's main revenues are earned from the carriage of petroleum, chemicals, grain, fertilizers, coal, metals, minerals, and forest products.[5]

Many analysts and business commentators have endorsed the "success" of the privatization[6] and have claimed that CN presents a highly attractive investment opportunity.[7] Much of the present optimism regarding CN stems from the discourse of its corporate leaders. In 2018, the chair of CN's board of directors (Robert Pace) claimed "CN has become an iconic brand, synonymous with innovation and operational excellence."[8] He reminded observers that "CN's dividend has increased on average by 16% every year since our IPO in 1995."[9]

Three Key Accounting-Speak Measures

Three accounting measures have been especially pertinent in the "before, during, and after" story of CN's privatization. These are net profit, operating ratio (OR), and free cash flow (FCF). Below we endeavor to make sense of how the accounting-speak associated with these measures was used and manipulated by a succession of CEOs of CN to support the company's rhetorical agenda. But first we conduct a brief and gentle "lesson" to explain these terms more clearly. Those not initiated into the rites of accounting should find this beneficial in lifting the veil of accountancy, even if just a little bit.

Net profit reported in a company's audited financial statements depends on (usually) thousands of accounting and operational decisions by management. For CN, these decisions were all made ostensibly within the framework of an often elastic set of "accounting standards." The standards CN applied could variously be Canadian generally accepted accounting principles (Canadian GAAP),[10] US GAAP, or international financial reporting standards (IFRS).

Net profit is reported in audited financial statements as if it is a precise, unique, and singular amount. But it is more prudent to regard net profit as elastic and prone to creative adjustment. This "elasticity" arises from the wide discretion allowable under whatever GAAP is applied to select the accounting practices and measurement methods used in its calculation. "Elasticity" is an enduring (if disguised) feature of reported accounting numbers even if management makes all operational and accounting decisions in good faith and the external auditor expresses an unqualified opinion on the financial accounts.

The *operating ratio* is defined by CN, consistent with practice in the railroad industry, as "total rail operating expenses as a percentage of total rail revenues."[11] In 1992, CN reported a very unflattering OR of 97.5 percent.[12] In 2018, CN reported an operating ratio of 61.6 percent. This OR figure was obtained by dividing total operating expenses of $8,828 million by total revenues of $14,321 million.[13] An OR of 61.6 percent implies that for every $1 of operating revenue earned, operating expenses were 61.6 cents. In other words, in 2018 CN made an operating profit of 38.4 cents on every dollar of operating revenue. Although the reported OR stems from calculations made in accord with GAAP, companies can choose from many allowable accounting methods when calculating their operating expenses and operating revenues. Rarely will any two companies rely on the same overall set of assumptions, policies, and methods in calculating operating expenses and operating revenues.[14]

Nonetheless, the accounting-speak of CN's senior executives seemed to overlook this. In an exchange of views with the first author of this book in the (Canadian) *National Post* newspaper in 2006, Claude Mongeau (then executive vice-president and chief financial officer of CN)[15] contended that the OR is a "testament" to CN's operating performance because "it is calculated from the company's audited financial statements."[16] However, the "testament" Mongeau mentions should be recognized as a fragile one because it ignores

> the amply allowable discretions under GAAP to produce a wide range of auditor-sanctioned component measures of the OR – that is, of operating expenses and operating revenues. Caution should therefore be exercised when using the OR to make comparisons between companies, because the likelihood that any two companies will define and measure operating revenue and operating expenses in identical fashion is remote.[17]

To evaluate reported OR figures (and the components thereof), and the accounting-speak that accompanies the presentation of OR figures, it is beneficial to answer three questions:

1. What variety of GAAP is used to calculate operating expenses and operating revenues?

   The differences in calculation of operating expenses and operating revenues arising from applying different sets of GAAP can be substantial. In 1998, CN switched its principal basis for measuring OR from Canadian GAAP to US GAAP. This change alone reduced the OR in that year from 79.6 percent to 75.3 percent.

2. Does the operating ratio include or exclude any special charges?

   In 2002, the exclusion of special charges reduced CN's operating ratio from 76 percent to 69.4 percent.

3. Is the operating ratio calculated using a definition of "operating items" and "non-operating items" that is unchanged from previous years?

Care should be exercised if the definition of these terms is not the same from year to year. A more conservative definition of operating expense and/or a more liberal definition of operating revenue than has been used in a prior year can make it easier to report a reduced OR. When ratios such as the OR are used to compare performance between companies, it is critical that the underlying basis of calculation in each company is identical. Otherwise, the outcome is akin to comparing apples with oranges. This caution also holds when assessing one company over time.

Free cash flow (FCF) is a more defensible (though far from perfect) accounting-based measure. It is not subject to quite as many discretionary treatments as are allowed in calculating net profit and OR. FCF measures how much cash a company has after paying for its ongoing activities and growth. CN calculates FCF as cash flow from operations less capital expenditures and dividends.[18]

CN claims that FCF is a "useful measure of performance as it demonstrates the company's ability to generate cash after the payment of capital expenditures and dividends."[19] Investors often look favorably on FCF as a measure of value and as a prelude to increased profits. When FCF is rising and a firm's share price is low, a rise in share price is often expected. Alternatively, a falling FCF is often thought to signal that a company is having trouble sustaining earnings growth and that it will have to incur additional debt, and will not have sufficient liquidity to survive in the long run.[20]

There is no accounting or regulatory standard governing the calculation of FCF. Consequently, companies can boost FCF "by stretching out their payments, tightening payment collection policies and depleting inventories,"[21] and by exploiting disagreements about "exactly which items should and should not be treated as capital expenditures."[22]

CEO Accounting-Speak and CN's Privatization

Pre-Privatization Phase (1992 to February 26, 1995)[23]

In 1993, in the prelude to the privatization, the (then) CEO of CN, Paul Tellier, presented a gloomy picture of the company in the employee newspaper, *Keeping Track*. He is quoted as saying that "CN has broken all possible records in corporate history – with the largest corporate loss ever recorded in Canada."[24] He indicated a strong intention to "communicate the urgency of CN's (financial) situation" to employees and to present them with "the company's plan of action."[25] On the front page of *Keeping Track*, Tellier used accounting-speak to highlight CN's total reported loss of $1,005 million for 1992.[26] This suited his privatization-positioning agenda nicely. The accounting measure of profit (in this instance, a "negative net profit" or large loss) helped him persuade employees to accept the privatization of CN. Tellier drew attention to the downward spiral in reported profits: a profit of $8 million in 1990, a $14 million loss in 1991, and the record loss of $1,005 million in 1992.

Tellier's accounting-speak was mischievous in its support of CN's overall privatization strategy. Most of the reported "bottom-line loss" of $1,005 million in 1992 was due to "one-off" "special charges" of $887 million for "workforce reduction." In that year, there was also a substantial extraordinary (accounting) item of $64 million for "post-retirement benefits other than pensions." These two items rendered a fair and reasonable comparison with the two prior years' results invalid. The special charges reduced profit in a way that assumed they had been incurred in 1992 – when, in fact, they were expended principally in the following three years. Further, the "one-off" extraordinary charge of $64 million (mainly for post-retirement benefits) was written off against 1992 revenues despite most of the payments involved being borne well into the future.

Such use of discretionary accounting practices suited Tellier's rhetorical agenda. His accounting-speak (and that of his successors as CEO) deserves scrutiny because it misconstrued and misled by entering highly contestable interpretations of accounting measures. The intent was to induce the various stakeholders of CN, including employees, to accept that the company's financial state was dire, and that the company needed to transform from its self-claimed "do or die situation"[27] in 1992.

During Privatization Phase (February 27, 1995, to November 17, 1995)

Much of the debate in this phase was directed to support the success of CN's IPO that was then being considered by the public and the investment community. A large part of the case to subscribe for shares was that the privatization would enhance CN's capacity to improve operating efficiency and attain lower OR targets. The OR had become ingrained as an integral part of the life world and performance management lexicon of CN's senior managers.

The prospectus for the IPO used projected OR measures to elaborate two elements of CN's intended post-privatization compensation policy. First, the basis for the calculation of annual variable cash bonuses to senior managers was "the achievement of ... targets based on the OR, pre-tax rail income and total operating expense reductions." Second, an attractive management stock option plan was proposed whereby options would be granted "to acquire common shares at a price equal to the IPO price." However, a proviso was that two-thirds of the options would vest only if CN's OR targets decreased from 85.6% to 82.0% between 1996 and 2000.[28] Thus, the OR was a critical element of projected incentive plans for managers. Investors who were considering subscribing to the IPO would have been warmed by the prospect that these OR-related incentives would spur managers to increase operating efficiency and, presumably, profits.

Post-Privatization Phase (November 17, 1995, to the present)[29]

In this phase, accounting performance measures and accounting language generally were invoked by CEOs to show that the decision to privatize had been wise. Many of the claims in this phase promoting the success of the privatization were supported by accounting language and measures. For example, in commemorating the tenth anniversary of the privatization, CN's annual report for 2005 began with a prominent 13-page section heavily laden with accounting-speak and headed: "A Great Run, A Great Future." Two full pages were devoted to highlighting impressive changes in each of five performance measures: OR, diluted earnings per share, market capitalization, FCF, and dividend increases. This seemed intended to show that the imagined future for the privatized CN in the early and mid-1990s had come to fruition. Although CN's post-privatization accounting-speak continues to the present day, our analysis in this chapter focuses on the years up to and including the tenth anniversary celebration in 2005.

Accounting-speak was used to tell and re-tell this "good tale" of success over time as a means of persuasion,[30] especially by Paul Tellier (CEO from 1992 to 2003) and E. Hunter Harrison (CEO from 2003 to 2009) in their letters to shareholders. Elements of the "good tale" of privatization success are evident in those letters at several levels.

The *heroes* at the macro level are market forces and the socially beneficial outcomes generated from a pursuit of profit and capitalism generally. At the micro level, the *heroes* include the CEOs and senior managers of CN and the politicians responsible for the decision to privatize. The *villains*, at the macro level, are bureaucrats and misguided national economic policy. They are demonized for placing government business entities in competitive markets but burdening them with community service obligations. At the micro level, the *villains* are entrenched and inefficient work practices, employees with a poor work ethic, and ineffective operating systems. The *audience*, at the macro level, includes the Canadian public and (more importantly from CN's perspective) the investment community. At the micro level, the *audience* includes shareholders, employees, and other immediate stakeholders in CN – and the CEOs themselves.

Accounting-Speak and the Narrative of Success

A high volume of perception-fashioning rhetoric emerged after the privatization. The ten CEO letters to shareholders in CN's annual reports for 1996 to 2005 highlighted accounting-related benchmarks. The accounting-related rhetoric that emerged relied on two strategic decisions by CN: first, to calculate OR using US GAAP rather than Canadian GAAP; and second, to prefer FCF to OR as the principal performance measure.

CEOs Tellier and Harrison engaged in unremitting hyperbole about the success of the privatization and its beneficial transformational effects. They invoked accounting-speak to describe the privatization "after story" as glorious and superior to the "before story." Such glorification of the "success" story ought to have prompted greater skepticism.

The targets set in the IPO in 1995 were to reduce OR from 85.6 percent to 82 percent by 2000. These were exceeded by 1997 (see exhibit 9.1). The company attributed this achievement to the incentives in its stock option plan for managers. In 1997, CN set revised OR targets for a new tranche of management stock options. The bulk of these were exercisable if there was a "specific and ambitious improvement of the Operating Ratio" from 76 percent (US GAAP) in 1998 to below 70 percent (US GAAP) in 2001.[31]

Since 1998, CN has adjusted its operating expenses and operating revenue (and hence its OR) to take account of the effects of adopting US GAAP. CN has also excluded special charges (mainly for workforce reduction costs, such as severance payments). But it has also recorded special charges for the "costs to redeem, repurchase or defease [annul] long-term debt" and for "asset impairment write-downs."[32] The typical effect of making adjustments for special charges is to lower the reported OR. As an example, in 2002, management removed a $120 million "workforce reduction charge" and a $281 million "personal injury charge" from railroad operating expenses. This caused that year's adjusted OR to be 69.4 percent,

Exhibit 9.1 Canadian National Railway's operating ratio and free cash flow, 1990–2004

(1) Year Ended December 31	(2) OR (exc. special charges) per Canadian GAAP Percent	(3) OR (exc. special charges) per US GAAP Percent	(4) OR (inc. special charges) per Canadian GAAP Percent	(5) OR (inc. special charges) per US GAAP Percent	(6) FCF ($CDN Mill)
Ronald E. Lawless *incumbent CEO*					
1990	98.2	98.0	98.2	98.0	n.d.
1991	96.8	96.8	96.8	96.8	n.d.
Paul M. Tellier *appointed CEO*					
1992	97.1	97.3	121.5	121.7	n.d.
1993	94.9	95.1	96.1	96.4	n.d.
1994	*89.4*	89.6	89.4	89.6	n.d.
1995	*89.3*	n.d.	n.d.	n.d.	n.d.
1996	*85.3*	84.7	n.d.	n.d.	n.d.
1997	*81.5*	78.4	n.d.	n.d.	n.d.
1998	79.6	*75.3*	n.d.	n.d.	228
1999	76.6	*72.0*	n.d.	n.d.	276
2000	74.6	*69.6*	n.d.	n.d.	386
2001	74.1	*68.5*	n.d.	n.d.	443
E. Hunter Harrison *appointed CEO*					
2002	75.2/75.5	*69.4*	82.0	76.0	*513*
2003	76.8	*69.8*	76.8	69.8	*578*
2004	n.d.	*66.9*	65.9	66.9	*1,025*
2005	n.d.	*63.8*	n.d.	n.d.	*1,301*

Notes: n.d. = not disclosed; italics indicate that this figure was mentioned in the CEO's letter to shareholders
Source: CN's Annual Reports, 1990–2005

whereas the year's OR (based on Canadian GAAP which included these charges in operating expenses) had been much higher (75.5 percent).

CN has endeavored to report a declining OR over time. The company wanted its OR to be lower than its competitors. However, its capacity to achieve these outcomes is affected by whether OR is calculated according to Canadian GAAP or US GAAP. Significant differences arise between the two: for example, CN's Canadian GAAP net profit for 2003 was reported as CDN$734 million, while its US GAAP net profit for the same year was CDN$1,014 million.[33]

Replacing Operating Ratio with Free Cash Flow

Management's discretion to deflate or inflate the annual reported OR figure means they can "gamesplay" by exercising their prerogative and allowable discretion under accounting rules to manipulate the operating revenue and operating expense of any reporting period. Given the equivocality surrounding the construction of the OR, managers subject to control by this ratio have short-term self-interest incentives (e.g., through stock option plans) to engage in gamesplay to construct an OR outcome that is amenable to them. CN's management had a keen interest in how OR was calculated because their compensation bonuses and ability to exercise performance share options were linked to whether they succeeded in reducing the OR to target levels.

Usually, CN placed discussion of the OR prominently at the beginning of the annual report CEO letter to shareholders. In 1999, CEO Tellier wrote that "our operating ratio was the best of all Class I railroads at 72.0 percent, an improvement of 3.1 points from our operating ratio of 75.1 in 1998." Thus, OR was a key benchmark that CN used to compare itself to its competition. In 2000, Tellier began his letter by reinforcing the importance of the OR as a fundamental measure of achievement for CN management:

> On November 17, 2000, CN celebrated the fifth anniversary of its IPO. It was a moment for all of us to pause and reflect on our accomplishments – the most successful privatization in Canadian history; going from worst to first among railroads in operating ratio and other performance measures.[34]

In 2001, Tellier wrote that

> despite the challenges presented by a significantly weaker economy, we continued to improve our operating ratio, reaching 68.5 percent, excluding the workforce adjustment charge. This was 1.1 points better than the 69.6 figure we achieved in 2000.[35]

On January 28, 2004, CN announced its financial results for the fourth quarter of 2003. This gave headline prominence to the OR: "CN Reports Q4–2003 performance, record operating ratio of 66.1 per cent."[36] CEO Harrison claimed that this OR result "and strong free cash flow ...

[demonstrated] the value of CN's proven business model focused on service, cost control, asset utilization, safety and people."

CN has sought to drive its OR down as low as possible. But the extent to which that is feasible depends on the technology in use, the type of freight carried, the nature of the terrain over which track passes, and other important contextual factors such as weather and labor relations. An ultimate goal of an OR equal to zero is nonsensical. Even a low OR of, say, 40 percent (if that were achievable) implies a profit of 60 cents in every dollar of revenue. Such an outcome would expose CN to accusations of price gouging, requests for price controls, demands for wage increases, and the entry of new competitors.

A minimum achievable level of OR is likely for a given mix of technology, competitive forces, collective bargaining agreements, and market circumstances. We call this OR_{MIN}. It is the minimum OR that will result if management uses existing factors of production in the most efficient manner. Because CN has long been making determined efforts to reduce OR, its actual OR is likely to approach OR_{MIN} asymptotically. We assess the OR_{MIN} for CN as being likely to fall in the range 55 to 65 percent. Assuming no major breakthroughs in technology or in other factors (such as abandoning relatively high-cost, low-profit rail lines), large reductions in OR become increasingly difficult to sustain repeatedly over time as OR_{MIN} is approached. This reduces the rhetorical appeal of the OR as a public and internal performance measure (see exhibit 9.2).

Exhibit 9.2 is consistent with CN's experience over time. The company's OR figures since 1990 evidence large reductions from the high 90s down to the low 60s. It is plausible that OR_{MIN} was being approached at times between 1995 and the early 2000s. During the early years after the privatization of CN in 1995, it made a good story to proclaim large year-to-year reductions in the OR. However, as time passed and relatively easy reductions in OR were achieved, a plateau was reached in the early 2000s and it would have been increasingly difficult to achieve further large reductions in OR.

This seems to have prompted Harrison, in his CEO letter of 2002 (when the OR was reported to be 69.4 percent) to introduce FCF as another accounting-related performance benchmark. FCF allows large percentage increases to be claimed from year to year. Furthermore, it has no upper bound – in contrast to the lower bound (OR_{MIN}) of the OR. The first sentence of Harrison's 2002 CEO letter states, "CN delivered growth and generated record free cash flow." In his 2003 letter, he claims, "CN has maintained the industry's ... best free cash flow performance in 2003." The silence in these letters with respect to the OR is revealing and understandable given

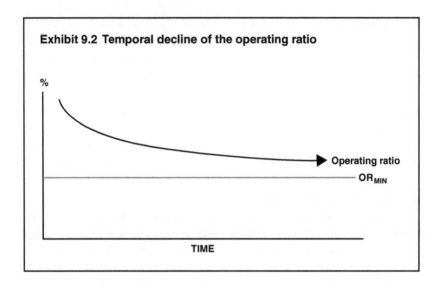

Exhibit 9.2 Temporal decline of the operating ratio

the rhetorical problem confronting CN. Although OR was touted widely as an indicator of efficiency in railroading, CN's OR had served its purpose and could no longer sustain CN's rhetoric of "privatization success." Nor was the OR as serviceable for CN's executive compensation incentive plan.

CN solved this rhetorical and practical problem in 2002 by shifting emphasis to FCF, an unbounded measure. However, since the public discourse of railroading incorporates widespread talk of the OR, acknowledgment of this accounting measure could not be ignored entirely. This is evident in the following excerpt from Harrison's 2004 CEO letter:

> It was a banner year for CN [...]
>
> Our Operating ratio for the year was a record 66.9 per cent ... performance in this key measure improved 2.9 percentage points when compared with the 69.8 Operating ratio we reported for 2003.
>
> Perhaps the most dramatic yardstick for CN financial performance in 2004 was in the area of free cash flow. Here, our business model and success in executing it delivered powerful results: record free cash flow in 2004 of $1,025 million, a significant increase over the $578 million we generated in 2003.[37]

Here Harrison acknowledges the OR, lauds it as "a record," and claims it is a "key measure." But his reference to FCF is much more potent. Harrison claims that FCF is "the most dramatic yardstick for CN financial performance in 2004." Indeed, 2004 showed there was a "record" FCF and "a significant increase" over the prior year. The OR results were said to be driven by operational factors whereas the FCF results were due more to strategic factors and "our business model and success in executing it." Insofar as strategic management success is valued more than operating management success, this shift from OR to FCF (and the associated shift in accounting-speak) combined to enhance the potency of CN's post-privatization narrative of success.

The FCF for 2000 to 2004 reveals a desirable steadily increasing FCF from 2000 to 2004, as follows:[38]

Year	FCF ($CDN Millions)
2000	386
2001	443
2002	513
2003	578
2004	1,025

However, in calculating FCF for 2004 ($1,025 million) and for 2001 ($443 million), CN adds back the cash outflow arising from acquiring major subsidiary companies in those years. This procedure was rationalized on the grounds that such acquisitions "are not indicative of normal day-to-day investments in the company's asset base." So, the FCF reported for 2001 and 2004 are distorted by the large cash flow effect of the added-back items in each of those years ($1,278 million in 2001 and $1,531 million in 2004). A more defensible approach in estimating annual FCF is to smooth large acquisition costs over several years. Had this been done, the resulting FCF figures would not reveal the desirable steadily increasing trend that CN reported. Moreover, it would not have been as helpful in sustaining a case to replace the OR with FCF as CN's prime yardstick of operating performance.

Concluding Comments

CEOs of large corporations often draw on accounting measures such as net profit, OR, and FCF to benchmark performance. The task of decoding CEO-speak will be aided if it is recognized that the accounting performance benchmarks relied upon can often be calibrated and changed at will. A skeptical outlook is needed in entering assessments of company financial and operating performance. Accounting-speak should be monitored closely by stakeholders because it is a complicit servant of the strategic and rhetorical ends of companies and their CEOs.

chapter ten

Autobiographical Vignettes

Another medium for CEO communication is short autobiographical narratives or vignettes that are included in a CEO's annual report letter. These can generate fresh insights to the CEO's personality and leadership. By "vignette" we mean "a brief evocative description, account, or episode."[1] Examples of autobiographical vignettes can be found by searching CEO narratives for phrases such as "I remember… ," "My first… ," and "When I … ." Autobiographical vignettes are "life stories as told in the present time."[2] They allow the past to be the "starting point for a story that fits the present circumstances … [and for it to be] a blend of author and audience, spatial and temporal context, and … the hopes, and often, failed aspirations of lived lives."[3]

Autobiographical vignettes are not a routine part of the written communications of CEOs. They are used occasionally, often prompted by strategic factors. Nonetheless, some CEOs (such as Warren Buffett of Berkshire Hathaway) use autobiographical vignettes frequently in communications with stakeholders. Buffett's annual report CEO letters to stockholders attract a high degree of interest in the business and broader community.[4] In part, this is because he uses autobiographical vignettes to recount candid personal stories of error, folly, imperfect learning, and ultimate redemption.[5] There is considerable potential for strategic use of autobiographical vignettes to elicit an emotional connection with stakeholders (especially employees) and for them to help fashion the landscape within which a firm proposes to develop, and possibly transform.[6]

Autobiographical vignettes in CEO letters are one of the "mechanisms by which management attempts to exert control."[7] Skillful use of autobiographical vignettes can help to control the behavior of other persons.[8] They can "shape and reinforce shared values, promote a common organizational identity, and frame issues, build legitimacy, or help to accomplish change."[9] Followers and stakeholders can draw on autobiographical vignettes to assess the accountability, personality, and leadership style of a CEO. For example, two weeks before Barack Obama's inauguration as president of the USA, Jonathan Raban reviewed Obama's 1995 autobiography *Dreams from My Father*.[10] Raban was (we believe) cannily accurate in predicting Obama's leadership style, concluding that Obama's presidency was likely to feature a

> watchful eye and patiently attentive ear; a proper humility in the face of the multiplex character of human society; and, most of all, a belief in the power of [Obama's] imagination to comprehend and ultimately reconcile the manifold contradictions in his teeming world.[11]

Because CEOs have "complex lived histories, social status, emotions and psyches,"[12] it is reasonable to believe that an autobiographical vignette in a CEO letter will reflect these factors and hold clues to the CEO's character, behavior, and ideology. By giving closer attention to autobiographical vignettes, we can obtain fresh insights to how CEOs conceive and enact leadership, perceive and manage followers, and exert management control.

In this chapter, we introduce examples of autobiographical vignettes from the CEO letters to shareholders of British Petroleum (CEO Dudley, 2010) and Walmart (CEO Duke, 2008). We also cite examples of vignettes presented to US Congressional committees by Dennis Muilenburg, CEO of Boeing, in October 2019 and by Jeff Bezos, CEO of Amazon, in July 2020. Although we offer some observations on each these vignettes, we do not delve into their deep context. Rather, we reserve analysis of deep context to three autobiographical vignettes that were embedded in CEO letters of Canadian National Railway (CN) during the tenure of E. Hunter Harrison as CEO from January 1, 2003, until December 31, 2009. We focus on these principally to highlight their strategic importance in the context of CN's adjustment to being a privatized entity. We demonstrate the capacity for Harrison's autobiographical vignettes to self-construct the image by which he wanted to be known. In particular, we highlight how he used appeals to emotion in several vignettes to build common ground and legitimacy with employees.

Autobiographical vignettes in a CEO letter can serve at least three purposes: strategic communication, self-legitimation, and belief forming. Each of these purposes is discussed below.

Strategic communication. BP used an autobiographical vignette strategically in its 2010 CEO letter as part of a strategy to repair trust after the *Deepwater Horizon* disaster. (For fuller discussion of this disaster, see chapter 6.) BP wanted to overcome the distrust and negative impressions held by the American public and other stakeholders. One way of doing this was for the (then) recently appointed CEO, Bob Dudley, to "put to the fore his American identity and strive to show that he personally care[d] for the areas and people hit by the spill."[13] Dudley's following autobiographical vignette was located near the beginning of his letter:

> [I]t all started in a part of the world that's very close to my heart. I grew up in Mississippi, and spent summers with my family swimming and fishing in the Gulf. I know those beaches and waters well. When I heard about the accident I could immediately picture how it might affect the people who live and work along that coast.[14]

This vignette shows Dudley's sense of belonging and emotional attachment. It promotes positive perceptions of him and BP's

> benevolence toward the inhabitants of the Gulf and … toward Americans. By stressing his American roots and portraying himself as a member of the community (he could immediately picture the impact the spill would have on the local people's lives), the CEO also seeks to establish his credibility as a trustworthy interlocutor, a task that his predecessor failed at.[15]

The vignette personalizes Dudley and his message to "fellow shareholders." It signals how intimate the tragedy was to him as BP's new leader.

No other autobiographical vignette appears in Dudley's subsequent seven post-*Deepwater Horizon* CEO letters in BP's annual reports for 2011 to 2017. In this regard, the autobiographical vignette in his 2010 letter stands alone. The vignette served a *strategic* communication purpose because it appeared in the first CEO letter after the *Deepwater Horizon* tragedy. Apparently, no such strategic communication purpose was felt to be needed in subsequent years. Thus, although autobiographical vignettes are not routine inclusions in CEO letters, occasional use of them makes their impact strategic and more potent. They do not need to be used frequently to have impact.

Self-legitimization. A study based on "life-history" interviews with members of the British business elite concluded that "business leaders use their storytelling as a vehicle for self-legitimization"[16] and as part of "an ongoing search for [personal] legitimacy."[17] A leader can invoke four modes of legitimacy-seeking:

1. *Defying the odds* (being heroic): demonstrating courage, fortitude and tenacity, and a capacity to triumph in adversity.

2. *Staying the course* (being steadfast): being resilient and committed. Thus, the leader can be regarded as trustworthy and loyal and as possessing the determination to be successful.
3. *Succeeding through talent* (being meritorious): making it clear that success comes from one's own efforts. This inspires confidence and support among followers and other stakeholders.
4. *Giving back to society* (being altruistic): highlighting the leader's accumulated material success and reputation while conveying the impression of being a compassionate individual who places society's well-being above self-interest.[18]

Belief-forming. Autobiographical vignettes are elements of "a battery of belief-forming institutions"[19] They are reminiscent of a "confessional" and a "romance (the hero overcomes daunting obstacles to attain the object of his affection); [and] epic (the hero overcomes daunting obstacles to realize his own and his people's destiny)."[20] Epic stories (with the CEO as hero) have an important role to play "in preserving a place [for the CEO] within the elite, demonstrating fitness to lead, warding off potential challengers and safeguarding control."[21]

Opinion is divided on whether a vignette should be true or not. One view is that the "narrative coherence and the believability of leaders' life stories is crucial for followers."[22] Another view is that in translating the life story "from event to memory and from memory to text" and coupling this with "the separation of the narrator from the narrative ... the inevitable conclusion is that alternative life stories, alternative interpretations of life, must be possible."[23] Thus, an autobiographical vignette should be considered a textual or symbolic attempt at control rather than a textual portrayal of "truth." For some, "the accuracy of *information* is nearly irrelevant, whereas accuracy of *feeling and experience* ... how it felt to be there while these concrete things were actually happening ... is critical to the storyteller."[24] The latter view accords more with post-truth thinking that condones "cherry-pick[ing] data [to] come to whatever conclusion you desire."[25]

Life-Story Vignettes and the CEO Letter

The identities projected by CEOs, and by which followers know them, can be bound intimately with their life stories. Steve Jobs emphasized this in his highly influential commencement speech at Stanford University in 2005. There is support for the idea that "[b]y reflecting on personal life stories, leaders develop unique perspectives and values that support their authentic leadership."[26]

Telling a "good [CEO life story] tale" is a means of capturing attention.[27] Such tales can be influential because of their power to constitute and configure the past and anticipate the future.[28] Reading or hearing a story told by a CEO (especially a story in which the CEO is the central character or hero) can be very persuasive. This is especially so if, as in many stories, "the problem is solved and everything works out well …"[29] Effectiveness in telling a company's story can be enhanced if the CEO is the central character in a heroic life-story vignette.

Life stories that reify a revered company founder, such as Walt Disney of The Walt Disney Company,[30] can be particularly effective in promoting images of a "friendly ghost," a "benign patriarch," or "utopian images of family, community, and work life."[31] The promotion of such images in the case of Walmart's founder, Sam Walton, have ignored claims that Walmart engaged in predatory business practices, adopted an aggressive anti-union stance, and had dubious integrity.[32]

We now introduce three brief examples, without contextualization, of illustrative autobiographical vignettes. We then move on to an in-depth analysis of three vignettes of E. Hunter Harrison when he was CEO of CN. The first non-contextualized example is from the annual report CEO letter to shareholders in 2008 of the (then) newly appointed CEO of Walmart, Michael Duke. He wrote:

> My first day in the new job fell on the first Sunday in February. So my wife Susan and I took a few hours to move some boxes and belongings into my new office. But we didn't replace the carpet, furniture, or even Sam Walton's old wood paneling. With the exception of a couple of pictures on the wall, we kept it as the same office in which Sam Walton, David Glass and Lee Scott made the decisions that built our great Company. I could not be more honored or more humbled to sit at their desk now.[33]

This story is located near the end of the CEO letter, just before the following sentence: "Although there will continue to be many changes at Wal-Mart, there is one thing that will never change – our culture." In this vignette, Duke does not disturb the physical setting in which prior generations of Walmart leaders "made the decisions that built our great company." Thereby, Duke strongly signals his respect for Walmart's history and culture. He is sitting "at their desk," not at his desk.

Duke lets us know that his "first day in the new job" was a Sunday, and he and his wife (and presumably not hired movers) "took a few hours to move some boxes and belongings into my new office." Working on a Sunday, and engaging one's spouse to assist, offers a lesson in commitment, teamwork, and cost savings. Thus, a strong work ethic and respect for tradition and culture are the vivid images conveyed. These are images that Duke and his top management team intend employees to emulate and shareholders to regard approvingly. This one short story seems to use symbolism to control Walmart employees and gain the approval of capital providers at the same time.

We now turn to an illustrative vignette in the opening statement of (then) Boeing CEO Dennis Muilenburg to the US House of Representatives Committee on Transportation and Infrastructure, on October 30, 2019. Muilenburg was appearing as part of the Committee's investigation into the crash of two Boeing 737 MAX airplanes. He said,

> Mr. Chairman, I've worked at Boeing my entire career. It started more than 30 years ago when Boeing offered me a job as a summer intern in Seattle. I was a junior at Iowa State University studying engineering, having grown up on our family farm in Iowa. It's beautiful land with rolling hills where my siblings and I milked cows and baled hay. Our parents taught us the value of hard work, integrity, and respect for others. Back then, I drove my 1982 Monte Carlo from Iowa to Boeing's operations in Seattle, crossing the Rocky Mountains for the first time. I was awestruck at the opportunities I had to work on projects that mattered at the company that brought the Jet Age to the world and helped land a person on the moon. I was amazed by the people of Boeing. Today, I'm still inspired every day by what Boeing does and by the remarkable men and women who are committed to continuing its legacy.[34]

Muilenburg evokes an idyllic personal story that is consistent with (idealized) American family values. He claims his family farm background spent baling hay and milking has taught him "the value of hard work, integrity, and respect for others." Further, and importantly, Muilenburg lauds his employer and "the remarkable men and women who are committed to continuing its legacy." This autobiographical vignette frames the testimony he gave to the committee charged with investigating a horrific set of events. Such framing seems intended to condition members of the committee to be softer in the assessments they make of Muilenburg's trustworthiness and integrity. However, Boeing's board of directors was not soft in its assessment of Muilenburg. In a press release on December 23, 2019, it announced that Muilenburg had resigned and that the board of directors had "decided a change in leadership was necessary to restore confidence in the company."[35]

The third illustrative vignette was submitted at the beginning of a 4,457-word written statement by Jeff Bezos, CEO of Amazon, to a hearing of the US House of Representatives Committee on Judiciary on July 29, 2020, titled "Online Platforms and Market Power, Part 6: Examining the Dominance of Amazon, Apple, Facebook, and Google."[36] This autobiographical vignette, comprising 885 words, is not reproduced in this chapter because of its length, but is shown in appendix E. It is likely that Bezos began with a highly personal story in such a high-powered setting because, as a sophisticated corporate leader, he understood the potential to exploit the rhetorical power of a good life tale in a hostile setting.

Bezos begins: "I'm Jeff Bezos. I founded Amazon 26 years ago with the long-term mission of making it Earth's most customer-centric company." He then immediately turns to his autobiographical tale, perhaps to help him explain and justify the company's "long-term mission." The opening paragraphs are devoted to the struggles of his mother, Jackie, and his father, Miguel. He tells an inspiring tale of how they, as marginalized people, were able to overcome adversity, aided by supportive family members and a commitment to education.

In a very personal way, Bezos praises hard work, education, persistence, family values, family responsibility, loyalty, and the importance of role models. His use of an extended autobiographical vignette to frame his appearance before the congressional committee helps him gain the moral high ground and to dilute criticism that would otherwise have been directed at him and Amazon.

We now provide deeper contextual analysis of three autobiographical vignettes attributed to the former CEO of CN, E. Hunter Harrison, in three of his CEO letters. As we explained in the preceding chapter, CN used language strategically after its privatization in 1995 to sustain a rhetoric of post-privatization success. The company wanted stakeholders to accept the strategy it had adopted[37] and to agree that the decision to privatize was sagacious. As part of this strategy, several CEOs engaged in "unremitting hyperbole about the success of the privatization and the transformational effect of the privatization on CN."[38]

Thus, the autobiographical vignettes in Harrison's 2004, 2005, and 2007 CEO letters are scenes within a long-running grand narrative of CN's alleged post-privatization success.[39] The vignettes are part of the array of management control devices CN marshalled to win support for the privatization strategy and the company's ensuing reforms of management control practices. In the analysis below, we look for language-related insights to Harrison's personality, leadership, and style of management control. We focus on the narrator (the CEO) because of the potential for a CEO's discourse "to reveal how they view the world and their company within it."[40]

Ewing Hunter Harrison was CEO of CN from 2003 until 2009. The three autobiographical vignettes of his that we examine are from CN's annual reports for 2004 (129 words), 2005 (167 words), and 2007 (203 words). Before using a close reading approach to analyze them, we first provide a brief biographical profile of Harrison.

Harrison (b. November 7, 1944 – d. December 16, 2017) was an American-born career railway executive who served variously as the CEO of Illinois Central Railroad, CN, Canadian Pacific Railway, and CSX Corporation. During his tenure at CN, Harrison was named Railroader of the Year for 2002 by industry trade journal *Railway Age* and as CEO of the Year for 2007 by the Canadian newspaper *The Globe and Mail*.

Harrison was known as a "hard-nosed" "hard-core red meat man" with "testicular fortitude."[41] He was characterized as a "crusty," "relentless," "impatient," and "no-nonsense" person but was also a "polarizing figure, admired and loathed in seemingly equal parts." He was described as an "innovator," "mind changer," and "brass-knuckle fixer," respected for his "ability to inculcate culture change." He preached the need for "continuous improvement," cost cutting, and streamlining. His five guiding principles as CEO were "service, cost control, asset utilization, safety and people."

Labor Relations at CN[42]

Harrison's three vignettes are explored in the context of CN's labor relations environment at that time. Of major note is that in early 2004, CN experienced its first major strike since privatization in 1995. Employees resented CN adopting "American business practices" that were aimed at cutting costs and boosting profits. The pervading work environment in many parts of CN was said to be hostile and intimidating because of the aggressive attitude to workers by an "American-style" management. CN's American managers were claimed to be "ruthless by Canadian standards" and to have instituted "some eyebrow-raising labour changes." They were criticized for increasing employee workloads and for treating Canadian employees in a derisory manner, including through such slurs as "snow niggers" and "overpaid Mexicans."[43] Many CN workers felt humiliated and disrespected by management.

Speaking in early 2004, Doug Olshewski, a national representative of CN's main union, the Canadian Auto Workers Union, stated that "a real big issue" was "… the lack of dignity shown to the workers …" [44] In 2004, in the *Globe and Mail*, CEO Harrison acknowledged that

> the strike was mostly a result of management's failure to do a better job at communicating the need for change … to workers [and that] the real issue was the management of change [and that] a key challenge for the company now is to try to repair the relations with the CAW [so that] we don't go through this experience again. [45]

Our analysis has firmly in mind the prospect that the three vignettes were part of an image-repair strategy to improve CN's labor relations environment and help CN and its CEO to be regarded as more respectful, less aggressive, more inclusive, and more understanding of workplaces and employees. In each vignette, Harrison recounts a tale from his lifetime experience of working in railroading. The vignettes are not drawn from his life *before* railroading. This helps him to garner legitimacy as the CEO of a railroad company such as CN. The emphasis on his railroader experience reinforces his right to speak authoritatively about CN's strategy, performance, and future operation.

Vignette 1 is a recollection of Harrison's time, early in his career, working in the Memphis rail yard of his (then) employer and meeting a "great railroader," W.F. Thompson. In the preamble to vignette 2, Harrison mentions his "40 years in [the railroad] business." Vignette 3 is a tale of Harrison's time "as a young railroader coming up in the business" and being taught how to inspect rail ties. Collectively, the three vignettes "lend consistency to otherwise fragmented experiences … [in a way] … that is community building." [46] They subtly encourage readers to subscribe to a mild form of epic tale in which Harrison is a hero whose railroading career progressed through hard work, commitment, and listening to the advice of "wiser heads."

Harrison projects himself as a CEO who knows what he is talking about. He constructs a self-image as a legitimate leader who has common work experience with employees. He demonstrates his believability and fitness to lead. He is not an outsider or a novice in the industry. Rather, he is a legitimate railroader who has inspected rail ties, walked rail yards, and met great railroaders. This is the image he wants to project to stakeholders, especially employees. The narrative implies that he attained the position of CEO by working hard and listening to the advice of more experienced railroaders. He seems keen to motivate employees to do the same – to comply with *his* (as a now "great" railroader) policies and management direction. Harrison's implicit message to employees is "you can improve yourself too by doing the same as me" and "you can become a better rail-roader" by being more accommodating of the changed workplace labor practices CN has implemented.

Harrison's three vignettes course over common ground with employees and are likely to appeal to them.[47] The subtle conditioning rhetoric directed to employees is "work hard and listen to me, even if it goes against the grain of your current work attitudes." Thus, Harrison's personal story becomes a symbol of what can be achieved by employees in a company, such as CN, that is committed to transformation. This symbolism is exploited in an endeavor to exert management control by changing the attitude of employees. The intent seems to be to have employees commit (if they have not already) to the management control changes (such as labor shedding and changed rostering practices) instituted at CN in the post-privatization era.

The picture that emerges of Harrison is of a hard-working, committed, and determined leader by example – one who is seeking followers (employees) to do as he has done.

Vignette 1

This autobiographical vignette appeared near the beginning of Harrison's CEO letter in CN's 2004 annual report:

> I remember one of the turning points of my career. I was a young man, in my first management job at BN's [Burlington Northern's] Memphis yard. W.F. Thompson, a great railroader who would eventually become a mentor of mine, was visiting the facility. He looked out at a rail yard packed with cars and asked me, "Son, what do you see out there?" I was young, and he was a big, intimidating man. I wanted to say the right thing. My answer was, "Sir, that's a lot of business out there in the yard."
>
> Mr. Thompson's answer changed forever my view of railroading. He said, "You know, that's the problem. You look at a crowded yard and see a lot of business. I see a lot of delayed trains."[48]

Two paragraphs later Harrison writes: "Since that moment in the Memphis yard long ago, getting the absolute maximum out of rail assets has been a major focus of mine." This autobiographical vignette is reinforced vividly elsewhere in CN's 2004 annual report. The front cover presents a simple stark photograph of an empty rail yard with the words: "This is excellence." On page 1, in a large, highlighted sidebar, the following text appears: "To CN, an empty rail yard represents excellence because it means our assets are out on the network – moving product, earning revenue and helping customers compete."

This autobiographical vignette is a confessional tale and a parable. It recounts a seemingly brief, but nonetheless highly memorable episode in the life of the CEO. Importantly, it reveals how Harrison conceives and enacts leadership. The vignette is framed as an epiphany or "narrative of self-realization."[49] Harrison, as a now mature and renowned CEO himself, recalls his (presumably) chance meeting many years ago (as "a young man") with "a great railroader" (W.F. Thompson). The latter communicated vividly to him (the future CEO) the importance of an empty rail yard. Both the future CEO and the "great railroader" saw the same "rail yard packed with cars." However, their respective interpretations were very different, prompting the future CEO's epiphany. Harrison basks in Thompson's aura, pays homage to him, and acknowledges him clearly as a mentor.

This vignette, and the epiphany it embodies, is a vivid way for the CEO to self-construct an identity with CN stakeholders, especially employees. Harrison enacts leadership for all who read his letter – and perhaps too for himself, as he makes sense of his world of corporate leadership. He reveres Thompson and acknowledges him as an "intimidating man." Harrison seems comfortable in endorsing a view that leadership can be enacted through intimidation.

The implicit message in vignette 1 was especially timely for CN. The vignette appeared at a time when CN wanted to convince the world of the merits of its privatization, resolve its post-privatization identity, calm labor unrest, and placate employee concerns about the lack of respect managers were showing them. The vignette is saying, in effect, that when Harrison was new to the industry his view of the railroading business was wrong. He changed and CN employees, especially those with entrenched pre-privatization "public servant" work attitudes and practices, can change too. Thus, we see "use of language to get people to do things"[50] – in this case to change their attitude and behavior.

Vignette 1 helps Harrison identify with his audience. Almost all of them are likely to have similarly embarked on a first relatively important job, feeling uncertain and harboring a desire to impress a high-profile superior. Most (if not all) employees can probably identify with Harrison in that situation. Further, since Harrison apparently learned an important lesson from this episode, CN employees and stakeholders can probably identify with him as someone open to development and change. This helps Harrison to construct the image of a legitimate leader.

However, Harrison's perspective on leadership has a curious twist. There is an ominous punchline in his assertion that "getting the absolute maximum out of rail assets has been a major focus of mine." Harrison's leadership manifesto seems to endorse a Tayloristic ideology of management control.[51] Followers ought to be interested in how such extreme declarations are implemented. This seems especially pertinent because elsewhere Harrison makes it clear that he regards "rail assets" to include human assets (that is, employees). Clearly, employees would want to know what performance measures Harrison intends to rely on to "get the absolute maximum" out of them.

Vignette 2

Harrison's 2005 letter began with five sentences that were laden with hyperbole, euphemism, and self-acclaim:

> What a great run. The accomplishments and results that CN has been able to achieve in its first 10 years as a public company are nothing short of spectacular. Some of the things we have done are beyond anything I have seen in my 40 years in this business. While our culture is never to be satisfied, there's a certain amount of pride among all of us at CN. Because it has been anything but easy.[52]

Throughout CN's 2005 annual report (and not just in the CEO letter) the company used self-eulogy and vivid graphics to celebrate its (alleged) "spectacular" "accomplishments and results" since privatization.

The fourth and fifth paragraphs of the 2005 CEO letter included the following autobiographical vignette:

> And as we entered a new period of rapid, profound change, people sometimes became emotional. I remember a meeting I had with the CN account manager for one of our largest customers. He was upset with some rightsizing and bureaucracy reductions we had made in our marketing group. He said, 'You've taken away my analyst here, you've taken away my sales person there, you've taken away this, you've taken away that. And you expect me to still manage this account?' This was the only account he managed. I got a little excited myself, and I might have raised my voice a little – I said, "Excuse me. Let me ask you a question. Exactly what is it that *you* do?"
>
> Long story short: that account manager became a believer. And we got one small step closer to the culture of precision and execution we were trying to build. Six months later, he was proud of how significantly the service he was able to offer his customer had improved.[53]

This reveals a powerful leader with an aggressive attitude. He is exercising top-down influence on a follower who seems to need enlightenment. The follower, as it transpires, eventually became enlightened and compliant. This vignette shows the CEO's determination to be steadfast and stay the course in spite of opposition from staff. Harrison uses language to "create worlds of understanding," show the "exercise of power," and "get people to do things."[54]

However, there is a touch of disingenuousness and a tone of evangelism in this leader's tale. The CEO denigrates the account manager by implying he is not pulling his weight as an employee. This is an intimidating exercise of coercive power. But such behavior is consistent with Harrison's characterization as a person who "prod[ded] a work force with a mix of fear and inspiration."[55] Harrison's actions are consistent too with those of his revered mentor, Thompson, who was known to be intimidating.

We read that the account manager has lost two hitherto valued support staff through "rightsizing" (a euphemism for sackings). He bravely remonstrates with the CEO about this. Yet, readers are informed that within six months, the account manager experienced an epiphany too – he became a "believer" in CN's ideology and restructuring and is proud of the improved service he is now offering. There is no hint of the verisimilitude that is required for successful sensegiving.[56]

Harrison has now graduated to become a (seemingly) "great railroader." He sees it to be his role to act as a sagacious business teacher to educate *his* student, the CN account manager, about the proper way to manage business within the sought-after "culture of precision and execution." Indeed, vignette 1 (2004) and vignette 2 (2005) work together. The first vignette casts Harrison as a student who has learned an apparently profound business lesson. In the second vignette, Harrison is now the GREAT RAILROADER AS TEACHER. He provides a tough-love education to a recalcitrant subordinate who "became a believer." Thus, the two autobiographical vignettes cohere in a rhetorically persuasive way to justify the wisdom of CN's strategy to privatize and to institute less amenable workplace practices for employees. Vignette 2 portrays a leader who shows strong unedifying vestiges of bullying and an apparent absence of regard for followers. This lends support to employee claims that they were being disrespected by managers.

The emerging picture is of a leader who classifies stakeholders using a binary matrix of believer or non-believer in the company's broad strategic direction and management control systems. Some stakeholders might identify readily with the image of leadership advanced, but many, including many employees, would probably recoil from it and engage in various resistance strategies, including strike action (as detailed earlier).

Vignette 3

In his 2007 CEO letter, Harrison mentions his "40 years in [the railroad] business" before likening employees who are performing unsatisfactorily to mud. He says: "We have plenty of room for progress in the people area, and progress is never permanent. It requires constant work to remove the 'mud' from an organization and keep it from coming back." Then he goes on to relate the following autobiographical vignette to explain what he means by "mud."

> When I was a young railroader coming up in the business, my supervisor was teaching me how to inspect rail ties and mark bad ones for replacement. We were moving along, and I was marking bad ties when I saw them, when the supervisor stopped me and asked me why I hadn't marked a particular tie. I told him that it looked good to me, and he said that I was right, it looked good. Then he had someone come and pull the spikes. We pulled the tie up from the ballast and turned it over. More than half the underside of the tie was gone. The middle, the most critical part of the tie, was rotted to the point that it was just a few inches thick.
>
> The cause? Mud. The tie looked fine on the surface, but the ballast underneath was not draining properly. That day I learned how to spot poor drainage, and I've since learned that the same principle applies to management. Problems under the surface – hidden "mud" – exist even in the best organizations. It's bureaucracy. It's resistance to change. It's lack of understanding or commitment. It's mud, and while it's not always visible, it always slows you down.[57]

Harrison presents himself as a leader who has learned from experience and can identify impediments to business success (such as bureaucracy and resistance to change). The implicit message is that all railroaders can learn from Harrison and resist being "slowed down" by such impediments. A striking metaphor system is evoked for reinforcement:

ORGANIZATIONAL BUREAUCRACY IS HIDDEN MUD.
RESISTANCE TO CHANGE IS HIDDEN MUD.
LACK OF UNDERSTANDING OR COMMITMENT IS HIDDEN MUD.

Harrison points out that two physical features of mud are inherent in these metaphors: mud is "not always visible" and mud "always slows you down." There is little question that mud is a harshly negative word. Harrison uses this word in a deeply pejorative way in connection with bureaucracy, resistance to change, and lack of understanding or commitment. The message he conveys is an important aspect of his use of language symbolically for management control. Given the strategic direction of CN since privatization, if any employee is hostile to bureaucracy, resists change, or lacks understanding and commitment, then that employee is making mud. Such behavior is "not always visible" and "always slows [CN] down." The implied message demeans many employees. The implication seems to be that many of them are engaging in unintended sabotage.

Concluding Comments

Autobiographical vignettes can be rhetorically potent parts of the paraphernalia of corporate control. They can be part of the public relations response to the exigencies of a company's immediate context (for example, BP's need to redeem its reputation after the *Deepwater Horizon* tragedy). They can offer important means of strategic communication and a way to legitimize leadership. By virtue of their capacity to reveal key aspects of leadership style, they can help fashion the beliefs of followers and other stakeholders.

Harrison's three vignettes have strong religious overtones of a leader who is capable of "knowing the way," seeing workforce members as "believers" and "non-believers," and drawing on a personal epiphany to transform followers' belief systems. The vignettes provide insight to Harrison as a person and to how he conceived and enacted leadership. The autobiographical vignettes discussed earlier (from the CEOs of BP, Walmart, Boeing, and Amazon) serve similar purposes.

Harrison promoted the idea that corporate leaders should respect and openly endorse the wisdom of their predecessors. Nonetheless, vignette 1 points to Harrison seeing merit in leaders and followers periodically changing their view of corporate endeavor. In enacting his leadership, Harrison seemingly condones intimidation as an acceptable way of transforming human behavior. The linguistic tropes of hyperbole, euphemism, and self-eulogy seem acceptable to him.

Harrison's three vignettes are used strategically, but none too subtly, to exercise management control. They are a call for followers to be more receptive to tough policies that endorse a program of retrenchments, cost reductions, and the prioritization of policies intended to maximize financial returns on equity capital. An important aspiration of control is the construction of an (allegedly) legitimate leader in a way that others can identify with. Such identification is at least partly influenced by the rhetoric of autobiographical vignettes embedded in a CEO letter and other media.

Autobiographical vignettes should be recognized as part of a pervasive "battery of belief-forming institutions"[58] that are available to leaders who want to influence the formation of beliefs by company stakeholders. However, they are comprehensible largely within a dominant ideology of corporate endeavor – one in which capital is privileged over labor and corporate leadership is privileged over followership. Autobiographical vignettes have strong capacity to be rhetorically potent and to frame attitudes and perceptions. Infrequent and strategic use of them adds to their potency.[59]

chapter eleven

Narcissism and Hubris

The following disturbing headlines are typical of many in the business press recently.

How narcissistic CEOs put companies at risk.[1]

Can a narcissistic CEO destroy their company?[2]

Elon Musk may not be the narcissist Tesla needs right now.[3]

Hubris is an ever-present risk for high-flying chief executives.[4]

CEO hubris costs millions.[5]

Here we explain how monitoring CEO-speak can help to identify language-based signs of narcissism and hubris. Such identification can yield early warning of harmful consequences for a company and indicate the need for remedial action.

Neither of the authors is an accredited psychiatrist or psychologist. Thus, neither can credibly or reliably diagnose dysfunctions such as narcissism and hubris. But what we can do, as we do here, is to critically analyze the language of corporate leaders with a view to proposing methods that will help identify linguistic signs of such dysfunctions.

Many companies are led successfully by CEOs who engage in narcissistic and hubristic behavior. This should not be surprising because it is often a person's grandiose sense of self-importance, preoccupation with success and power, and arrogant behavior that is instrumental in their appointment as CEO. However, an excessive level of narcissism in a CEO is dangerous because it is often associated with self-delusion and detachment from reality. There is a fine line between assertive confidence (desirable) and excessive narcissism (undesirable). The hubris of high-profile business, political, and military leaders has become a major public concern too, so much so that it has prompted the creation of the *Daedalus Trust* by Lord David Owen.[6] The aim of this trust is "primarily to raise awareness of hubris and Hubris Syndrome in public and business life."[7]

Describing a CEO as narcissistic and/or hubristic are common pejorative terms. They are often used as a catch-all diagnosis for what corporate observers deem to be dangerously inapt leadership behavior. But naming and shaming in this way has a serious side because of the potential dangers the CEOs involved pose to their company and its stakeholders.

Admiration for charismatic leaders has encouraged "the proliferation of narcissistic leaders" who exude overconfidence, a sense of entitlement, and massive egos.[8] But even when narcissistic CEOs attain success, they are often ineffective and deficient because they

> overpay when they acquire firms, costing their shareholders dearly. Their firms tend to perform in a volatile and unpredictable fashion, going from big wins to even bigger losses. They are often involved in counterproductive work behaviors, such as fraud. They are also more likely to abuse power and manipulate their followers, particularly those who are naïve and submissive.[9]

Systematic means of identifying hubristic CEOs is necessary because of the failure to address what has been described as the biggest risk facing companies – the risk that

> the chief executive gets so high on power that he or she loses the plot. Nowhere on a risk register [is] "hubristic CEO" [listed] as a specific danger to the business … [this] is a bit of an oversight when you consider [it] is the common denominator in every corporate catastrophe you've ever heard of.[10]

The dangers of leaders with hubris syndrome are that they

> often take action first, especially those actions that make them look good, then think about the consequences later. Their restless and reckless way of acting along with their messianic way of talking makes them look action oriented … [They] have an overwhelming arrogance – a feeling that they are entitled to bully and intimidate anyone less powerful, verbally and physically, especially women and those in lower positions. They think that they are always entitled to more and don't even need to listen to others, even those who are serving their needs.[11]

In this chapter, we demonstrate how analysis of CEO-speak using close reading and DICTION can elicit linguistic signs that suggest narcissism and hubris in a CEO. We begin by describing narcissism and hubris more fully. We use the definition of narcissism in the American Psychiatric Association's *Diagnostic Statistical Manual* (2000, fourth edition, text revised version) known commonly by the acronym *DSM-IV-TR*.[12] In 2009, the *DSM-IV-TR* Narcissism Personality Disorder (NPD) construct in this manual was claimed to be "the gold standard by which all other conceptualizations of narcissism should be judged."[13]

Narcissism

DSM-IV-TR defines narcissism as "a pervasive pattern of grandiosity (in fantasy or behavior), need for admiration and lack of empathy." The condition is said to exist when five (or more) of the following criteria (stated in abridged form) are present in a person:

1. Has a grandiose sense of self-importance
2. Is preoccupied with fantasies of unlimited success, power, brilliance, and beauty
3. Believes that he or she is special and unique and can only be understood by, or should associate with, other special or high-status people (or institutions)
4. Requests excessive admiration
5. Has a sense of entitlement to especially favorable treatment
6. Is interpersonally exploitative
7. Lacks empathy and is unwilling to identify with the feelings and needs of others
8. Is envious of others or believes that others are envious of him
9. Shows arrogant and haughty behaviors and attitudes

Many people err in regarding narcissism as axiomatically and necessarily bad. Indeed, narcissism "has become a linguistic garbage pail piled so high with entirely negative characteristics that it has lost its descriptive power."[14] So, it is important to recognize that all humans show signs of narcissistic behavior[15] and it is possession of too little or too much narcissism that is likely to lead to an unstable personality. Although "a healthy dose of narcissism is essential for human functioning … it is the danger of excess, particularly in the case of leaders, which gives narcissism its often derogatory connotations."[16] CEOs who have a "healthy dose" of narcissistic tendencies (and not an excess or absence) can be "very talented and capable of making great contributions to society."[17] Indeed, narcissists are often suited to lead organizations during rapid social and economic change.[18]

Constructive Narcissism and Destructive Narcissism

The difference between *constructive narcissism* and *destructive narcissism* is important. The former is potentially desirable. The latter is likely a recipe for corporate disaster.

Constructive narcissists[19] can be "quite ambitious and can be manipulative and hypersensitive to criticism."[20] They also have a positive vitality, a secure sense of self-esteem, and a capacity for introspection and empathy.[21] Constructive narcissists identify with followers, consult with them, and advance their causes.[22] Quite often, they have a vision for a better organization. They want to realize this vision with the help of others. Constructive narcissists are likely to possess the following five elements of "strategic intelligence." They will probably be able to

- predict "how social and economic forces will interact [to] change the business climate";
- "conceptualize the whole rather than … separate parts";
- combine foresight and systems thinking holistically;
- "get people … to embrace a common purpose"; and
- make personal and strategic alliances fit a vision for a company.[23]

A *constructive narcissist* is suited to an innovative, change-oriented business. There they are more likely to have scope to take risks and "to realize visions in new technologies, globalization and the information age."[24] But constructive narcissists are not well-suited to retailing and manufacturing companies "where success is measured by doing the same thing over and over again more efficiently."[25]

Destructive narcissists often enter "adulthood with a legacy of feelings of deprivation, insecurity, and inadequacy" and see life as a "zero-sum game [with] winners and losers."[26] They wield power to buttress a grandiose self-image. Destructive narcissists reign in an environment of orchestrated adulation, rash and volatile behavior, and offer paranoiac defense of themselves.[27] They are more prone to unethical behavior than constructive narcissists and are likely to be "cold, ruthless, grandiose, and exhibitionistic" and "fixated on issues of power, status, prestige, and superiority."[28] Destructive narcissists are preoccupied with having their "very inflated self-views ... continuously reinforced."[29] Many rely on ego-defense mechanisms to maintain their excessive levels of self-esteem.[30]

Fantasy is often an important component of a narcissistic personality disorder, especially for destructive narcissists. This is unsurprising because people "learn that 'getting ahead' in organizational life comes from dramatizing a fantasy about the organization's perfection."[31] CEOs who are destructive narcissists "can become intolerant of criticism, unwilling to compromise and frequently surround themselves with sycophants,"[32] such as acquiescent auditors[33] and compliant chief financial officers. They often live in a fantasy world and have a faint understanding of reality. "They are happy to find themselves in a hall of mirrors that lets them hear and see only what they want to hear and see."[34] To this we would add, "and to write what they want to see written – especially if it reflects well upon them and their leadership."

Hubris

"Hubris ... [is] not just narcissism; it's much more dangerous than that."[35] Hubris is "insolence or arrogance caused by inordinate pride ... [and] exaggerated self-confidence."[36] It is "... often associated with a lack of humility."[37] Persons with hubris tend to have lost contact with reality and are prone to overestimate their competence or capabilities. Indeed, the concept of management itself is "easily given to hubris ... [since it] ... has often lapsed into the hubris of total control – the belief that everything is, can be and must be predicted, planned for and controlled."[38]

Hubristic leaders are those

> who become excessively confident and ambitious in their strategic decision choices ... [and who] show contempt for the advice and criticism of others ... they often end up over-reaching themselves and inflicting damage, both financial and reputational, on themselves and their organizations.[39]

CEO hubris is a dysfunction[40] that leads to "overestimat[ing] the correctness of one's own judgment."[41] Such a view ignores emotionally vital aspects of hubris suggested by the observation that "hubris is a vicious response to fear."[42] The concept of hubris is "elusive and contested"[43] and needs to be clarified.

There is considerable overlap between hubris and narcissism.[44] To clarify this overlap, Lord David Owen (former UK cabinet minister, and a trained neurologist) and Jonathan Davidson proposed 14 criteria (listed below) by which to identify the hubris syndrome. They pointed out that

> 7 of the 14 possible defining symptoms are also among the criteria for Narcissistic Personality Disorder [specifically, criteria 1, 2, 3, 4, 7, 8 and 9]. Criterion 11 is associated with Antisocial Personality Disorder. Criterion 14 is associated with Histrionic Personality Disorder. The five remaining symptoms are unique [criteria 5, 6, 10, 12 and 13].

The five criteria that are unique to hubris are shown in italics in exhibit 11.1.

These 14 attributes point to the diagnostic overlap between hubris and narcissism. However, several ways in which hubris is distinct from narcissism are stressed, as follows:

> Narcissism is a personality trait characterized by self-absorption, grandiosity and a sense of entitlement. Narcissists believe that they are uniquely special and deserving of praise and admiration. They can become arrogant and hostile if their grandiose yet shallow and fragile self-concept, which they need to constantly maintain, is threatened. Hubris on the other hand is not a personality trait; it is a transitory state which develops in the wake of prior successes and the acquisition of significant power, and which may abate once power is lost. Narcissists are intoxicated with themselves, whilst hubrists are intoxicated with power and success.[45]

Thus, a key distinction between hubris and narcissism is that hubris is likely to be triggered by one's acquisition of power and attendant success, whereas narcissism is likely to be an enduring personality trait. This raises the important question of whether the presence of narcissism in an individual is a necessary precursor of hubris that becomes evident once power is acquired. Below, we canvass the potential links between narcissism, hubris, and CEO-speak.

**Exhibit 11.1 Attributes of hubris proposed by
Owen and Davidson**[46]

1. A narcissistic propensity to see their world primarily as an arena to exercise power and seek glory
2. A predisposition to take actions that seem likely to cast the individual in a good light to enhance image
3. A disproportionate concern with image and presentation
4. A messianic manner of talking about current activities and a tendency to exaltation
5. *An identification with the nation or organization to the extent that the individual regards his or her outlook and interests as identical*
6. *A tendency to speak in the third person or use the royal "we"*
7. Excessive confidence in the individual's own judgment and contempt for the advice or criticism of others
8. Exaggerated self-belief, bordering on a sense of omnipotence, in what they personally can achieve
9. A belief that rather than being accountable to the mundane court of colleagues or public opinion, the court to which they answer is history or God
10. *An unshakable belief they will be vindicated by history or God*
11. Loss of contact with reality that is often associated with progressive isolation
12. *Restlessness, recklessness, and impulsiveness*
13. *A tendency to allow their "broad vision" about the moral rectitude of a proposed course of action to obviate the need to consider practicality, cost, or outcomes*
14. Hubristic incompetence. Things go wrong because too much self-confidence has led the leader not to worry about the "nuts and bolts" of policy

Language Signals of Destructive Narcissism and Hubris

Four actions have been proposed to contain the emergence of hubris in organizations. These are "(1) high reliability organizing (2) cooperative decision-making processes (3) listening for faint signals (4) diagnosing, grounding and de-isolating the CEO."[47] We focus here on the third of these actions: listening for faint signals.

Word choices of CEOs can offer faint signals that enable hubris and destructive narcissism to be identified at a distance.[48] The words CEOs use offer "early warning signs [that] might make it easier to fix the problem rather than leaving it until disorder becomes incurable."[49] Below, we illustrate the potential for close reading and DICTION to provide faint signals of narcissism and hubris. First, we show how Enron's 2000 CEO letter reveals language signals of destructive narcissism.[50] Then we explore whether there are traces of narcissism in the CEO letters to shareholders of Starbucks and General Motors (GM). We conclude by illustrating some of the strengths and weaknesses of DICTION in assessing CEO language for linguistic signs of hubris.[51]

The annual report CEO letter is a good source from which to identify destructive narcissistic and hubristic language.[52] This is because of its privileged status as a showcase of a company and its CEO. Many CEOs are prone to believe that when the spotlight is focused on them (such as on what they write in their annual report CEO letter) they have opportunities for self-validation through gaining admiration from others. This is consistent with the view that "the performance of narcissists [is] highly sensitive to changes in self-enhancement opportunities" and that "narcissists perform well when they perceive that high performance will bring self-glorification."[53]

Enron's CEO Letter to Shareholders for 2000

We begin by applying the *DSM-IV-TR* criteria for narcissism personality disorder to the language used in Enron's annual CEO letter to shareholders for 2000.[54] This was the last such letter before Enron collapsed on December 2, 2001. The letter was signed jointly by Jeffrey Skilling (as president and CEO) and (the late) Kenneth Lay (as chair). The joint signing does not present a potential problem for the case we are advancing, because we are interested in the language of leadership and not the clinical diagnosis of specific individuals. Analysis of the letter yields insights to leadership and prevailing corporate culture. The letter's first 186 words are reproduced in exhibit 11.2,[55] with line numbers added.

The language in this extract is mesmerizing. Enron is portrayed as big, successful, growing fast, and with nothing that can impede it. Superlatives throughout the letter seem directed to give readers a clear sense of a company to envy (criterion 8; see *DSM-IV-TR* criteria listed earlier in this chapter). A persistent use of powerful hyperbole presents Enron (and Skilling and Lay) as invincible. Readers seem invited to believe that nothing

Exhibit 11.2 Opening of Skilling and Lay's letter to shareholders of Enron for 2000

[1]   Enron's performance in 2000 was a success by any measure, as we
[2]   continued to outdistance the competition and solidify our leadership in
[3]   each of our major businesses. In our largest business, wholesale ser-
[4]   vices, we experienced an enormous increase of 59 percent in physical
[5]   energy deliveries. Our retail energy business achieved its highest level
[6]   ever of total contract value. Our newest business, broadband services,
[7]   significantly accelerated transaction activity, and our oldest business,
[8]   the interstate pipelines, registered increased earnings. The company's
[9]   net income reached a record $1.3 billion in 2000.
[10]   Enron has built unique and strong businesses that have tremendous
[11]   opportunities for growth. These businesses – wholesale services, retail
[12]   energy services, broadband services and transportation services – can
[13]   be significantly expanded within their very large existing markets and
[14]   extended to new markets with enormous growth potential. At a mini-
[15]   mum, we see our market opportunities company-wide tripling over the
[16]   next five years.
[17]   Enron is laser-focused on earnings per share, and we expect to
[18]   continue strong earnings performance. We will leverage our extensive
[19]   business networks, market knowledge and logistical expertise to pro-
[20]   duce high-value bundled products for an increasing number of global
[21]   customers.

could conceivably go remiss with Enron. In the first 186 words, "strong" and "large" (and derivatives thereof) are used five times each. Readers are assured that earnings are (or will be) "strong" (line 18); that Enron has "tremendous opportunities for growth" (lines 10–11); that things are "enormously" good at Enron, and service deliveries have increased by "59 percent" (line 4); and that the company's new markets have "enormous growth potential" (line 14).

Implicitly, readers are encouraged to believe that Enron (through its leaders Skilling and Lay) has impeccable judgment and could not possibly fail. Later in the letter (in extracts not reproduced in exhibit 11.2) competitors are dismissed contemptuously for being incapable, unlike Enron, of "providing high-value products and services"; for not possessing "the skill, experience, depth and versatility" of Enron; and for being unworthy of comparison with Enron. Such language is consistent with a lack of empathy for others (criterion 7) and an arrogant and haughty behavior and attitude (criterion 9).

Enron is depicted as a quintessentially successful company that has exemplary leaders who will continue to "outdistance the competition" (line 2) and achieve "strong earnings" (line 18). Enron's portrayal as a company that will grow, become more intelligent and more formidable, and be the epitome of perfection, was egregious. Within 12 months, the company had to seek bankruptcy protection. The leadership duumvirate of Skilling and Lay camouflaged Enron's underlying decay. Their knowledge of Enron's imminent demise, and the grandiosity displayed in their text, could be characterized as a form of countervailing psychological puffery, driven by a sense of vulnerability and helplessness.[56]

Through use of the sport metaphor "outdistance the competition" (line 2), Enron and its leaders associate sporting fantasy with commercial brilliance. Their bold assertion that "Enron's performance in 2000 was a success by any measure" (line 1) is arrogant hyperbole and self-reification. Their claim of success was based on measures that were shown subsequently to be bogus and reliant on highly dubious accounting. The blatant self-touting of "success," "leadership," and achieving a "record" reveals a strong theme of egocentricity. A grandiose sense of self-importance (criterion 1) is on display, together with an arrogant and haughty behavior and attitude (criterion 9) and a preoccupation with fantasies of unlimited success, power, and brilliance (criterion 2).

Disconcertingly, Skilling and Lay's joint letter asserts that Enron "is laser-focused on earnings per share" (line 17). This public declaration is rife with overtones of individual and corporate narcissism. The almost irrational obsession alluded to by this metaphor reflected the ambient profit-driven culture at Enron. Presumably, no other goals or targets deserved management's attention. To be "laser-focused" on the conventional financial accounting-based measure, earnings per share (EPS), suggests a perverse fixation that is likely to bias managers' behavior. Indeed, the dysfunctional outcomes of preoccupation with a single quantitative measure have been known for many years.[57] The fixation on EPS is even more surprising because this ratio can be manipulated easily due to the vagaries of the profit calculation on which its numerator relies. This raises the possibility that EPS is invoked in a deliberately exploitative fashion (consistent with criterion 6) to take advantage of the financial naivety of others. The declaration of a "laser focus on EPS" is unequivocal, permitting no uncertainty or debate. Whether EPS is a sensible object on which an entire corporation should concentrate its cognition so pointedly is ignored.

The words in the letter point to Skilling and Lay being consumed by their egos and the company's pervading culture. They present Enron as being so influential and financially strong that it is immune to the effects of recession or market downturn. The letter helps them to fantasize that they were responsible for the (alleged, but as it turned out, mythical) unlimited success, invincibility, and infallible commercial judgment of Enron (criterion 1). The letter invites belief that Enron is a unique company, blessed with advantage, capable of prospering unimpeded, and immune to the economic perils experienced by its mortal (and unworthy) competitors.

Starbucks' CEO Letter to Shareholders for 2005

Exhibit 11.3 reproduces the first 192 words of the letter to shareholders for 2005 of Starbucks.[58] This was signed jointly by Howard Schultz (Chair) and Jim Donald (President and CEO).[59] The letter evidences traces of at least five of the nine diagnostic criteria for narcissism.

Exhibit 11.3 Opening of Schultz and Donald's letter to shareholders of Starbucks for 2005

[1] The human connection – it's the foundation of everything we do at Star-
[2] bucks. One customer, one barista, one community, one great cup of coffee
[3] at a time. That seemingly simple relationship, which today develops in more
[4] than 10,500 Starbucks stores around the world, inspires millions of people
[5] to embrace us as their neighborhood gathering place. That same connec-
[6] tion is at the heart of our passion to innovate and grow in new markets, with
[7] new tastes, new sounds and new experiences.
[8]   Every day, more than 100,000 Starbucks partners (employees) strive
[9] to exceed the expectations of every one of our customers – to achieve
[10] that delicate balance between touching people's daily lives while build-
[11] ing a thriving and multifaceted business. Regardless of our individual
[12] differences, people around the world share a common desire to be
[13] treated with respect and dignity, and to feel a sense of community,
[14] belonging and inclusion. We believe that Starbucks helps fulfill these
[15] needs by providing a welcoming environment and a place of comfort,
[16] while serving the world's finest coffees. This has resulted in Starbucks
[17] establishing a unique third place between home and office: first in North
[18] America and now around the world.

Criterion 1: Has a grandiose sense of self-importance.

Schultz and Donald are portrayed as remarkably grandiose and self-important. They profess to know, unequivocally, the "common desire" of "people around the world" (line 12). They claim grandly that Starbucks outlets have "inspire[d] millions of people to embrace [them] as their neighborhood gathering place" (lines 4–5). The grandiosity continues later (in text not reproduced in exhibit 11.3) where we read of Starbucks' "outstanding ability to achieve financial targets" (para 3) and the claim that "the Starbucks Experience resonates around the world" (para 4).

Criterion 2: Is preoccupied with fantasies of unlimited success, power, brilliance, and beauty.

Several delusional fantasies are evident. Schultz and Donald fantasize that every cup of coffee made by Starbucks is "great" (line 2) and that Starbucks (presumably because of their leadership) has "establish[ed] a unique third place between home and office: first in North America and now around the world" (lines 17–18). We are invited to accept the absurd proposition that, throughout the world, the key locations in most people's lives are their home, their place of work, and their Starbucks outlet. Seriously.

Criterion 3: Believes that he or she is special and unique and can only be understood by, or should associate with, other special or high-status people (or institutions).

Starbucks is conceived as special because of its "passion" (line 6), its "striv[ing] to exceed the expectations of every one of our customers" (lines 8–9); and its desire to "touch ... people's daily lives" (line 10).

Criterion 7: Lacks empathy and is unwilling to identify with the feelings and needs of others.

Schultz and Donald regard all of their employees as "partners" (line 8) in creating a "human connection" (line 1). They seem unwilling to recognize the feelings of a preponderance of their employees who are non-unionized and receiving minimum wage rates. If their baristas and servers were truly "partners" in a legal sense, they would be entitled to a share in the company's profits. The text contains many silences: for example, it does not allude to the widespread criticism of the company's anti-competitive tactics, or of its alleged generally anti-labor union stance.[60]

Criterion 9: Shows arrogant and haughty behaviors and attitudes.

Schultz and Donald appear to be arrogant in asserting that Starbucks has "helped transform the way people discover and experience music" (para 7; not reproduced here).

General Motor's CEO Letter to Shareholders for 2005

Exhibit 11.4 reproduces the first 287 words of the letter to shareholders for 2005 signed by Rick Wagoner, CEO of General Motors (GM).[61] We compare the language used in this letter with that of Enron and Starbucks. We conclude that Wagoner's letter falsifies any axiom that CEO letters are, by their very nature, destructively narcissistic.

Exhibit 11.4 Opening of Wagoner's letter to shareholders of General Motors for 2005

[1]   2005 was one of the most difficult years in General Motors' 98-year history.
[2]   It was the year in which GM's two fundamental weaknesses in the U.S.
[3]   market were fully exposed: our huge legacy cost burden, and our inability
[4]   to adjust structural costs in line with falling revenue. The challenges we
[5]   cited in this space a year ago – global overcapacity, falling prices, rising
[6]   health-care costs, higher fuel prices, global competition – intensified and
[7]   significantly weakened our business. The result was a loss of $3.4 billion,
[8]   excluding special items, and a reported loss of $10.6 billion, on revenues
[9]   of $192.6 billion. Obviously, that is unsustainable. Though we are confident
[10]   that GM has time and sufficient cash to see itself through a turnaround,
[11]   I want you to know that we are working diligently to get things moving in
[12]   the right direction – quickly. Essentially, we are changing our business
[13]   model to deal with the larger phenomenon of globalization and the com-
[14]   petition it has brought to the U.S. economy. We already have made some

---

significant moves to improve our competitiveness in the long term. We   [15]
need to do more – and we will.   [16]

Financial Reporting   [17]
We also have a renewed commitment to excellence and transparency   [18]
in our financial reporting. The recent discovery of prior-year account-   [19]
ing errors has been extremely disappointing and embarrassing to all   [20]
of us. Credibility is paramount, for GM as a company and for me per-   [21]
sonally. While I will not offer excuses, I do apologize on behalf of our   [22]
management team, and assure you that we will strive to deserve your   [23]
trust. The fact is that errors were made, and we can't change that. What   [24]
we have done is disclose our mistakes and work as diligently as we can   [25]
to fix them.   [26]

The choice of this letter to exemplify non-narcissistic language might seem curious. In November 2008, Wagoner arrived in Washington, DC in his company's Gulfstream jet to appear before the US Senate Committee on Banking, Housing and Urban Affairs. He was in Washington to argue GM's case for an immediate $15 billion federal government loan to help prevent the company from sliding into insolvency. The mode of Wagoner's arrival was viewed as an ostentatious display of power and wealth and as insensitive, haughty, unthinking, and egregiously offensive. It prompted demands by the chair of the Senate Banking Committee, Senator Dodd, for Wagoner to resign.[62]

This episode seems likely to promote mental characterizations of Wagoner as a destructive narcissist – and he could well be such. But the language in his letter to shareholders for 2005 does not suggest this. Rather, it contrasts starkly with that of Skilling and Lay (Enron) and Schultz and Donald (Starbucks). This would probably not surprise prominent author and journalist, William Holstein. He offers a sympathetic and countervailing view of Wagoner:

> in all the times that I have [spoken] with Wagoner, he has never appeared to be an imperial CEO, however grand his trappings. His personality, operating style, and values are those of a humbler man, serious and focused on his business. Many people find that he actually listens when they talk to him.[63]

If Wagoner's CEO letter were to evidence destructively narcissistic language it would need to reflect grandiosity, self-importance, fantasies of

unlimited success, belief in uniqueness and entitlement to special treatment, arrogance, haughtiness, exploitation, lack of empathy for others,
and a quest for admiration from others. There are slight traces of some of
these characteristics in the text. For example, Wagoner claims that GM has
"undergone tremendous structural change," that it is "absolutely committed to trend setting design," and that GM is "doing exactly what is needed
to position [it] for success."

However, in the main, Wagoner's language is the antithesis of most characteristics of narcissism. The pervading tone reflects an absence of grandiosity, self-importance, arrogance, or haughtiness. Parts of the letter are
self-effacing, self-critical, and apologetic. There is no arrogance or grandiosity in Wagoner's admissions that "errors were made" by GM (line 24)
and that "the recent discovery of prior-year accounting errors has been
extremely disappointing and embarrassing to all of us" (lines 19–21).

Wagoner frankly admits to making mistakes and to GM's inadequate
performance ("we need to do more," lines 15–16). He does not fantasize
about brilliance or seek admiration from others. Rather, he is candid in
drawing attention to GM's "fundamental weaknesses" (line 2) and "inability to adjust" (lines 3–4). Wagoner admits that GM has been "significantly
weakened" (line 7) and writes: "While I will not offer excuses, I do apologize on behalf of our management team" (lines 22–4).

Wagoner's language does not convey a sense that he believes GM
is entitled to special treatment. He makes it clear that GM has identified the problems it is facing and is "working diligently to get things
moving in the right directions – quickly" (lines 11–12). The letter is
neither exploitative nor lacking in empathy. The language is inclusive,
considerate, and re-assuring: "I assure you that we will strive to deserve
your trust" (lines 23–4); and "we recognize that our stockholders have
shared the pain … we appreciate your patience and advice" (final
sub-section, p. 7).

Identifying "Faint Signals" of Hubristic Language

Here we briefly illustrate how DICTION and close reading can be used to
identify "faint signals" of hubristic language by a CEO.

There is emerging evidence that computer-assisted, corpus-based methods can provide some insight to whether a CEOs' language contains hints
of hubris.[64] Nonetheless, "close reading … analysis ought to be preferred
in seeking a deeper understanding of leadership language and its subtleties,

nuances, and context."[65] Academic Amanda Murphy agrees with such an assessment:

> analysis of key words and key semantic domains needs to be complemented by close phraseological analyses, since it is in the phraseology of the texts that the nuances of a message are to be found.[66]

Nevertheless, it is important to investigate the potential for computer-assisted text analysis software such as DICTION to identify signs of hubristic CEO-speak.

We now briefly compare a computer-assisted text analysis (using DICTION) of the first 500 words of Boeing CEO Dennis Muilenburg's letter to shareholders in 2017 with a brief close reading analysis of that part of his letter. Our aim is to tease out any hubristic language. As a framework for analysis, we employ the five clinical features that Owen and Davidson[67] claim are unique indicators of hubris. A hubristic person will

- regard their outlook and interests as identical with those of the nation or organization;
- have a tendency to speak in the third person or use the royal "we";
- have an unshakeable belief that they will be vindicated by history or God;
- be restless, reckless, and impulsive;
- have a tendency to allow their "broad vision" of the moral rectitude of a proposed course to obviate the need to consider practicality, cost, or outcomes.

Muilenburg's letter (see exhibit 11.5)[68] was released in February 2018, well before the two fatal crashes of the company's 737 MAX aircraft.[69] Here we explore whether there were language hints of hubris in its first 500 words.[70]

Our analysis uses DICTION's "Corporate Financial Reports" norm and is restricted to exploring the five master variables reported by DICTION.[71] We do not explore DICTION's four calculated variables and 31 dictionary variables. (For a fuller explanation of the various types of DICTION variables, see appendix A). Results are as follows:

Master Variable	DICTION Score	Normal Range	Out of Range?
Activity	52.25	46.26–53.97	No
Optimism	55.35	47.92–52.50	Yes, high side
Certainty	50.38	38.62–50.26	Yes, high side
Realism	54.79	41.14–46.85	Yes, high side
Commonality	52.55	47.94–55.30	No

Exhibit 11.5 Extract from Boeing's CEO letter to shareholders for 2017

[1]   TO THE SHAREHOLDERS AND EMPLOYEES OF THE BOEING
[2]   COMPANY
[3]   In the first full year of our second century, we worked together with
[4]   accelerated pace and purpose to be the best in aerospace and an
[5]   enduring global industrial champion. For a company that dreams big
[6]   and delivers on those dreams, a bold, bright future is ours to seize– and
[7]   we will do so, together.

[8]   2017 in Review
[9]   In 2017, more than 140,000 dedicated Boeing employees around the
[10] world delivered record company financial and operational performance,
[11] strengthened our businesses for profitable, long-term growth, and drove
[12] additional productivity and quality gains across the enterprise. Our
[13] strong performance trend–underpinned by our sizeable backlog, a large
[14] and growing aerospace and defense market, and our positive future
[15] outlook–helped make Boeing the Dow's top-performing company in
[16] 2017, as measured by stock price and total shareholder returns. Com-
[17] pany revenue in 2017 was $93.4 billion, fueled by record commercial
[18] airplane deliveries, growth in our services business, and solid defense,
[19] space and security performance. We also won $110.2 billion in net new
[20] orders for our market-leading and innovative products and services, rais-
[21] ing our companywide backlog to $488 billion. Core earnings per share
[22] of $12.04* for the year, also a company record, reflected our strong
[23] operating performance and a favorable tax reform impact of $1.74 per
[24] share. Core operating earnings rose 64 percent over 2016 to a Boeing-
[25] record $9.0 billion* and operating cash flow grew to an all-time high of
[26] $13.3 billion, enabling us to return significant value to our shareholders
[27] while investing for the future in our people and our business. Keeping
[28] with our balanced cash deployment strategy, in 2017 we repurchased
[29] 46.1 million shares of Boeing stock for $9.2 billion and paid $3.4 billion
[30] in dividends. In December, the Boeing Board of Directors signaled its
[31] continued confidence in our financial strength and long-term outlook,
[32] authorizing a new $18 billion share repurchase program and increas-
[33] ing the quarterly dividend by 20 percent. Over the past five years, we
[34] have raised our quarterly dividend by more than 250 percent. Boeing

Commercial Airplanes reported $56.7 billion of revenue in 2017 and led   [35]
the industry in deliveries for the sixth consecutive year with a record 763   [36]
airplanes. With net new orders for an additional 912 airplanes, we grew   [37]
our commercial airplanes backlog to a company record of 5,864 jets.   [38]
This strong order book, worth $421 billion, is equal to approximately   [39]
seven years of production at current rates. Full-year operating margins   [40]
were 9.6 percent. The 737 family continues to exceed expectations in   [41]
the single-aisle market, with 745 net new orders received and a com-   [42]
pany record of 529 airplanes delivered in 2017. Our 737 backlog now   [43]
stands at more than 4,600 airplanes. In 2017, we also transitioned our   [44]
production system smoothly to the 737 MAX, allowing us to deliver the   [45]
first 74 737 MAX 8 airplanes while increasing overall 737 production   [46]
to 47 aircraft per month. We continued to make progress building out   [47]
the MAX family, including the start of production on the 737 MAX 7, the   [48]
rollout and first flight of the ...   [49]

Below we explain how these results can be interpreted in the light of Owen and Davidson's[72] five unique hubris features (see italicized points in exhibit 11.1).

Five Unique Features of Hubris	*DICTION* Analysis
1. Outlook and interests regarded as identical with those of the nation or organization	The very high OPTIMISM score seems likely to be associated with overconfidence and hubris.[73] This score is suggestive, but not determinative. The slightly high CERTAINTY score supports this suggestion.
2. A tendency to speak in the third person or use the royal "we"	None of the DICTION master variable scores pertain to this criterion.
3. An unshakeable belief that they will be vindicated by history or God	The slightly high CERTAINTY score is mildly suggestive of this "unshakeable belief."
4. Restlessness, recklessness, and impulsiveness	None of the DICTION master variable scores pertain to this criterion.
5. A tendency to allow their "broad vision" about the moral rectitude of a proposed course of action to obviate the need to consider practicality, cost, or outcomes	The REALISM score is very high when compared to the norm. When combined with the slightly high CERTAINTY score and the very high OPTIMISM score, it suggests an "I'm right" attitude. This weak hint indicates further investigation would be insightful.

In this example, using just the first 500 words of a single CEO letter and DICTION's five master variables only, there are some intriguing "faint signals" of the language of hubris. A much richer DICTION (or other computer-assisted text analysis software) investigation of the entire corpus of Muilenburg's CEO letters, speeches, and earnings conference call transcripts would yield more substantive and reliable hints. Further analysis should not be limited to the five master variables but should extend to the 35 other DICTION variables.

DICTION analysis provides a high-level view of text that misses nuance and therefore needs to be complemented by a close reading, as we do below. However, when faced with the large amounts of CEO-speak that merit a preliminary screening for hubristic-like language, computer-assisted approaches such as DICTION are useful. For example, in analyzing the 332,847 words in the 125 speeches that BP's CEO Lord Browne delivered between 1997 and 2007, we used DICTION to assist in locating hints of hubristic language (Craig & Amernic 2014).

Illustrative comments from our close reading of the first 500 words of Muilenberg's 2017 CEO letter appear below. A substantive close reading would analyze the entire letter.

Five Unique Features of Hubris	Close Reading: Illustrative Comments
1. Outlook and interests regarded as identical with those of the nation or organization	The two sentences in lines 3–7 include words and phrases that are consistent with this feature. Muilenberg claims Boeing aspired to be "an enduring global champion."
2. A tendency to speak in the third person or use the royal "we"	"We" appears eight times in the 500-word excerpt. Most usages are akin to a royal "we." For example, the first sentence presumes a unitary, top-down approach to management and leadership. The "we" in this sentence implies that everyone at Boeing is in a special and superior category.
3. An unshakeable belief that they will be vindicated by history or God	The introductory paragraph evokes images of superiority and arrogance. The means of "vindication" mentioned in the first 500 words are financial, production, and growth-based performance measures. These are mainly lagging, abstract indicators. There is no mention of the communities and safety issues affected by Boeing. An analysis of the full letter would provide much more here.

4. Restlessness, recklessness, and impulsiveness	There is evidence of an apparent impulsive obsession with growth, size, and winning. Growth for its own sake seems injudicious at best and reckless at worst. The absence of mentions of employees, other than as compliant automatons, hints of impulsiveness and perhaps recklessness (lines 9–13).
5. A tendency to allow their "broad vision" about the moral rectitude of a proposed course to obviate the need to consider practicality, cost, or outcomes	Lines 9–16 contain a stunning use of hyperbole, and a top-down unitary assumption of leadership. The text assumes that the restricted list of performance measures mentioned are plausible ways to judge the performance of a huge, risky, enterprise such as Boeing. Where does "safety" fit in? Indeed, "safety" is mentioned only once in the letter, but this is far removed from the first 500 words.[74]

The preceding analysis is tentative and illustrative. Nonetheless, it reveals the depth a close reading can provide in investigating links to indicators of hubris.

Concluding Comments

The language of CEOs should be investigated for "faint signals" of narcissism and hubris. This could stimulate further investigation and, perhaps, the intervention of appropriate specialists who are competent in diagnosing and treating narcissism and hubris. Boards of directors and other key stakeholders in a company should be very interested in continuous and respectful monitoring of CEO language. But in doing so, they should be alert to the challenge of ensuring a balance between encouraging a CEO's entrepreneurial, creative zeal on one hand and, on the other, of not ignoring faint (or stronger) linguistic signs that such zeal may have gone terribly wrong.

chapter twelve

Monitoring CEO-Speak

The insights offered in this book will help in monitoring the quality, tone, and effectiveness of CEO-speak. This, in turn, should help to improve leadership-through-language. We have drawn attention to the importance of CEOs choosing their language carefully and of being conscious that what they write and say is what they want to communicate. Their exercise of such care is important because the public discourse emanating from the top of a company reflects the company's values, branding, and future – as well as the attitudes and values of the CEO.

CEOs and those who advise them should be conscious that public scrutiny of the language of CEOs has increased due to the widespread use of the internet and various forms of social media. When the words of a CEO are posted on the internet, they become widely accessible almost immediately and can reach an audience of billions instantaneously. Those words can be located easily using search engines. They can be downloaded quickly, forwarded, tweeted and retweeted, and analyzed using sophisticated text-analysis software and close reading techniques. This enhanced capacity for analysis facilitates scrutiny of a CEO's language by a wide range of interested parties, such as competitors, regulators, financial analysts, lobbyists, journalists, bloggers, and activists.

The various communications of CEOs simultaneously strive to satisfy, and seek legitimacy from, three broad sets of diverse audiences. First are those who are internal to the organization, such as employees and managers. Second are those external to it, such as shareholders, governments, customers, competitors, and the public. Third is the CEO himself or herself. These three audiences are not separate and distinct. Exponents of CEO-speak, and monitors of it, should be conscious that CEO language not only permeates a company internally but also gains broader currency externally. Although CEO-speak has many formal and informal guises, it is a dominant means by which a company engages with its many external and internal stakeholders.

The CEO letter to shareholders of IBM for 2018, signed by Virginia M. Rometty as chair, president, and CEO, demonstrates the use of CEO-speak to address these three audiences. A brief look at this letter shows that although it is addressed to "Dear IBM Investor" (one part of the external stakeholder group), the letter has a wider audience. The CEO-speak used reflects the obvious importance the letter was conceived to have with many other parties in the external stakeholder group and with employees and managers of IBM. The carefully crafted, specific, and very detailed letter explains the company's business model and strategy in forthright but clear terms. It offers insight to Rometty's thinking about IBM's complex business and has a broad focus on "clients."

We should not overlook that Rometty herself is also an audience for the letter. She ends it by confiding: "I am honored to steward this great company…" thereby signaling a level of humility and a lack of entitlement. Her use of "steward" is an enlightening signal to both herself and to all audiences that she sees her role mainly in terms of accountability. The company is not *her* company; she is acting as a steward and so (apparently) she must lead the company in an ethical and responsible manner.

The Subtleties of Language

CEOs and their advisers should think closely about the subtleties of the specific words and phrases that comprise CEO-speak. If language is imprecise or poorly chosen, companies risk sustaining damage. CEOs should contemplate closely the intended and unintended consequences of the words and literary tropes they use. Failure to do so can lead to *mis*communication and unintended negative outcomes.

CEOs should be very conscious to not distort their intended message inadvertently, make unintended revelations, or encourage undesirable responses. Wherever possible, they (and their advisors) should carefully edit and re-edit the text of their communications or have them separately vetted for unintended implications, prior to release. There should be a high degree of coherence and consistency between the various forms of CEO-speak and a company's other communications (including in its financial reports and regulatory filings). It is very important too that those charged with corporate governance, such as the board of directors, monitor CEO-speak routinely. They should be alert to the tone at the top that the CEO's language fashions and to any "faint signals" of dysfunction.

Monitoring of written and oral manifestations of CEO-speak by external stakeholders of a company is equally important. Such monitoring is a useful way of assessing business leadership risk and the company's culture, strategy, and prospects. It can also help to identify whether the CEO is exaggerating his or her proficiency, ability to command events, and claims of success. As we have demonstrated, such monitoring (e.g., through close reading and text analysis software) can also provide insights to an organization's safety culture and ethical conduct, and to the CEO's personality. An often-overlooked benefit of monitoring CEO language is that it will help develop better understanding of issues that a CEO regards as important and worthwhile – the CEO's strategic priorities.

Below we emphasize several matters that are often overlooked but that should be regarded as very important when composing, reading, and reviewing various forms of CEO-speak.

Metaphor Choice

Metaphors play a strong role in leadership language. They can be constructive or damaging. CEOs need to closely consider the nature and entailments of the intentional and unintentional metaphors they use. Stakeholders who monitor CEO-speak should closely review the metaphors used. This will help them to more fully understand a CEO's thinking.[1] CEOs should give close attention to whether the metaphors they use will do what they intend and whether they will be interpreted as intended.

Jack Welch, the communication-savvy CEO of General Electric (GE) (1981–2000), used metaphors extensively to self-construct a favorable view of himself, sustain key strategic themes, and win support for his transformational agenda. A study of Welch's 20 annual report letters to stockholders identified five root metaphors through which he self-constructed the identity he wanted to be known by, and to heighten persuasive impact. These were WELCH AS PEDAGOGUE, WELCH AS PHYSICIAN, WELCH AS ARCHITECT, WELCH AS COMMANDER, and WELCH AS SAINT.[2]

Consider the SAINT metaphor. Welch fortified his view of GE and the business world by projecting himself as a saint and adopting a saintly pose. This metaphor helped sustain his implicit and explicit assertions that his leadership was based on positive human values and that "Saint Jack" articulated the best interests of affected stakeholders. Welch claimed that not only could he distinguish goodness from evil, but that he could deal with sinners and other wicked influences too. He used terms laden with religious imagery to express his commitment to management techniques that he felt would ensure every product was of near-perfect quality.

The following subtle but insidious metaphor that CEOs and many other members of senior management use, seemingly with little thought, has gained widespread currency: FINANCIAL STATEMENTS ARE A TRUTH-TELLING LENS. This metaphor should be avoided because it reinforces the falsehood that a single set of financial statements is unimpeachably true and offers the one (and only) faithful lens that portrays the objective financial reality of a company. Such a view is unjustified because of the vagaries of accounting rules, assumptions, and cost-allocation techniques. At best, externally published financial statements provide an opaque portal to a company's financial health.

CEOs should not display insensitivity in their choice of metaphor and imagery. The CEO letter published in Southwest Airlines' annual report for 2001 likened the hard financial times experienced in the airline industry after "9/11" to the "holocaustic economic catastrophe that afflicted the airline industry from 1990–94." This imagery exhibits a peculiarly unthinking and offensive trivialization of "holocaust" – a term that when capitalized is regarded universally to signify the gross inhumanity suffered in the 1930s and 1940s.[3] Though this probably was unintended, selection of this term was likely to cause serious offense to many.

Cultural Keywords

Cultural keywords are words that carry common knowledge that is accepted by society at large. Examples include words such as "democracy," "patriotism," "integrity," and "technology."[4] Cultural keywords should not be overused and must always be chosen carefully. CEOs should be aware of the implications of borrowing cultural keywords from other spheres, such as politics, religion, and morality. The meaning a CEO intends for any cultural keyword will not necessarily be identical to the meaning ascribed by others. Thus, there is a risk that cultural keywords can have wider, harmful effects. Nonetheless, CEOs seem to use cultural keywords in the hope that by doing so, they will be perceived positively by the public. CEOs should avoid using cultural keywords repeatedly, as a self-validating mantra, in the hope this will reflect favorably on them and the company they lead.

CEOs must have a justifiable and coherent rationale for using a cultural keyword. They should not use ineffective cultural keywords or use them in a counterproductive fashion. The latter was demonstrated for the cultural key-word "integrity" in May 2005, when GE released its first *Citizenship Report*. CEO Jeffrey Immelt was anxious to establish a reputation for GE as a good corporate citizen. The introductory paragraph of his letter to sharehold-ers mentioned "integrity" seven times, including three mentions of GE's commitment to "integrity." Immelt thereby reinforced "integrity" as a focal aspect of GE's "citizenship." Through overuse, the word "integrity" was ren-dered an almost meaningless, self-serving, hollow platitude – the opposite of the desired response. Immelt's use of "integrity" neutered the word.

Framing

Framing of a text can make an aspect of perceived reality seem more salient. CEOs need to be more alert to how framing can help them define problems, diagnose causes, make moral judgments, suggest remedies, and organize their belief systems.[5] Frames can be constructed through the pres-ence or absence of particular keywords, stock phrases, images, and informa-tion sources, and by thematically reinforced sentences or clusters of facts or judgments.

Metaphor can be an effective way of framing a text. For example, the use of a pervading root metaphor early in a CEO letter serves an important framing function. A COMMANDER metaphor might be used promi-nently in the opening paragraphs when "downsizing" or "rightsizing" (laying off staff) is management's intent. If a particular transformational change involves negative outcomes for key stakeholders, then an astute, rhetorically sophisticated leader might begin with a more socially sensitive metaphorical persona (say, of a PHYSICIAN). This could be followed later by the persona of a COMMANDER who must do their harsh work to effect the prescription of the PHYSICIAN for (corporate) healing.

American International Group (AIG) CEO Martin Sullivan dealt with a major leadership challenge in his stockholders' letter issued on June 10, 2005, just after the company experienced a massive accounting and gov-ernance crisis. Sullivan framed his letter deftly through a skillful combina-tion of two pervasive metaphors. In the opening paragraphs, he used a JOURNEY metaphor to depict himself as "leading this great company embarking on a new era of marked changes." Thereby, he established the image of strong and decisive movement forward under his direction. Con-currently, he also used the metaphor of BALANCE. This enabled him to couple needed change with the desirability of preserving core values. In the final paragraphs Sullivan reinforced this metaphorical BALANCE by "summariz[ing] what will, and will not, change under AIG's new leadership." The factors that *will change* are that the company will now offer full cooperation with regulators, rigorous accounting, greater transparency, and no conflicts of interest. The factors that *will not change* are financial strength, global reach, market leadership, customer focus, and a family feeling.

The JOURNEY and the BALANCE metaphors jointly frame the letter effectively. They provide sought-after "balance" too because they open and close the letter. The use of metaphor in this way to frame a crucial stockholders' letter during a crisis signals strong and nuanced leadership. In a profoundly stressful time for his company, Sullivan's letter marshals language, partly through framing, to signal his worthiness as a corporate leader.

Precision, Coherence, Consistency, and Transparency

CEO-speak should be checked for consistency and coherence with the other key components of a company's broader disclosure regime: that is, with its published financial statements, management discussion and analysis, corporate social responsibility reports, regulatory filings, press releases, and speeches and disclosures on social media platforms.

CEOs should strive to write in a way that is understandable, relevant, complete, and honest. They should avoid silences that impair accountability, transparency, and credibility. They should make a concerted effort to disclose the good news and the bad news objectively and without hyperbole. Reporting bad news is often not easy. The consequences of doing so may be highly unfavorable and be a daunting deterrent. They may have reputational consequences for the CEO and be responsible for downward pressures on the company's share price. Nonetheless, reporting bad news can have the beneficial effect of enhancing a CEO's credibility and "softening" any inflated stock market expectations. Wherever possible, the reporting of bad news should be accompanied by a credible plan to alleviate the adversity.

The potency of CEO-speak can be enhanced by identifying and removing unwarranted ambiguities, buzzwords, clichés, and euphemisms. The language used should avoid exaggeration, hubris, or deceit; it should expunge gibberish, technical jargon, inappropriate metaphors, and trite platitudes.

Company websites are largely unregulated. But CEOs should monitor their design and operation carefully. Does the website facilitate full and objective accountability, including through narrative disclosures? Or is the design principally directed at manufacturing consent for corporate activity? CEOs should appreciate how easily public attitudes and behaviors can be influenced by the positioning, content, size, shape, and color of hyperlinks on their company's website. Some sites seem to conceal hyperlinks in order to make bad news difficult to find. Others design hyperlinks in a way that attracts users to navigate through the website using one desired path. Thus, among the matters CEOs and their advisors should consider are

> the positioning and content of hyperlinks … the order of items within a menu, the persuasive properties of defaulted "drop down" menus, ambiguous titles of items within a menu, the use of hyperlinks in disrupting sequential information processing, and the overall navigation technique (e.g., ambiguous direction vs. a clear-cut path).[6]

The use of social media such as Twitter and Facebook needs close monitoring too. One important matter to check is whether CEOs publicly disclose market-sensitive information in their personal social media accounts before disclosing such information to share markets through official corporate channels.

Concluding Comments

CEOs are powerful individuals whose words and communications generally are very important and deserve serious scrutiny. This is particularly true for the CEOs of companies that have economic and social clout. Stakeholders need to ensure that CEOs are more accountable publicly for what they write and what they say. CEOs should set an appropriate, principled tone at the top through their language. They should strive to be honest, consistent, complete, relevant, understandable, and accountable to all stakeholders. They should dispense with trite platitudes and exaggerations.

However, such normative goals for CEO-speak are likely to be unattainable in the real world of all-too-human leaders and advisors, lapses in corporate governance, and business and social crises. What CEOs *should do* and what they *actually do* in any given communication setting, whether formal or informal, seem likely to differ considerably. And, of course, what they should do or have done in any given situation may be rife with value judgments and the bias of hindsight. All of this makes close monitoring of CEO-speak crucial in striving to attain a more equitable society.

The audiences for whom this book is intended (CEOs and those who advise them, students of business and communication, and a general business audience interested in understanding the language of CEOs) comprise everyday citizens as well as CEOs. Those consuming CEO-speak, as well as those creating it, need to pay more attention to language now than perhaps they ever did before. This book provides a timely alert to the importance of CEO-speak and its many channels and manifestations as a socially potent language genre.

No matter how experienced or esteemed CEOs are, they should be reflective and diligent critics of their own communications. They should venture beyond the advice of public relations "spin doctors" and solicit critical comment from other members of the top management team – especially from the CFO, internal and external auditors, and, possibly, a trusted in-house contrarian. Close review of CEO-speak should be a formal protocol in audit processes too. A crucial part of the monitoring role of a company's board of directors should be to critically assess their company's CEO-speak.

Everyday citizens, external stakeholders in a company, and analysts have a right to investigate a company's CEO-speak. Economic systems will work more fairly if rigorous checks and balances on corporate endeavor are adopted. An integral part of such checks and balances will be to have informed consumers of CEO-speak.

In its various forms, CEO-speak can be revealing, manipulative, enlightening, frustrating, inspiring, shocking, and many other things as well. The "raw power" of the language of leaders of companies deserves close monitoring. This book has drawn attention to ways of going about this important task.

Pandemic

We submitted this book for publication in March 2020, just as the COVID-19 pandemic began to take hold globally and before the depth of its profound implications were widely apparent. Since then there have been some insightful uses of CEO-speak as the effects of the pandemic were felt more fully. By early May 2020, approximately 265,000 deaths had been attributed to the COVID-19 virus across the world. Many countries were in various stages of lockdown. Unemployment was increasing rapidly and many employees were working remotely. By then, the pandemic had demonstrated a clear capacity to "eviscerate a business, its workforce, and its profitability within a single month."[1] The pandemic's effects were already significant because they had extended beyond causing economic consequences for individual businesses and industries to posing a calamitous threat to humanity, the global supply chain, and social stability worldwide.

In this epilogue, we explore some features of the language CEOs used as COVID-19 began to make its presence felt. We critique some examples of pandemic-related CEO-speak that emerged. We refer to these examples as *pandemic-speak*. We draw attention to selected aspects of the pandemic-speak of two CEOs whose communications have been admired in media reports. These are Jamie Dimon (JPMorgan Chase) and Arne Sorensen (Marriott). As counterexamples, we cite instances of the much-criticized leadership language of prominent "political CEOs," such as (former) US President Donald Trump. Thereby, we offer fresh insights to the language CEOs have used to communicate during the early stages of a profound crisis.

In the early months of the pandemic, some leaders used their communications with stakeholders to exercise accountability, effect transparency, and develop a tone at the top that was intended to promote trust. Some well-known CEOs spoke and wrote with candor, compassion, and seemingly authentic positivity. They encouraged followers to have confidence in their leadership actions in a time of crisis. But this pandemic, with its "known unknowns" and its "unknown unknowns," made uninformed positivity – often in defiance of expert medical knowledge – a potentially compromising approach. As the seriousness of the virus became apparent and the death toll grew, uninformed optimism was clearly an inappropriate communications strategy for leaders.

Many CEOs used language to set a strategic tone for their followers – variously of brutal honesty, compassion, or positivity. They sought to encourage followers to have faith in their leadership. Some succeeded. Others failed. Some were dishonest.[2] What was clear is that no amount of confected positivity, often in defiance of medical knowledge and advice, could guarantee that followers would also adopt a similar *faux* positive attitude. In many instances, a positive tone in language was driven by hubristic leaders who were implacably convinced that they knew better than epidemiologists and medical experts. In the case of (former) US President Donald Trump, his unremittingly positive claims and musings reflected an air of "I know it all" and have been derided widely.

The economic and social crisis of the pandemic is distinctive. Whereas the effects of many crises in the past have been felt largely by a company entity itself (and to a greater or lesser extent by its immediate stakeholders), the impact of the COVID-19 pandemic has been much more pervasive. The pandemic has not just had economic effects for individual business entities but has posed a serious threat to the economic and social welfare of broader society and the lives of all persons. The pandemic's effects contrast starkly with those of many prior crises in which more than a single business entity was affected. Many of those prior crises were neither global nor did they have profoundly toxic consequences for public health worldwide.[3]

A distinctive feature of the oral and written communication by CEOs during the pandemic has been their change in mode of delivery. In periods of "lockdown," CEOs resorted more to online and oral modes of communication: through formal meetings with staff who were working remotely or through orchestrated online meetings involving communications software technologies such as *Zoom*, *Teams*, and *Skype*. Many CEOs used informal online meetings to share information and experiences as a way of maintaining morale: for example, through virtual "happy hours," "town hall" meetings of employees, and weekly all-company videoconferences. Many CEOs "ramp[ed] up communication with employees to address confusion, anxiety and isolation among the rank and file."[4]

The tone of the communications of many CEOs has variously been emotional, self-serving, and/or upbeat. Metaphors have been invoked for effect, including the now clichéd WHEN WE GET TO THE OTHER SIDE. This alludes to the anticipated time when the crisis will end. Hyperbole and misinformation have abounded. The spoken words of many national political leaders (in effect, their country's CEOs) seem intended to deliberately paint a rosy picture, often contrary to the expert opinion of epidemiologists, the findings of peer-reviewed medical research, and dire public health statistics.[5] When confronted with the reality that the news is bad, CEOs are better advised to be completely honest and transparent and not engage in discourse that raises expectations falsely. Acknowledging bad news, plainly, pointedly, and calmly, along with at least some aspects of a strategy TO GET TO THE OTHER SIDE seems to be the best communication policy.

(Former) President Trump made confident statements promoting untested drugs and proposing his recommended treatments to eradicate the virus. These have been ridiculed for offering false hope. At a press conference on April 24, 2020, Trump suggested that the coronavirus might be treated by injections of disinfectant:

> And then I see the disinfectant where it knocks it [the virus] out in a minute. One minute. And is there a way we can do something like that, by injection inside or almost a cleaning? … I'm not a doctor. But, I'm, like, a person that has a good you-know-what.[6]

The following day, Trump claimed he was "being sarcastic." His statements and overall language of leadership in the pandemic exhibit traces of the leadership and personality dysfunction known as hubris (discussed in chapter 11). Trump's excessively optimistic pronouncements in press briefings were intended to convey the message "I know what we can expect, and I'm in control." Trump wanted the spotlight to be on him. Instead of exhibiting any doubt by preparing for a worst-case scenario, Trump chose to act as Optimist-in-Chief, ostensibly to calm an anxious public. His "happy talk" or "boosterism" appears to have been intended to promote the well-being of the economy and financial markets – an outcome that was a critical element of his re-election strategy in 2020.

Other political leaders also exploited the power of incumbency to use language in a way that recklessly set an unrealistic tone of positivity for followers. In a statement on March 3, 2020 (three weeks before his

COVID-19 diagnosis), UK Prime Minister Boris Johnson was apparently blithely and arrogantly unaware of the potential for his actions to lead to infection:

> I was at a hospital the other night where I think there were actually a few coronavirus patients and I shook hands with everybody, you'll be pleased to know, and I continue to shake hands.[7]

Brazil's President Jair Bolsonaro has also adamantly denied the reality of bad news. He frequently described COVID-19 as a "little flu," thereby raising expectations falsely.

CEOs have made their share of inappropriate declarations too. One of Australia's richest persons, Gina Rinehart, executive chair of Hancock Prospecting, in a letter to staff in May 2020, suggested a remedy involving "intravenous injections of vitamin C and regular consumption of ginger, turmeric and lemon water."[8] Tesla CEO Elon Musk, on March 19, 2020, predicted that there would be "close to zero new cases in the U.S. by the end of April."[9]

There were some laudable examples of CEO-speak during the early months of the pandemic. The CEO of Marriott, Arne Sorensen, was praised widely for the honesty, clarity, and transparency of his 6-minute video address on March 20, 2020. In this he displayed strong emotion. He was visibly upset when announcing staff layoffs and in concluding that the pandemic's economic effects would be greater than 9/11 and the 2007–9 global financial crisis combined. Sorensen backed his calls for strong financial control measures by announcing that he and other executives would take a 50 percent salary cut. His address (available at https://www.youtube.com/watch?v=SprFgoU6aO0) has been described as inspirational and as "a powerful lesson in leading during a crisis."[10]

A clear feature of the language of the pandemic has been that many terms, expressions, metaphors ("flattening the curve," "lockdown," "the new normal") and acronyms (PPE for personal protective equipment) have entered the lexicon as a part of pandemic-speak. Some neologisms have appeared (e.g., quarantini, doomscrolling, covidiot). Some terms have become ideographs (e.g., COVID-19, "social distancing") or cultural key words (unprecedented). The unintentional (we think) "mixed messaging" has been remarkable too. Many CEOs have urged followers to "stick together." This was an odd call in an era in which the mantra of the global pandemic was to engage in "social distancing."[11] Jamie Dimon, CEO of JPMorgan Chase, for example, in his CEO letter for fiscal 2019 (published April 6, 2020) impressed on his fellow shareholders the "need to come together."[12]

Hyperbole has been rife. This is evident in the use of the adjective "unprecedented." There are no shades or degrees of "unprecedented*ness*." Yet, many CEOs have found many things unprecedented – and some may well be so. But many are not. The overuse of "unprecedented" reflects little understanding of the H1N1 influenza virus pandemic (commonly referred to as the Spanish Flu pandemic) of 1918–19. According to the US Centers for Disease Control and Prevention,

> [i]t is estimated that about 500 million people or one-third of the world's popu-
> lation became infected with this [Spanish Flu] virus. The number of deaths was
> estimated to be at least 50 million worldwide with about 675,000 occurring in
> the United States.[13]

Similarly, the fact that the bubonic plague of the mid 1300s killed "more than 20 million people in Europe – almost one-third of the continent's population"[14] seems to have been ignored too. The Plague of Justinian (541 CE–542 CE, with recurrences to 750 CE) left a deadly legacy too.[15] Thus, in the COVID-19 pandemic setting, the word "unprecedented" no longer means "this has never happened before in the course of history." Rather, the word has assumed the meaning "this has never happened before in the (limited) understanding of history possessed by the author" or "this event is extraordinary and worth pay-ing attention to."[16] Through such misuse and overuse, "unprecedented" loses its effect and impact. CEOs would be well advised to follow the advice of the *New York Times* stylebook: "Use the term [unprecedented] rarely, and only after verifying the history. Then carefully specify the aspect that qualifies."[17]

What have CEOs claimed was unprecedented? BlackRock Chairman Larry Fink, in his letter to shareholders on March 29, 2020, asserted that the "coronavirus ... [was] ... an unprecedented medical, economic and human challenge." The "economic challenges" posed by the Great Depression of 1929 to 1933 clearly did not seem to figure in Fink's assessment.[18]

Quite often the use of "unprecedented" is associated with gross overuse of other extreme adjectives, such as "extraordinary." But why? Is this just sloppiness on the part of the authors? Or is it part of a broader rhetorical agenda of CEOs? Do they want to condition readers to their impending announcement of poor operating and financial results that have been fos-tered by the pandemic? Is it part of a strategy to deflect attention from the unpreparedness of companies and CEOs to assess risk and the effects of a "Black Swan" event,[19] such as the spread of the COVID-19 virus?

Through overuse, JPMorgan Chase CEO Jamie Dimon diminishes the power of the words "extraordinary" and "unprecedented." He invests those words with new meanings. He uses "extraordinary" 24 times (9 times in a running heading) in his letter to shareholders dated April 6, 2020. Among the matters described as extraordinary are "things"; "lengths" [to which the company has gone to help customers] (n = 2); "efforts" [to lift up our communities] (n = 2); "times" (n = 2); "crisis" (n = 9); "extension of new credit"; and "team." "Unprecedented" is used four times variously to describe the "environment," "challenges," "times," and "situation."

Warren Buffett, CEO of Berkshire Hathaway, has been an exception to the broader unpreparedness of CEOs (and their companies) to cope with disaster or catastrophe. His 2019 letter to shareholders was dated February 22, 2020 (before the full implications of the pandemic were apparent). In his letter, Buffett was prescient (and perhaps deserving of his sobriquet "Oracle of Omaha") in observing that:

A major catastrophe that will dwarf hurricanes Katrina and Michael *will* occur –
perhaps tomorrow, perhaps many decades from now. "The Big One" may
come from a traditional source … or it may be a total surprise involving say,
a cyber attack having disastrous consequences beyond anything insurers now
contemplate.[20]

Indeed, consistent with Buffett's view, there had been ample forewarnings of an impending global pandemic. The world confronted HIV/AIDS in the 1980s and 1990s, avian flu in 1997, Sudden Acute Respiratory Syndrome (SARS) in 2003, N1H1 (swine flu) in 2009, Middle East Respiratory Syndrome (MERS) in 2012, and Ebola in 2013. The pandemic-speak associated with COVID-19 seems to have been used to deflect attention from the brutal fact that many companies and their CEOs were poorly prepared to cope with a damaging pandemic or other catastrophic event.

The letter to shareholders of Jamie Dimon, CEO of JPMorgan Chase, published in early April 2020, has been praised because it (metaphorically) threw out the usual template for a CEO letter "to address the coronavirus crisis."[21] Before exploring some of the details of this letter, we first draw attention to how Southwest Airlines (SWA) enlisted "9/11" as an ideograph, immediately after the September 11, 2001, terrorist attacks in New York. An ideograph is

an ordinary language term … that warrants the use of power, excuses behaviour
and belief which might otherwise be perceived as eccentric or antisocial, and

guides behaviour and belief into channels readily recognized by a community as acceptable and laudable.[22]

SWA seemed to use the phenomenon of "9/11" and phrases related thereto (such as "LET'S ROLL!") strategically and symbolically as rhetorical currency to promote its own virtuosity.[23]

Cynical observers in 2020 might have questioned whether the terms "coronavirus" and "COVID-19" were being used in a similar way: that is, as an ideograph or as a universal whipping post with strongly negative connotations. For CEO Dimon, COVID-19 was the cause variously of "hardships," "fears," "turmoil," and "further inequities in society" (p. 14 of his CEO letter). Dimon's attribution of agency here lay not with human executives and their lack of preparedness for a pandemic, but with the inanimate "virus."

Dimon used "COVID-19" as an ideograph with the apparent intent of absolving his leadership from any possible blame. This is consistent with a broad range of CEO communication that seemed directed to blame COVID-19 for the misfortunes of companies – and do so while overlooking that many companies had vulnerable business models and pre-existing financial ills. Rarely have CEOs confessed to the pre-pandemic reality that their management of capital, cash flows, risk, and long-term planning left much to be desired.

Commendably, Dimon's letter to shareholders is very frank in stating that the US "was not adequately prepared for this pandemic" and that Americans "need to demand more of ourselves and our leaders if we want to prevent or mitigate these disasters" (p. 18). He makes a heart-felt plea for higher levels of "civility, humanity [and] empathy" (p. 18) to improve America.

We focus on Dimon's framing of Section 7 of his letter, titled "We need to come together: My fervent hope for America." In the middle part of this section, Dimon criticizes the failure of America's political leaders to adequately address a range of social ills: the quality of inner-city schooling, an increasingly costly healthcare system, the scourge of obesity, ineffective infrastructure planning, misplaced immigration policies, and poorly designed social safety nets. He frames these criticisms with references to the "American Dream" and constructs himself and JPMorgan Chase metaphorically as genuine patriots. His text invokes ideographs such as "liberty," "equality," and "freedom." However, what emerges is a smarmy sugar-coated nationalistic eulogy that "reads as if it were a deliberate parody of the worst excesses of an advertising copywriter."[24]

Dimon begins with references to the "greatness" of America's prosperity and asserts that America is blessed with "extraordinary [and unequaled] gifts" of freedoms bequeathed by the "Founding Fathers" and their promise of "equality and opportunity." One can scarcely remonstrate with the public policy critique that follows, given the virtuosity of such a framing and the way it "softens up" the reader to Dimon's following assessment. Dimon adopts the high moral ground by calling for "non-partisan solutions" and urges readers not to lay the blame by "finger pointing." He channels the rhetoric of John F. Kennedy by exploiting Kennedy's famous expression in which he balanced two or more clauses against each other by reversing their structures – a rhetorical trope known as chiasmus. Dimon writes: "Ask not what your country can do for you – ask what you can do for your country."

Dimon is unrelenting in the back-end framing of his critique. Whether or not this is effective probably depends on whether one is an American patriot and is keenly disposed to such rhetoric. He calls for "America to roll up its sleeves," to "strengthen America's role in the world," and to preserve "the freedoms ascribed by our Founding Fathers" (p. 19). Dimon sees an inseparable link between "happiness, our freedoms, and free enterprise" (p. 19). He ends by casting himself as a true patriot, declaring his "deep and abiding faith in the United States of America and its extraordinary resiliency and capabilities" (p. 19).

Dimon's language invokes sentiment to disguise intent, yet elsewhere his letter features socially acceptable "authentic-talk." So, we have a mixed bag from Dimon: some good things and some not-so-good things. However, unlike the language of most people, the important difference is that the CEOs of major companies are persons with power. They exercise material influence over those they lead and at times have profound broader political influence. The overriding impression is that Dimon's recipe for rallying his stakeholders in the midst of a pandemic seems to be this: confer agency (blame) on the disease, cite the need for progressive solutions, and add a heavy dose of American patriotism.

In a crisis, CEOs should be calm and selfless and avoid intemperate language. Such advice seems to have been lost on Tesla CEO Elon Musk. In a series of tweets in March and April 2020, and in the company's first quarter 2020 earnings call on April 29, 2020, Musk used extreme and offensive language to express his strong disdain for government stay-at-home orders.[25] He delivered a rant, presumably because he was frustrated at being prevented from resuming production at his Northern California manufacturing plant. He set an egregious example for the broader community by claiming these state health orders were "fascist" and tantamount to "forcible imprisonment." He called for people to be given back "their Goddamn freedom" and completed his tirade with the offensive expression "What the f★★★." Such language is grossly insensitive in the stressful environment of a pandemic when workers and community members have good reason to be especially worried about their lives and those of their loved ones.[26]

What we observe is that some CEOs have taken the opportunity to use pandemic-speak to impress audiences and to serve their personal rhetorical and strategic agendas. The best overall communications policy for CEOs in a pandemic is to acknowledge bad news plainly, humbly, and calmly – and to present a narrative that includes some aspects of a strategy to survive such an existential crisis.

Throughout this book, we have stressed that CEO-speak is never innocent. We need to be alert to the motives that often drive CEO-speak. We urge readers to be ever more conscious that CEO-speak is "not merely words that evaporate into thin air … [but that they should] monitor the language used by CEOs and hold them accountable for [it]."[27]

DICTION Text Analysis Software Explained

DICTION "is a dictionary-based package that examines text for its verbal tone." DICTION deploys 10,000 search words divided into 31 word lists or dictionaries that were compiled after the analysis of 20,000 texts of several different types. No search word is present in more than one dictionary. DICTION's main strength is its capacity to detect signs of five master variables that are thought to be good indicators of the pervading tone of a text: ACTIVITY, OPTIMISM, CERTAINTY, REALISM, and COMMONALITY. There is almost no statistical relationship among these five master variables. They are constructed after combining various subaltern variables that mostly represent semantic fields (such as PRAISE, SATISFACTION, INSPIRATION, BLAME, HARDSHIP, and DENIAL) and four non-semantic fields: INSISTENCE (the degree to which a text relies on the repetition of words), EMBELLISHMENT (ratio of descriptive to functional words), VARIETY (type-token ratio), and COMPLEXITY (word length).

The five master variables are claimed to "provide the most robust understanding" of a text. They are defined as follows:

ACTIVITY: language featuring movement, change, the implementation of ideas, and the avoidance of inertia
CERTAINTY: language indicating resoluteness, inflexibility, and completeness and a tendency to speak *ex cathedra*
OPTIMISM: language endorsing some person, group, concept, or event or highlighting their positive entailments

---

All quoted material is from Hart (2001). The other principal source is Murphy (2013).

REALISM: language describing tangible, immediate, recognizable matters that affect people's everyday lives

COMMONALITY: language highlighting the agreed-upon values of a group and rejecting idiosyncratic modes of engagement

DICTION calculates frequency scores for the occurrence of words in the dictionary lists for each of its semantic variables. These scores are assessed as being within, above, or below a normal range that is calculated based on the type of text being analyzed. Of the six available comparative dictionaries in the class designated as "Business" (Corporate Financial Reports; Corporate Public Relations; Financial News; Legal Documents; Magazine Advertising; TV Advertising), we select the Corporate Financial Reports on most occasions because it is compiled exclusively of words from samples of written text in annual financial reports. Occasionally, we use the Corporate Public Relations dictionary because it includes non-written text, such as speeches and public pronouncements drawn from sources other than annual financial reports. Care needs to be exercised with DICTION because its standard word lists have restricted capacity to capture the subtlety of the language used by CEOs.

Much of the analysis we conduct with DICTION identifies the pervading tone of text as evidenced by its scores for the five master variables (ACTIVITY, OPTIMISM, CERTAINTY, REALISM, and COMMONALITY); and any common patterns in the four calculated variables (INSISTENCE, EMBELLISHMENT, VARIETY, and COMPLEXITY). For each of its variables, DICTION highlights out-of-range scores that are more than +1 standard deviation above the expected mean score or more than −1 standard deviation below the expected mean score. Our analysis usually focuses on results for the DICTION master variables that are "extremely out-of-range": that is, language use indicated to be statistically significant in two-tailed terms at the 5% level or better.

Statement of Tim Sloan to the US Senate Committee on Banking, Housing and Urban Affairs

Chairman Crapo, Ranking Member Brown, and members of the [1]
Committee, thank you for your invitation to today's hearing, "Wells Fargo: [2]
One Year Later." I appreciate the opportunity to discuss the progress Wells [3]
Fargo has made. [4]

    The past year has been a time of great disappointment and transition at [5]
Wells Fargo because we recognized too late the full scope and seriousness [6]
of the problems in our Community Bank. When my predecessor testified [7]
here last year, we had not fully grappled with the damage the sales practices [8]
scandal had done to our customers, our team members, and their trust in [9]
the bank. We came to Congress without a good plan and all of you were [10]
right to criticize us. But I heard you – and I heard our customers and our [11]
team members – loud and clear. You expect us to do better, and so do we. [12]

    So let me be very clear about this: I am deeply sorry for letting down [13]
our customers and team members. I apologize for the damage done to all [14]
the people who work and bank at this important American institution. [15]
When the challenges at Wells Fargo demanded decisive action, the bank's [16]
leaders acted too slowly and too incrementally. That was unacceptable. [17]

    I also want to be clear about another thing: Wells Fargo is a better bank [18]
today than it was a year ago. And next year, Wells Fargo will be a better [19]
bank than it is today. That is because we have spent the past year deter- [20]
mined to earn back the public's trust. Since I became CEO eleven months [21]
ago, my team and I have been focused on the three tasks you have invited [22]
me to discuss today. [23]

This statement, titled "Wells Fargo: One Year Later," was presented on October 3, 2017.
Retrieved February 10, 2018, from https://www.banking.senate.gov/public/index.cfm/2017
/10/wells-fargo-one-year-later. Available January 8, 2020, at https://www.govinfo.gov/content
/pkg/CHRG-115shrg28111/html/CHRG-115shrg28111.htm.

[24]   First, in response to the sales practices problems announced in 2016,
[25]   we are transforming our Community Bank. Our retail bank has strong
[26]   new leadership, more effective organization, and incentives that reward our
[27]   team members for doing what is right for the customer. This is a funda-
[28]   mentally different organization from the one that existed in 2016.

[29]   Second, we are looking beyond our Community Bank to review our
[30]   operations across the entire company, including in our indirect auto lend-
[31]   ing business. That review is still in progress, but it has already identified
[32]   several ways in which we can improve. I am committed to confronting
[33]   these problems head-on, and fixing them.

[34]   Third, we are working diligently to make things right for every customer
[35]   who was harmed by any of our practices and, to that end, we will compen-
[36]   sate every customer who suffered because Wells Fargo made mistakes. I am
[37]   pleased to report that these remediation efforts are well underway.

[38] Transforming Our Community Bank

[39]   No part of our company better reflects the difference between Wells Fargo
[40]   in 2016 and Wells Fargo in 2017 than our Community Bank. We have
[41]   dramatically overhauled its leadership, its organization, and its incentives.
[42]   At every level of the bank, our efforts focus squarely on the needs of our
[43]   customers, not on achieving product sales goals.

[44]   I appointed a new leader, Mary Mack, to transform the Community
[45]   Bank. Mary has worked tirelessly to improve our approach to meeting cus-
[46]   tomer and team-member needs. Together, we have eliminated product sales
[47]   goals for retail bankers. Those goals contributed to a high-pressure sales envi-
[48]   ronment that failed our customers. In some cases, these goals even resulted
[49]   in customers receiving products they never requested or realized they had.

[50]   The old sales goals and pressure failed our team members, too. Our new
[51]   compensation and performance plan rewards retail team members for excel-
[52]   lent customer service and team performance, not for selling products. The new
[53]   goals place a priority on risk management and compliance, demonstrating to
[54]   team members that they all have a role to play in ensuring that Wells Fargo
[55]   is serving customers with integrity. This begins with revamped hiring and
[56]   training programs, as well as increased base pay for entry-level team members.

[57]   In addition, we have made dramatic changes in the way our team mem-
[58]   bers interact with our customers by adopting a new customer-service
[59]   approach across our Community Bank. We have simplified complicated pro-
[60]   cesses, replaced required questions with relevant tips, and enabled bankers

and tellers to better meet their customers' needs by offering them the [61]
right products, services, or referral. Managers have also been empowered to [62]
immediately resolve some customer issues, like fees, at the branch rather than [63]
through a call center. These changes have led to a more personalized experi- [64]
ence for our customers and more fulfilling jobs for our team members. [65]

We are equally committed to the former Wells Fargo team members [66]
who were affected by the Community Bank's old ways of doing things. [67]
I am proud to report that since last September we have hired back more [68]
than 1,780 team members who left the bank during those years. [69]

I have also now made clear that, when team members have concerns, [70]
I want to know. I have traveled the country, visiting more than 100 offices, [71]
to meet personally with thousands of team members. Our senior leader- [72]
ship team has done the same. We have also improved our ethics protections [73]
to ensure that every team member feels empowered to speak up without [74]
any fear of retaliation when he or she sees a problem. [75]

Accountability [76]

I know that responsibility for Wells Fargo's shortcomings reaches well [77]
beyond our bank branches. That is why our review and our changes have [78]
not stopped there. We started by holding executives accountable. Over the [79]
past year, Wells Fargo eliminated a record $180 million in senior-executive [80]
compensation: [81]

- No member of the Operating Committee who served before [82]
  September 8, 2016, including me, received a bonus for 2016. [83]
- Every member of the Operating Committee who served before [84]
  September 8, 2016, had his or her long-term incentive awards for past [85]
  performance reduced by up to 50%. [86]
- Neither former CEO John Stumpf nor former head of the [87]
  Community Bank, Carrie Tolstedt, received a bonus for 2016. [88]
- Mr. Stumpf forfeited $69 million in compensation and equity. [89]
- Ms. Tolstedt forfeited $67 million in compensation and equity. [90]
- And, finally, we terminated four senior leaders of the Community [91]
  Bank, which cost them their 2016 bonuses, their unvested equity [92]
  awards, and their vested outstanding stock options. [93]

Looking forward, we have made oversight and compliance much [94]
more effective than a year ago. These are fundamental changes to the way [95]

[96]   the company runs. We have reviewed and adjusted the roles of tens of
[97]   thousands of our team members. We have moved away from a decentralized
[98]   "Run It Like You Own It" structure, where business leaders had the discre-
[99]   tion to run their operations independently. Now we follow a more central-
[100]   ized model in which risk, compliance, and human resources leaders have
[101]   far greater visibility into, and accountability for, issues across the individual
[102]   business lines. In addition, I established a Conduct Management Office
[103]   with company-wide responsibility for investigations and complaints. This
[104]   new team assesses complaints across the company, reports every month to
[105]   our executive team – including me – and helps leaders "connect the dots"
[106]   in ways we never could before. Now when a problem emerges, we can
[107]   identify it quickly, escalate it promptly, and address it fully.
[108]   These changes are consistent with, and designed to address, the findings
[109]   of our Board's independent investigation into the root causes of our retail
[110]   sales practices issues. That investigation found, and I agree, that our previ-
[111]   ous structure contributed to a failure to see the threat that high-pressure
[112]   sales goals posed to our Community Bank and our customers. This struc-
[113]   ture also contributed to our slow and insufficient response to that threat.
[114]   My job as CEO is to ensure that never happens again.
[115]   One important way I have exercised that responsibility is by calling for a
[116]   comprehensive review of sales practices and other customer-facing opera-
[117]   tions across the bank. We decided to go beyond the requirements of our
[118]   regulators and conduct a company-wide review, leaving no stone unturned.
[119]   That review has consumed a big portion of the past year and continues
[120]   today. This has been, and continues to be, a massive undertaking. It has
[121]   involved our own team members, as well as regulators, independent direc-
[122]   tors, lawyers, and independent consultants. The mandate is to identify any
[123]   failures or practices that could harm our customers.
[124]   We expected to find more shortcomings through this effort, and we did.
[125]   You have undoubtedly heard about some of these problems in the news.
[126]   Last fall, we reviewed 93 million accounts opened between 2011 and 2015.
[127]   That review raised concerns regarding whether approximately 2 million
[128]   accounts had been properly opened. We told you and others that we would
[129]   look at even more accounts, and we did. We searched across 2009, 2010,
[130]   and 2016 – nearly doubling the time frame to eight years. We also looked
[131]   at other types of accounts or services, such as online bill pay, that may have
[132]   been initiated improperly.
[133]   In August, we announced the result of this broader look at 165 million
[134]   accounts opened between 2009 and 2016. Our estimate of potentially
[135]   unauthorized accounts grew by about 1.5 million. This is a substantial

number, but it is important to note that these are not "new" instances of [136]
possible misconduct since last fall; they are newly revealed instances of pos- [137]
sible misconduct based upon our own expanded investigation of the years [138]
before 2017. Of the total of 3.5 million accounts, approximately 190,000 [139]
incurred fees and charges. Wells Fargo will provide a total of $2.8 million [140]
in additional refunds and credits on top of the $3.3 million previously [141]
refunded as a result of the original account review. Our commitment is to [142]
refund all fees and all charges imposed with respect to any accounts and [143]
services that proved to be unauthorized. [144]

During the past year, we also confronted problems in our auto-loan [145]
business. We explained in August that some of our auto loans involved [146]
insurance that had been placed by a vendor when the customer was already [147]
insured. This issue is quite different from the previous sales-practices issues [148]
in our Community Bank, because this insurance was not a product that [149]
Wells Fargo team members were given an incentive to sell. Also, this is an [150]
issue we found and addressed ourselves. The improper insurance charges [151]
occurred because of flaws in our process for verifying the customer's insur- [152]
ance status and disclosing the premiums added. It was a significant mistake [153]
that harmed a lot of people, and we are making it right. Last month, we [154]
began issuing checks to affected auto-loan customers, all of whom we [155]
expect to reimburse by the middle of 2018. [156]

Making Things Right with Our Customers [157]

The entire Wells Fargo team, all 270,000 of us, is committed to making [158]
things right for customers the bank let down. This is a big job, and we will [159]
get it right. [160]

To ensure our changes to the Community Bank are working for our [161]
customers, we dramatically enhanced our monitoring and compliance. As [162]
an example, we are closely monitoring the opening of new accounts. Every [163]
new account now generates an email within an hour, or a letter within a [164]
day, to confirm the account holder's authorization. In our branches, we are [165]
on pace to conduct 16,000 visits by "mystery shoppers" this year, so that [166]
these anonymous reviewers can test and examine the practices and service [167]
that our customers experience. These visits will help ensure we are pro- [168]
actively identifying any improper sales practices and delivering customer [169]
service that is consistent with our mission. [170]

We also are reaching out to customers all across America to determine [171]
if they were affected by the bank's practices and, if so, how we can fix it. [172]

[173]   During the fourth quarter of 2016, we contacted more than 43 million
[174]   individual and small business customers. We are issuing refunds to every
[175]   affected customer who has responded or has been identified by our
[176]   third-party review. Wells Fargo has already paid millions in refunds and
[177]   credits to Community Bank customers we spoke with between September
[178]   2016 and July 2017. In addition, customers harmed by our discontinued
[179]   sales practices will receive a total of $142 million in compensation (after
[180]   deducting plaintiffs' attorneys' fees and administration costs) under our
[181]   class-action settlement. This will compensate customers for claims dating
[182]   back to 2002, including claims by customers for increased borrowing costs
[183]   resulting from credit-score impact.
[184]   Beyond these formal reimbursement mechanisms, I want to be clear
[185]   that Wells Fargo is committed to addressing every concern any customer
[186]   may have about an unwanted product or service – no matter where or
[187]   when it may have occurred.

★ ★ ★

[188]   The past year has been humbling and challenging. We are resolving
[189]   past problems even as we make changes to ensure nothing like this hap-
[190]   pens again at Wells Fargo. We are doing this by strengthening our culture,
[191]   holding leaders accountable, and improving our business practices and risk
[192]   management. I want to thank all our team members for their hard work in
[193]   this transformation.
[194]   Together, we will do whatever is necessary to put our customers first.
[195]   I see the improvement every day, and so do the team members I visit in
[196]   our bank branches. I think our customers have noticed the improvement,
[197]   too. I pledge to you that we will not stop until we restore our reputation
[198]   and our customers' trust, and make Wells Fargo the finest and most ethical
[199]   company it can be.
[200]   Thank you again for the opportunity to address this Committee. I look
[201]   forward to your questions.

Tony Hayward's Speech to BP's AGM in 2010

Good morning ladies and gentlemen. It's great to see so many of you here [1]
today and thank you for your support over the past year. [2]

I'd like to start by welcoming Carl-Henric to BP and to his first AGM. [3]
As an international business leader, Carl-Henric has brought a fresh per- [4]
spective and a wealth of experience to the company, and I am very much [5]
enjoying working with him. [6]

BP has made a lot of progress over the last three years, but there's still [7]
more to do. We now have a real opportunity to make our asset base work [8]
harder for our shareholders and today I'd like to explain how we plan to [9]
make that happen. [10]

But first let me begin by looking at the broader environment and how [11]
it is shaping our priorities. In the short term, the global downturn has [12]
reduced energy demand although we expect oil demand to grow again in [13]
2010, probably by about a million barrels a day. And over the longer term, [14]
driven by industrialization and rising living standards in the developing [15]
economies, global energy consumption will continue to rise. [16]

Of course a number of big challenges lie ahead, especially in the realm of [17]
policy, where the question of how to meet rising energy demand in an afford- [18]
able and sustainable way has risen to the top of the global political agenda. [19]

For a long time now, BP has advocated a proactive approach to climate [20]
change and supported action to curb carbon emissions. And we continue [21]
to believe that the world needs a diverse energy mix that incorporates [22]
all available sources from oil sands to solar and leverages investment in [23]
technology. [24]

Key to this is a need to promote efficiency to minimize the environ- [25]
mental impact of fossil fuels and to ensure we maximize best use of the [26]
world's energy resources. This will help to provide secure supplies of energy [27]
as well as addressing climate change. [28]

[29]   We also believe that encouraging free and open energy markets is the
[30] best way to induce change. A carbon price, preferably created by capping
[31] emissions, would provide a strong incentive to encourage energy efficiency
[32] and investment in alternatives to fossil fuels.
[33]   BP is supporting the transition to a low-carbon economy in a number
[34] of ways: firstly by improving energy efficiency within our own operations,
[35] as well as by developing more efficient products such as BP Ultimate and
[36] Castrol lubricants.
[37]   Secondly, by using an internal cost of carbon when making investment
[38] decisions about fossil fuel projects. This encourages investment in technol-
[39] ogy to reduce carbon emissions.
[40]   And thirdly by promoting the lowest-cost energy pathways to reduce
[41] emissions a good example being the use of natural gas to generate power.
[42] Gas is easily the cleanest-burning fossil fuel – it's efficient, versatile and
[43] abundantly available.
[44]   We also continue to invest in our low-carbon businesses; since 2005 we
[45] have invested more than $4 billion in Alternative Energy, and focused our
[46] activity in four key areas:

[47] • In Biofuels we're converting sugar cane to ethanol in Brazil. In the UK
[48]   we're constructing an ethanol manufacturing plant and a technology
[49]   demonstration plant for biobutanol with DuPont. And in the US we
[50]   are working on the conversion of ligno-cellulosic material to biofuels.
[51] • In Wind we've focused the business in the US where we already have
[52]   more than 1.2 gigawatts of gross capacity spinning. We expect this
[53]   business to become cash flow positive this year.
[54] • In Solar we've focused the business and we're repositioning our
[55]   manufacturing footprint to lower-cost locations, principally in India
[56]   and China.
[57] • And in Carbon Capture and Sequestration we're concentrating on two
[58]   major projects – one in California, the other in Abu Dhabi.

[59] All this is underpinned by our continuing investment in research and tech-
[60] nology. BP currently has 20 major technology programs underway. Around
[61] two thirds relate to existing businesses and the remainder to new forms of
[62] energy and ways of making today's energy more efficient.
[63]   Our priorities which lie at the heart of all our operations remain safety,
[64] people and performance. This is what we call our Forward Agenda. Our
[65] focus on safe and reliable operations is now strongly embedded in all our
[66] businesses; we are continuing to build the on the core capabilities of our

people; and we have started to see the benefits of improved operational [67]
performance flowing through to the bottom line. [68]

Let me address each of these in turn. [69]

Safety remains our number one priority and I'm pleased to report we [70]
can see clear progress. There has been a significant reduction in the fre- [71]
quency of recordable injuries and the number of major incidents related to [72]
integrity failures has also fallen. At the same time we're reducing contain- [73]
ment losses in our operations. [74]

We are continuing to improve our skills and capabilities as we roll out [75]
a common Operating Management System across our business. By the [76]
end of 2009 we'd fully implemented this at 70 sites – covering around 80 [77]
percent of our operations and the remainder will be completed this year. [78]

But implementation is just the beginning. Our Operating Management [79]
System provides the framework to now drive continuous improvement [80]
across all of our operations. [81]

Our people have been fundamental to the company's transformation [82]
over the last few years. Not only have we refreshed the highest levels of [83]
leadership within BP, but we have also reviewed our whole approach to the [84]
organization. We are focusing on deepening our capability by putting the [85]
right people with the right skills in the right places. And we are ensuring [86]
they can reinforce their technical and functional expertise through devel- [87]
opment programs like our Operations Academies. [88]

We are continuing our drive to create a diverse and inclusive workplace [89]
to ensure that we can attract and retain the best talent. And we have linked [90]
reward more closely to performance. [91]

These changes have been clearly reflected in improved operational [92]
performance. [93]

Over the last two years we have closed the competitive gap that we [94]
identified in 2007, and restored momentum in our core businesses. In 2009 [95]
we grew production by 4 percent, building on the track record of momen- [96]
tum relative to our peers since 2000. In refining we have brought our US [97]
network back to full operation, and our system is now back to pre-2005 [98]
levels of availability. [99]

The drive to increase efficiency and reduce costs remains a key focus [100]
for everyone at BP. We started more than two years ago in our effort to [101]
counter cost inflation and drive much greater efficiency into our business. [102]

In the upstream we are leading our peer group in driving down produc- [103]
tion costs, with BP's unit costs in 2009 12 percent lower than in 2008. We [104]
will maintain this momentum through activity choice and in the way we [105]
manage the supply chain. In the downstream our efficiency initiatives have [106]

[107] reduced cash costs by more than 15 percent in 2009 and our goal over the
[108] next 2 to 3 years is to return costs to 2004 levels. For the group as a whole
[109] we reduced our cash costs last year by more than $4 billion.
[110]   In 2009, lower oil and gas prices and weak refining margins created
[111] a challenging environment for the whole sector. But the operational
[112] momentum in our business and our steadfast focus on efficiency has clearly
[113] improved our performance relative to our peers.
[114]   Despite a challenging year, this performance meant we could distrib-
[115] ute $10.5 billion to shareholders and increase our dividend to 56 cents
[116] per share. It's also been reflected in our relative share price performance
[117] since the beginning of last year; we have outperformed ALL our major
[118] competitors.
[119]   As well as delivering a good operational performance in 2009, we saw
[120] significant strategic progress across the company.
[121]   In E&P we achieved major new access to resources and made a series
[122] of significant discoveries. We have maintained our strong track record of
[123] reserve replacement. This is our 17th consecutive year in which we are able
[124] to report a reserves replacement above 100 percent. Year-on-year produc-
[125] tion growth was 4 percent. We started up seven major projects and sanc-
[126] tioned two notable new developments.
[127]   In R&M, our refining system has been fully restored. We decapitalized
[128] our US convenience retail business and reduced the geographic footprint
[129] of our international businesses. At the same time costs have come down by
[130] 15 percent.
[131]   Alternative Energy is more focused and disciplined. And we have
[132] furthered our corporate simplification agenda, reducing headcount by
[133] around 7500.
[134]   Let me give you a little more detail on how we strengthened our port-
[135] folio of oil and gas reserves in 2009. Our discoveries included the giant
[136] Tiber oil field in the Gulf of Mexico – the deepest well ever drilled in the
[137] industry. Indeed it lies further below the Earth's surface than the summit of
[138] Mount Everest does above it.
[139]   A particular highlight was our return to Iraq where we signed a contract
[140] to redevelop the supergiant Rumaila field in partnership with the Chinese
[141] National Petroleum Company. The project will help Iraqis to develop new
[142] skills as well as generate income to assist in rebuilding the country.
[143]   In the US we expanded our shale gas portfolio by securing a new posi-
[144] tion in the Eagle Ford Shale. We established a Coal Bed Methane position
[145] in Indonesia. And in Jordan we agreed to join with the National Petroleum
[146] Company to exploit the Risha gas field.

And we have continued to add resources in 2010, most notably through [147] the acquisition of $7 billion worth of assets from Devon Energy that we [148] announced last month. These include significant deepwater interests in [149] Brazil and the Gulf of Mexico. [150]

Over the last two years, through exploration, appraisal and access, we [151] have added a total of around 7.5 billion barrels of new resources that's five [152] years' worth of production replaced in just two – and that excludes Iraq. [153]

Our strong resource base reinforces the prospects for future production [154] growth. Last year I said that we expected to grow production between 1 [155] and 2 percent a year to 2013. We are now confident that at a $60 per barrel [156] oil price we can sustain average production growth from 2008 at 1 to 2 [157] percent a year out to 2015. [158]

This production profile is underpinned by 42 new projects, which will [159] start up between now and 2015. Together they will contribute around [160] 1 million barrels a day to total production by 2015. They are concentrated [161] in the Gulf of Mexico, the North Sea, Azerbaijan, and Angola, which are [162] all high margin production areas. [163]

The strategic progress that we made in 2009 is part of a longer track [164] record. Over the past decade our strategy has allowed us to build a port- [165] folio of great quality and huge potential: equal in our view to any in our [166] industry in terms of the key measures shown here. [167]

We have a long history as both an efficient and successful explorer. This [168] has given us a reserve replacement track record which is among the best in [169] the industry, and a long-lived asset base with a bias to conventional oil. We [170] have confidence in robust medium term growth and considerable potential [171] to apply new technologies to further improve recovery. [172]

In R&M despite a difficult environment – we have less overall exposure [173] to refining than our peers. We have high-graded our portfolio over the past [174] decade to end up with, on average, larger and more advantaged refineries [175] than the other super-majors. We believe we also have the best supply opti- [176] mization capability and a set of world class international businesses. [177]

However while our portfolio ranks amongst the best in the industry, our [178] financial performance has yet to fully reflect this. There is now a real oppor- [179] tunity to make this portfolio work harder for us and we intend to do just that. [180]

So how do we define the opportunity? There are many ways to view it: [181] from company-wide issues such as the gap in earnings versus our peers, to [182] return on capital employed versus the competition; and from segment-level [183] issues such as improving refining efficiency and closing the gap in fuels [184] value chain performance in the US to improving efficiency in our drilling [185] and in the execution of projects in the upstream. [186]

[187]   Whichever way you look at it, there are significant opportunities for
[188]   improvement and in every case firm plans are in place to close those gaps.
[189]   Our goal over the next few years is to realize the latent potential of
[190]   our asset base by improving the efficiency and effectiveness of everything
[191]   we do.
[192]   We will vigorously drive cost and capital efficiency whilst at the same
[193]   time maintaining our first priority of safe and reliable operations.
[194]   In E&P, we will drive efficiency through a new organizational struc-
[195]   ture. This will provide clearer accountabilities and a centralized approach
[196]   to project management. For example, it will ensure that we use standard
[197]   designs and equipment for similar projects in different parts of the world.
[198]   In R&M, we will focus on efficiency, quality and integration as we start
[199]   to realize the potential of our refinery network and restructured fuel value
[200]   chains.
[201]   All of this will be underpinned by our continuing investment in tech-
[202]   nology and by the new culture we are establishing at BP.
[203]   So to sum up, our strategy remains unchanged but we are now embark-
[204]   ing on a new phase in which we intend to realize the full potential of the
[205]   portfolio we've built up over the past decade. We have considerable scope
[206]   to pursue sector leadership, particularly in costs, capital efficiency and mar-
[207]   gin quality.
[208]   Of course the future looks challenging. It always does. But we have
[209]   emerged from 2009 in great shape and with renewed confidence and
[210]   determination. We can see the prize and we believe we are well positioned
[211]   to capture it.
[212]   I want to thank the employees of BP for their commitment – and I want
[213]   to thank each of you as shareholders for your loyalty and support. I hope
[214]   you will continue to support us on the journey that lies ahead. Thank you.

Appendix D

The "Drivers" Theme in Khosrowshahi's First 100 Tweets at Uber

Tweet Number	Date	Tweet Text	Comments
4 (themes 1, 2, and 6)	Sept. 6, 2017	#respect to the ones away from home to support family or follow their dreams. I know the feeling. #takemehome #uber	https://youtu.be/BZui4H91IZI Link to UberFreight on Youtube, with one of their drivers describing Uber's "Take me home" feature that creates schedules so that Uber freight drivers can spend more time at home. The video was published Sept. 6, 2017, and has the following tagline: "The Uber Team met Frank in December of 2016. He's a career driver who's constantly on the road. When we asked him what one feature he wished we could create for him, he responded: [follow the link and see the video]"
6 (themes 2, 3, and 6)	Sept. 13, 2017	Week 2 and I got to meet some of the awesome #drivers who make @Uber what it is. Lots of honest feedback and even more opportunity!	A photo in the tweet shows Khosrowshahi, along with nine "awesome drivers," posing against what looks like an office wall with "UBER" prominent behind and above them. Four of the drivers are in an informal front row, and the remaining five are on either side of Khosrowshahi. Everyone seems to be dressed casually. They are all smiling. Two of the four drivers in the front row are women. Two of the drivers in the back row alongside Khosrowshahi are giving the "thumbs-up," as is Khosrowshahi (but his seems more modest).

(continued)

All tweets retrieved from Dara Khosrowshahi's verified Twitter account, @dkhos.

Tweet Number	Date	Tweet Text	Comments
7 (themes 2, 3, and 6)	Sept. 20, 2017	So proud of our @ Uber_MEX team for offering free rides in impacted cities and contribution to @CruzRoja_MX - #FuerzaMexico #giveback	This tweet is a retweet of Uber Mexico Link to Uber Mexico tweet
8 (themes 2, 3, 5, and 6)	Sept. 22, 2017	Dear London: we r far from perfect but we have 40k licensed drivers and 3.5mm Londoners depending on us. Pls work w/us to make things right	
14 (themes 2, 3, 4, 5 and 6)	Oct. 3, 2017	Great meetings in London, including w some of the drivers who rely on our app. Determined to make things right in this great city	In a photo in the tweet, Khosrowshahi poses, facing the camera and smiling. Fourteen "London drivers" surround him. Everyone appears to have at least a slight smile, with Khosrowshahi's being the biggest. He is dressed casually in what seems to be an open-necked white shirt, with no jacket. The location seems to be Uber's London office.
15 (themes 2 and 6)	Oct. 4, 2017	We can never forget that drivers represent the heart of our service #UberEATS #nicesurprise	This tweet contains a photo screenshot of a letter from an UberEats customer, with the customer's address blacked out.
17 (themes 2, 3, and 6)	Oct. 13, 2017	Great Q&A with our #Uber Seattle team. Working on some big projects on our rider, driver, CRM and platform side. #lookingfortalent.	This tweet includes a photo showing Khosrowshahi posing, in casual attire, in what looks like a large room at the Uber Seattle office. He is smiling and surrounded by about a hundred younger men and women, all in casual dress and, like him, facing the camera.
19 (themes 2, 3, 4, and possibly 6)	Oct. 26, 2017	Honored to meet inspiring Saudi women today. Excited and proud to	A photo in the tweet shows Khosrowshahi in open-neck white shirt and dress jacket, seated and smiling at a small round table, with

Tweet Number	Date	Tweet Text	Comments
		hear how our technology can provide more economic opportunities for all.	fourteen smiling women standing behind him in a semi-circle. Everyone in the shot is facing the camera; all of the women are dressed modestly, with ten wearing head coverings. A vase of white flowers is placed on the small round table, accompanied by six smaller vases.
22 (themes 2, 3, and 6)	Oct. 31, 2017	Getting our message out in #Brazil. 500k drivers, 17mm users, 100 cities #LeiDoRetrocesso	This tweet includes a photo of newspaper pages, apparently Brazilian, attached to a rectangular pinboard. A large headshot of Dara Khosrowshahi appears on one of the pages.
23 (themes 2, 3, and 6)	Oct. 31, 2017	Standing up with our partners. #driverappreciation #LeiDoRetrocesso	A photo in the tweet shows Khosrowshahi, dressed very casually and smiling broadly, holding up his left arm with his left hand seemingly clenched. Or perhaps he is holding a camera and taking a selfie of himself surrounded by what appears to be several hundred smiling people looking into his camera.
42 (themes 2, 3, and 6)	Jan. 16, 2018	Great convo with drivers from all over at our very first Driver Advisory Forum. Awesome feedback that will feed into our product roadmap and business strategy going into 2018. #BuildingTogether	A photo in the tweet shows Khosrowshahi, on one knee and in casual attire, smiling and looking at the camera, surrounded by about thirty-five attendees at Uber's Driver Advisory Forum. Twelve are women. Khosrowshahi has placed his arms around the two people on either side of him, and they in turn seem to have placed their arms around him. Just Khosrowshahi and the four people adjacent to him are kneeling or sitting. At least one person, a woman, who is standing behind him to his right, has placed her hand on his shoulder.

(continued)

Tweet Number	Date	Tweet Text	Comments
49 (themes 2, 4, and 6)	Jan. 29, 2018	It all starts with awareness, and ours came from our driver partners. Now, together, we move – Uber enlists its drivers in the fight against sex trafficking –https://usat.ly/2FqsYIM via @usatoday	Link to https://www.usatoday.com/story/tech/2018/01/29/uber-enlists-its-drivers-fight-against-sex-trafficking/1066530001/. (Mardo della Cava, "Uber enlists its drivers in the fight against sex trafficking with new national campaign," *USA Today*, Jan. 29, 2018)
64 (themes 2, 3, and 6)	Feb. 23, 2018	Spent the morning meeting with a group of our drivers – great to hear about their experiences with Uber and get feedback on safety, support and much more.	A photo included in the tweet shows Khosrowshahi, smiling in casual business attire, apparently taking a selfie with about ten male Indian drivers, who are giving the "thumbs-up" sign and smiling.
86 (themes 2, 4, and 6)	Apr. 4, 2018	Tough news all around, but there are everyday heroes around the corner (or behind the wheel in this case) - @Uber driver helps people fleeing YouTube shooting	Tweet includes link to *LA Times* article by Tracey Lien: https://www.latimes.com/local/california/la-me-ln-youtube-shooter-live-updates-uber-driver-outside-youtube-office-1522793354-htmlstory.html ("Uber driver helps people fleeing YouTube shooting," Apr. 3, 2018). "Lucacio Simoes, 40, an Uber driver from San Bruno, learned of the shooting when a friend texted him about it while he was having lunch at the nearby Tanforan shopping center. Simoes said he drove his Ford Explorer toward YouTube headquarters to see if he could help. 'There were people running down the street,' he said."
88 (themes 2 and 6)	Apr. 10, 2018	Excited to introduce the new Driver app—built for and with drivers, and designed to meet	Tweet includes link to video with DK using the new app: https://youtu.be/9UrTVTiG6pg

Tweet Number	Date	Tweet Text	Comments
		their needs on their journey. Had a blast taking it for a spin. Driving is harder than it looks, but hopefully the new app makes the experience a lot less stressful.	
89 (themes 2, 4, and 6)	Apr. 10, 2018	When you see pics of parades in Ho Chi Minh and Hanoi, convoys in Jakarta, drivers bringing their families, waving goodbye and signing each other's jackets, you realize how much a part in everyday lives we play. #Respect	This tweet includes a photo of what appears to be several hundred people, with helmets, on motorcycles.
98 (themes 2 and 6)	Apr. 22, 2018	Enjoyed sitting down with and listening to female @Uber driver-partners in Cairo, followed by selfies! Favorite comment: "I love reading positive comments from riders saying things like 'great trip,' it makes me happy to wake up in the morning!"	This tweet is a retweet of Barney Harford (@barneyh, verified account) The photo in this tweet shows about nine women drivers in Cairo, and one man (who does not seem Egyptian), apparently in an office taking many selfies.

Statement of Jeff Bezos to the US House of Representatives Committee on the Judiciary

Thank you, Chairman Cicilline, Ranking Member Sensenbrenner, and members of the Subcommittee. I'm Jeff Bezos. I founded Amazon 26 years ago with the long-term mission of making it Earth's most customer-centric company.

My mom, Jackie, had me when she was a 17-year-old high school student in Albuquerque, New Mexico. Being pregnant in high school was not popular in Albuquerque in 1964. It was difficult for her. When they tried to kick her out of school, my grandfather went to bat for her. After some negotiation, the principal said, "OK, she can stay and finish high school, but she can't do any extracurricular activities, and she can't have a locker." My grandfather took the deal, and my mother finished high school, though she wasn't allowed to walk across the stage with her classmates to get her diploma. Determined to keep up with her education, she enrolled in night school, picking classes led by professors who would let her bring an infant to class. She would show up with two duffel bags—one full of textbooks, and one packed with diapers, bottles, and anything that would keep me interested and quiet for a few minutes.

My dad's name is Miguel. He adopted me when I was four years old. He was 16 when he came to the USA from Cuba as part of Operation Pedro Pan, shortly after Castro took over. My dad arrived in America alone. His parents felt he'd be safer here. His mom imagined America would be cold, so she made him a jacket sewn entirely out of cleaning cloths, the only

---

This statement from the founder and chief executive officer of Amazon was given on July 29, 2020, to the Judiciary Subcommittee on Antitrust, Commercial, and Administrative Law. The first 885 words of the statement are reproduced here.

material they had on hand. We still have that jacket; it hangs in my parents' dining room. My dad spent two weeks at Camp Matecumbe, a refugee center in Florida, before being moved to a Catholic mission in Wilmington, Delaware. He was lucky to get to the mission, but even so, he didn't speak English and didn't have an easy path. What he did have was a lot of grit and determination. He received a scholarship to college in Albuquerque, which is where he met my mom. You get different gifts in life, and one of my great gifts is my mom and dad. They have been incredible role models for me and my siblings our entire lives.

You learn different things from your grandparents than you do from your parents, and I had the opportunity to spend my summers from ages four to 16 on my grandparents' ranch in Texas. My grandfather was a civil servant and a rancher – he worked on space technology and missile-defense systems in the 1950s and '60s for the Atomic Energy Commission – and he was self-reliant and resourceful. When you're in the middle of nowhere, you don't pick up a phone and call somebody when something breaks. You fix it yourself. As a kid, I got to see him solve many seemingly unsolvable problems himself, whether he was restoring a broken-down Caterpillar bulldozer or doing his own veterinary work. He taught me that you can take on hard problems. When you have a setback, you get back up and try again. You can invent your way to a better place.

I took these lessons to heart as a teenager, and became a garage inventor. I invented an automatic gate closer out of cement-filled tires, a solar cooker out of an umbrella and tinfoil, and alarms made from baking pans to entrap my siblings.

The concept for Amazon came to me in 1994. The idea of building an online bookstore with millions of titles – something that simply couldn't exist in the physical world – was exciting to me. At the time, I was working at an investment firm in New York City. When I told my boss I was leaving, he took me on a long walk in Central Park. After a lot of listening, he finally said, "You know what, Jeff, I think this is a good idea, but it would be a better idea for somebody who didn't already have a good job." He convinced me to think about it for two days before making a final decision. It was a decision I made with my heart and not my head. When I'm 80 and reflecting back, I want to have minimized the number of regrets that I have in my life. And most of our regrets are acts of omission – the things we didn't try, the paths untraveled. Those are the things that haunt us. And I decided that if I didn't at least give it my best shot, I was going to regret not trying to participate in this thing called the internet that I thought was going to be a big deal.

The initial start-up capital for Amazon.com came primarily from my parents, who invested a large fraction of their life savings in something they didn't understand. They weren't making a bet on Amazon or the concept of a bookstore on the internet. They were making a bet on their son. I told them that I thought there was a 70% chance they would lose their investment, and they did it anyway. It took more than 50 meetings for me to raise $1 million from investors, and over the course of all those meetings, the most common question was, "What's the internet?"

Notes

Chapter 1: Introduction

1 Ms. Morrison was described as "…a much-honoured truth-teller who through celebrated novels and essays illuminated the Black experience in America" (p. IN6).
2 Jaques (2002, p. 9).
3 Denning (2006).
4 Silberstein (2002, p. 1).
5 Guerin (2003, p. 253).
6 Hart et al. (2013, p. 3).
7 Vignone (2012).
8 Slagell (1991, p. 156).
9 Ron (2008, p. 291).
10 Professor Roderick Hart, the software's developer, provides a catalog of published DICTION-based research on the website https://www.dictionsoftware.com /published-studies/.
11 In doing so, we draw, in part, from the explanation provided by Murphy (2013, pp. 60–1).
12 https://www.blackrock.com/us/individual/larry-fink-ceo-letter
13 Amernic et al. (2007).
14 Ibid., p. 1845.
15 Ibid.
16 Ochs & Capps (1996, p. 34).
17 Scott & Lyman (1968).
18 Ochs & Capps (1996, p. 32).
19 Ibid.
20 Kendall (1993); Fiol (1989); Hyland (1998); Prasad & Mir (2002); Palmer et al. (2004); Amernic & Craig (2006).
21 Amernic et al. (2007).
22 Staw et al. (1983).
23 Westphal & Zajac (1998).
24 Fiol (1989, p. 278).
25 Lyons (2011, p. 100).
26 Amernic & Craig (2006, p. 44).
27 Fanelli & Grasselli (2005).
28 The terms "shareholder" and "stockholder" are used synonymously in this book. "Stockholder" is more common in the USA, while "shareholder" is more common in Australia, Canada, Europe, and the UK.

Chapter 2: Tone at the Top

1   Edersheim (2007, p. 43).
2   Schein (2004, p. 225).
3   Amernic et al. (2010, p. 162).
4   Rittenhouse (2019).
5   https://www.sec.gov/news/speech/spch120304smc.htm.
6   OFHEO (2006, p. 3).
7   Cunningham (2005, p. 6).
8   Salter (2008).
9   Sheeder (2005, p. 35).
10 Mahadeo (2006, p. 1).
11 Schein (2004).
12 Jönsson (1998, p. 11).
13 Segars & Kohut (2001).
14 The letters of French CEOs, unlike those of CEOs in other countries, are characterized by "seduction, charm and obfuscation" (Bournois & Point, 2006, p. 46).
15 Tourish & Vatcha (2005).
16 These were proposed by (then) Stanford University Professor of Education, Alan Peshkin, in 2001.
17 All quoted material in this section is from Peshkin (2001, pp. 243–50).
18 Lakoff (1996).
19 Putnam & Boys (2006, p. 542).
20 Collins (2001).
21 This view was informed by the theme identification method outlined by Ryan and Bernard (2003).
22 BP Annual Report (1998), Letter to shareholders, page 7, paragraph 2. Available January 2021 at http://library.nioc.ir/free-e-resources/BP%20Annual%20Report%20and%20Accounts/Annual_Report_1998.pdf.
23 Gabriel (2000).
24 Cuno (2005, p. 205).
25 Bergmann (1982).
26 Gramm (1996).
27 Smith & Eisenberg (1987).
28 Heracleous (2004, p. 176).
29 Alvesson & Deetz (2000).
30 Oswick et al. (2004).
31 Postman (1996, p. 174).
32 The seven paragraphs quoted in this section are from BP Annual Report (1998), Letter to shareholders. http://library.nioc.ir/free-e-resources/BP%20Annual%20Report%20and%20Accounts/Annual_Report_1998.pdf.
33 For fuller discussion of the use of DICTION to analyze tone at the top, see Amernic et al. (2010, chapters 7 and 8).
34 For a full report on this study (including details of the companies sampled) see Amernic et al. (2010).
35 The formatting excised all non-text items such as tables, diagrams, logos, photographs, headers and footers, notations such as "continued on the next page," foreign symbols, and accents.
36 Merrill Lynch Annual Report (1997), Letter to shareholders.

Chapter 3: Ethicality

1   Arsenault & Castells (2008, p. 488).
2   One source for this in the popular press is *BBC News* (July 19, 2011), https://www.bbc.com/news/av/uk-14205909.

3 Hargie et al. (2010); Mallick (2011).
4 Lane (2011).
5 http://www.corporatewatch.org.uk/?lid=357 (URL no longer valid).
6 House of Commons Culture, Media and Sport Committee (2012, p. 70; italics added).
7 Vo (2010).
8 Egan (2012).
9 In companies in which the roles of CEO and board chair are vested in a single individual, especially a long-serving one, the possibility of insidious dysfunctions such as groupthink and its handmaiden, willful blindness, are ominously present (Heffernan, 2011). This seems likely to be ever more so here given that Murdoch founded the present News Corporation as a major global company. Centralizing power in the hands of one person is problematic. Because Murdoch is elderly, the possibility of cognitive impairment becomes an especially salient issue, and a strongly independent board would be more crucial.
10 Murdoch's letter is also accessible in the *Journal of Business Ethics*, vol. 118, pp. 389–93.
11 Amernic & Craig (2006, pp. 56).
12 Craig & Amernic (2011).
13 See, for example, Bettman & Weitz (1983); Salancik & Meindl (1984); Jones & Shoemaker (1994); Abrahamson & Amir (1996).
14 Scheff (1997, p. 54).
15 This use of "I" is replicated in sidebar text. We do not count this use twice.
16 See, for example, Bettman & Weitz (1983); Salancik & Meindl (1984).
17 Raskin & Shaw (1988, p. 393).
18 http://media.corporate-ir.net/media_files/irol/70/70972/Request-AR2010.pdf
19 Collins (2001). See also Morris et al. (2005).
20 Petersoo (2007, p. 419).
21 Lakoff (1996).
22 Ibid.
23 Amernic & Craig (2006, p. 8).
24 Van Dijk (2006).
25 Owen & Davidson (2009); Owen (2011).
26 Terms with the root stem "disrupt" are used three times (lines 25, 27, and 202).
27 Owen & Davidson (2009); Russell (2011); Craig & Amernic (2011).
28 Lakoff & Johnson (1980); Lakoff (1993); Werth (1994).
29 Amernic & Craig (2006, ch. 8).
30 Amernic et al. (2010, p. 157).
31 Ibid.
32 Amernic & Craig (2006, p. 7).
33 Clark (2012, p. 121).
34 Ibid., p. 123.
35 Amernic et al. (2010, p. v).

Chapter 4: Reputation

1 Executive Summary (2020, March). "The Real Wells Fargo: Board and Management Failures, Consumer Abuses, and Ineffective Regulatory Oversight." *Report Prepared by the Majority Staff of the Committee on Financial Services*, U.S. House of Representatives. https://financialservices.house.gov/uploadedfiles/wells_fargo_staff_report_final_mm .pdf.
2 Ashforth et al. (2008).
3 Bouilloud et al. (2019).
4 Bachmann et al. (2015); Kodish (2017).

5 Timothy Sloan, prepared testimony to the U.S. Senate Banking Committee, 3 October 2017, www.banking.senate.gov/public/index.cfm/hearings?ID=FE4441A6-5D3B-4C88-9637 -16F9BD71DCAC.

6 Letter to the committee's chair, October 4, 2018, https://www.banking.senate.gov/imo /media/doc/Wells%20Fargo%20Letter%2010.4.2018.pdf.

7 The material cited in this paragraph is drawn from a Wells Fargo press release retrieved from https://newsroom.wf.com/press-release/corporate-and-financial/wells-fargo -ceo-and-president-tim-sloan-retire-board.

8 Opening statement to the United States House Committee on Financial Services. https://financialservices.house.gov/uploadedfiles/hhrg-116-ba00-wstate-scharfc -20200310.pdf.

9 The source of information in this paragraph is the Wells Fargo Annual Report for 2016. https://www08.wellsfargomedia.com/assets/pdf/about/investor-relations/annual -reports/2016-annual-report.pdf.

10 Flitter, Appelbaum, & Cowley (2018). For another profile of Wells Fargo, see Anderson & Guo (2020, p. 214).

11 https://stories.wf.com/getting-know-tim-sloan/.

12 McLannahan (2016).

13 Berman (2018).

14 https://newsroom.wf.com/press-release/corporate-and-financial/wells-fargo-chairman -ceo-john-stumpf-retires-board-directors.

15 Hanlon & Mandarini (2015, p. 413).

16 Conger (1991, pp. 43–4, footnotes omitted).

17 Ochs (2016).

18 http://www.latimes.com/business/la-fi-wells-fargo-sale-pressure-20131222-story.html.

19 https://www.banking.senate.gov/hearings/an-examination-of-wells-fargos -unauthorized-accounts-and-the-regulatory-response

20 Wells Fargo Annual Report 2016 (p. 3). https://www08.wellsfargomedia.com/assets/pdf /about/investor-relations/annual-reports/2016-annual-report.pdf.

21 Glazer (2017).

22 Gray (2017).

23 Ochs (2016).

24 https://newsroom.wf.com/press-release/wells-fargo-reports-completion-expanded-third -party-review-retail-banking-accounts.

25 Glazer (2017).

26 https://www.govinfo.gov/content/pkg/CHRG-115shrg28111/html/CHRG-115shrg28111 .htm. The transcript of his reading varies slightly, but in non-consequential ways, from the previously posted version.

27 https://www.govinfo.gov/content/pkg/CHRG-115shrg28111/pdf/CHRG-115shrg28111 .pdf.

28 The source for this and the subsequent three sentences is "Banking Committee Democrats Call for Hearing to Hold Wells Fargo Accountable for Consumer Abuses." Press release, October 4, 2018. https://www.banking.senate.gov/newsroom/minority /banking-committee-democrats-call-for-hearing-to-hold-wells-fargo-accountable -for-consumers-.

29 Bouilloud et al. (2019, p. 8).

30 Rohrer & Vignone (2012, pp. 8–9).

31 Tourish & Hargie (2012).

32 Hargie et al. (2010).

33 https://newsroom.wf.com/press-release/consumer-lending/wells-fargo-announces-plan -remediate-customers-auto-insurance.

34 Benoit (2001, p. 72). Framing has been studied in politics (Iyengar, 1990), decision making (Tversky & Kahneman, 1981), US Senate interrogations of Clarence Thomas and Anita Hill (Simons, 1994), and accounting and auditing research (Emby & Finley, 1997).

35 Entman (1993, p. 52).

36 Ibid.

37 Ibid., pp. 52–3.

38 This framework of questions was proposed by Lye (1997, slightly abridged).

39 Alvesson & Spicer (2011).

40 Kalmoe et al. (2017).

41 This has been demonstrated in the context of Nazi discourse (Harrington, 1995), in tacit aspects of narrative in organizational research (Steger, 2007), in leadership (Amernic et al., 2007), and in accounting-related discourse (Amernic & Craig, 2009; Thornton, 1988; Walters-York, 1996; Young, 2013).

42 Landau (1961, p. 351).

43 Tinker (1986, p. 365).

44 Paparone (2008).

45 These were suggested by Duffy (2013).

46 Sims & Brinkmann (2002).

47 Amernic et al. (2010).

48 Oberlechner & Mayer-Schoenberger (2002).

49 Barilli (1989); Lanham (1993).

50 McCloskey (1985, p. 29).

51 Lanham (1993, p. 227; 2006).

52 Crespo-Fernández (2018, p. 1).

53 Tenbrunsel & Messick (2004, p. 226).

54 Bandura (1999).

55 Tenbrunsel & Messick (2004, p. 227).

56 "Sales Practices Investigation Report April 10, 2017," Independent Directors of the Board of Wells Fargo & Company. https://www08.wellsfargomedia.com/assets/pdf/about/investor -relations/presentations/2017/board-report.pdf.

57 See, for example, Sloan's open letter to the bank's customers, dated April 4, 2017. https:// newsroom.wf.com/press-release/wells-fargo-reiterates-commitment-building-better-bank -open-letter-customers.

58 Tourish & Hargie (2012).

59 Ibid.

60 Duffy (2013).

61 See Question 9 in the previously presented list of questions we abridged from Lye (1997).

62 The JOURNEY metaphor is apparent in various company press releases. For example, those dated March 28, 2017 (https://newsroom.wf.com/press-release/wells-fargo-announces -agreement-principle-settle-class-action-lawsuit-regarding) (URL no longer valid); April 21, 2017 (https://newsroom.wf.com/press-release/wells-fargo-expands-class-action-settlement -retail-sales-practices-142-million-adds); and August 4, 2017 (https://newsroom.wf.com /press-release/corporate-and-financial/wells-fargo-ceo-shares-updates-companys-rebuilding -trust). See also business periodical reporting at https://www.forbes.com/sites /maggiemcgrath/2017/03/28/wells-fargo-to-pay-110-million-to-settle-class-action-suit -over-phony-account-scandal/?sh=7eebad8567e6.

63 https://www.wellsfargo.com/about/corporate/stagecoach/.

64 Biel (1993, p. 73).

65 Peltz (2018).

66 Wells (1993).

67 Duffy (2013).

68 Lye (1997, question 6).

69 https://newsroom.wf.com/press-release/corporate-and-financial/wells-fargo-ceo
    -shares-updates-companys-rebuilding-trust.
70 Cheney (1998, p. 29).
71 Ibid.
72 Tourish & Hargie (2012, p. 1062).
73 Conger (1991).

Chapter 5: Deception

 1 See for example, Amernic et al. (2010); Bournois & Point (2006); Churyk et al. (2009);
    Dando & Bull (2011); Keila & Skillicorn (2005); Loughran et al. (2009); Porter & Brinke
    (2010); Sydserff & Weetman (2002); Vrij (2008); Vrij et al. (2000); Zuckerman et al. (1981);
    Zhou et al. (2004).
 2 Larcker & Tayan (2010).
 3 Raju's confession letter is accessible at https://trak.in/tags/business/2009/01/06/satyam/
    -head-raju-admits-fraud-letter-board-directors/. URL links to his annual report CEO letters
    are no longer operative.
 4 Donohue (2013).
 5 Purda & Skillicorn (2014).
 6 Zuckerman et al. (1981).
 7 Pennebaker et al. (2003).
 8 Zuckerman et al. (1981).
 9 Vrij et al. (2010, p. 9).
10 Porter & Brinke (2010).
11 Vartapetiance & Gillam (2012); Newman et al. (2003).
12 Pennebaker et al. (2003).
13 Newman et al. (2003).
14 Craig et al. (2013); Newman et al. (2003); Keila & Skillicorn (2005); Hancock et al. (2007);
    Henry (2008); Larcker & Tayan (2010); Larcker & Zakolyukina (2012); Zhou et al. (2004).
15 Carter (2015). See also Gupta & Skillicorn (2006); Newman et al. (2003).
16 Vartapetiance & Gillam (2012). Care must be taken in interpreting the frequency of
    instances of the personal pronoun "I." IBM's CEO Samuel Palmisano used "I" numerous
    times in his 2005 CEO letter. This was not to make boasts about personal responsibility for
    the company's achievements but to assert personal responsibility for providing accountability
    information to readers. In assessing CEO-speak, close reading is required rather than
    exclusive reliance on automated word searches and frequency counts.
17 Alli et al. (2018).
18 See Gupta & Skillicorn (2006); Craig et al. (2013); Pennebaker et al. (2003); Zhou et al. (2004).
19 Morrow (2008, p. 20).
20 See also Craig & Amernic (2010, p. 79).
21 Gupta & Skillicorn (2006).
22 Larcker & Tayan (2010).
23 Ibid., p. 2.
24 Larcker & Zakolyukina (2012).
25 Larcker & Tayan (2010). Nonetheless, the frequency of negative words was the *least*
    consistent indicator of deception in the emails of Enron executives prior to the company's
    collapse in 2001 (Keila & Skillicorn, 2005).
26 Zuckerman et al. (1981).
27 Larcker & Zakolyukina (2010).
28 Picornell (2013).
29 Johansson et al. (2006, p. 683).
30 Colwell et al. (2002, p. 289).
31 Nicolaides et al. (2018).

32 Carbone (1975, p. 105) is the source of this quotation and the following two quotations in this paragraph.

33 An extensive list of research works employing DICTION is posted to the website dictionsoftware.com.

34 Knapp et al. (1974, p. 21).

35 The sources for the material in this paragraph are Bhandari et al. (2009) and Leone (2009).

36 Nag (2009, p. xii).

37 The full text of this letter is accessible at https://www.firstpost.com/business/full-text-this -letter-ramalinga-raju-wrote-uncovered-the-rs-4676-cr-satyam-scam-2190559.html.

38 In the Indian numbering system, 1 crore = 10 million.

39 The sums involved are calculated based on foreign currency exchange rates at the time.

40 Leone (2009).

41 Agarwal (2009).

42 Reuters (2009).

43 Chandran (2009). See also Raghavan (2009).

44 Nag (2009).

45 All assessments of Raju's personality in this paragraph are from Bhandari et al. (2009, pp. 27, 2, viii, 30–1).

46 http://www.hindu.com/thehindu/holnus/002200711202070.htm.

47 Bhandari et al. (2009, p. 12).

48 Nag (2009, p. 75).

49 These forms are completed by those earning insufficient income to be classified as taxable income. By filling out the form, people instructed banks not to deduct income tax on the interest they earned on deposits.

50 Bhandari et al. (2009).

51 This raised speculation that Raju had used high-profile contacts and intimidation to abort Padmaja's investigation and to thwart exposure of his misdeeds (Bhandari et al., 2009; Nag, 2009, p. 122).

52 Vohra (2009).

53 Bhandari et al. (2009, p. 18).

54 Ibid., p. 25.

55 The sources for this paragraph are Bhandari et al. (2009) and Leone (2009).

56 The results draw on Craig et al. (2013). We do not explore changes in tense or some other techniques that were mentioned earlier.

57 Craig et al. (2013).

58 Henry (2008) advocated this technique.

59 Henry (2008, p. 388).

60 Smith & Taffler (2000).

61 Henry (2008).

62 Navarro (2010, n.p.).

63 The study used the Corporate Public Relations dictionary in DICTION 5.0 as the norm. For fuller details of this study see Craig et al. (2013).

64 For example, Raju stated that he had acted alone when inflating earnings and asset totals in the financial statements. However, it was revealed subsequently that Raju's brother, together with the CFO (Vadlamani Srinivas) and the vice president of finance (G. Ramakrishna), had also aided and abetted the alleged fraud. Other material discrepancies arose over the following months between what Raju stated was the total value of the misrepresentation in the confession letter and the amounts actually determined by investigators (Agarwal, 2009; Bloomberg News, 2009).

65 For details of the meaning and construction of these variables, see Hart & Carroll (2013).

66 NUMERICAL TERMS are "Any sum, date, or product specifying the facts in a given case. This dictionary treats each isolated integer as a single 'word' and each separate group of integers as a single word. In addition, the dictionary contains common numbers in

lexical format (one, tenfold, hundred, zero) as well as terms indicating numerical operations (subtract, divide, multiply, percentage) and quantitative topics (digitise, tally, mathematics). The presumption is that Numerical Terms hyper-specify a claim, thus detracting from its universality." See Hart & Carroll (2013).

67 See, for example, Brennan et al. (2009); Merkl-Davies & Brennan (2007).
68 For example, Zuckerman et al. (1981); Vrij et al. (2010).

Chapter 6: Safety Culture

1   Elkind et al. (2011).
2   Obama (2010).
3   Evidence supporting such a view is available from several sources. When questioned about this matter, Hayward admitted, "The industry norm would be … that the Operator would take that [safety] risk" (Questioning about Hayward Deposition, New Orleans US District Court, pp. 558–9, http://www.mdl2179trialdocs.com). BP's responsibility for the *Deepwater Horizon* disaster is also evident in Judge Barbier's decision in the US District Court on September 4, 2014. He found that BP was grossly negligent in the disaster, even under the restrictive rules of general maritime law, and deemed BP was 67% responsible (Gilbert & Scheck, 2014).
4   Rasmussen (2011).
5   Ocasio (2005, p. 118).
6   Perelman & Olbrechts-Tyteca (1969, p. 320).
7   Hart et al. (2005); Williams (1976).
8   Guldenmund (2000, p. 252).
9   This statement is from p. 14 of the subcommittee's proceedings published at https://www.govinfo.gov/content/pkg/CHRG-111hhrg77914/html/CHRG -111hhrg77914.htm.
10 Baker Report, accessible at www.bp.com.
11 Ibid., pp. 66–7.
12 Ibid., p. xii.
13 Ibid., p. 244.
14 CSB (2007, May 16).
15 Turner & Gray (2009, pp. 1259, 1261).
16 Haukelid (2008, p. 417).
17 Such as Edwards et al. (2013, p. 77).
18 Craig & Amernic (2017, p. 63).
19 Blazsin & Guldenmund (2015, p. 18).
20 Schön (1993).
21 Scheff (1997, p. 28).
22 Crooks (2010).
23 Baker Report (2007, p. xii).
24 Sissell (2010, p. 39).
25 CSB (2007, p. 179).
26 Steffy (2011, p. 160).
27 Reilly (2010, p. 9, lines 14–20, transcript, Day 2 of fifth meeting).
28 Edwards et al. (2013).
29 Schein (2004, p. 225).
30 Edwards et al. (2013).
31 Ibid.
32 Hopkins (2006, p. 876).
33 Ocasio (2005).
34 Hopkins (2006, p. 876).

35 Apostolides (2010, p. 140).
36 Schneider (1998, p. 294).
37 Weick & Sutcliffe (2007).
38 Catasús & Johed (2007, p. 173).
39 These speeches were downloaded from the BP website, www.bp.com, in 2007.
40 Rittenhouse (2019).
41 Sindreu (2019, p. 16).
42 Guldenmund (2000, p. 252).
43 Haukelid (2008, p. 417).
44 This sits oddly with the concepts of safety culture suggested by Silbey (2009) and Antonsen (2009).
45 Edwards et al. (2013).
46 Blazsin & Guldenmund (2015).
47 Ocasio (2005).
48 Ibid.
49 Rasmussen (2011, p. 474).
50 It is possible that this asset base included the company's workforce: that is, its human assets.
51 Craig & Amernic (2004).
52 Breeze (2012, p. 15).
53 Martin (1990).
54 Amernic & Craig (2006, p. 60). For description of this metaphor in the context of industrial relations, see Dunn (1990).
55 Dudley (2012, p. 94).
56 Elkind et al. (2011).
57 Dudley (2012, p. 94).
58 Fears (2020).
59 Breeze (2012, p. 11).
60 See http://www.prnewswire.com/news-releases/bp-shareholders-file-lawsuit-over-gulf-oil-spill-96037319.html.
61 Amernic et al. (2010, ch. 5).
62 Steffy (2011, p. 117, p. 258).
63 For example, the *Report of the Financial Stability Board to G20 leaders* (Sept, 2009, par 25) called for "more intense and internationally coordinated regulation and supervision of firms [in the banking industry] presenting greater risk."
64 The full text of ISA 315 is available at https://www.ifac.org/system/files/downloads/a017-2010-iaasb-handbook-isa-315.pdf.
65 Elkind et al. (2011).
66 Steffy (2011, p. 255).

Chapter 7: Twitter

1 Cooper (2019).
2 O'Leary (2015).
3 "The Most Followed Accounts on Twitter." Retrieved from Brandwatch.com.
4 On January 8, 2021, Twitter announced that Donald Trump had been permanently suspended from Twitter "due to the risk [his tweets posed] of further incitement of violence." https://blog.twitter.com/en_us/topics/company/2020/suspension.html.
5 "Donald J. Trump." https://www.socialtracker.io/twitter/realdonaldtrump/.
6 Stolee & Caton (2018).
7 Ott (2017).
8 Shane (2018).

9   Etter et al. (2019).
10 Lei et al. (2019).
11 Malhotra & Malhotra (2016).
12 Khosrowshahi's personal Twitter account can be found at https://twitter.com/dkhos ?lang=en.
13 Malhotra & Malhotra (2016).
14 McGill (2016).
15 Locander & Ladik (2017); see also Hwang (2012).
16 Antil & Verma (2019). We consider tweets from the time of his appointment as CEO of Uber in August 2017 until Uber's initial public offering on May 11, 2019.
17 Shane (2018, p. 3).
18 Ibid.
19 Ibid.
20 Ibid., p. 5.
21 Khosrowshahi's tweets can be accessed at https://twitter.com/dkhos.
22 Malhotra & Malhotra (2016).
23 Balick (2017).
24 Chen et al. (2019).
25 Girginova (2013).
26 Malhotra & Malhotra (2016).
27 Holmes (2016).
28 The leader of India's main opposition party, Rahul Gandhi, has used Twitter as a brand-building communication mechanism (Antil & Verma, 2019). Other Twitter users with large followings include former US President Barack Obama, Indian Prime Minister Narendra Modi, and Turkey's President Recep Tayyip Erdoğan.
29 Holmes (2016).
30 Capriotti & Ruesja (2018).
31 Men & Tsai (2016).
32 Guthey & Jackson (2008).
33 Acevedo (2013).
34 Cooper (2019).
35 Malhotra & Malhotra (2016).
36 We do not reproduce any photo that appears in any tweet because of the difficulties in obtaining permissions from legal rights holders to those photos and legal releases to display images of the (mainly) unknown subjects they contain.
37 Cooper (2019).
38 Hwang (2012).
39 Civil Action No. 1:18-cv-8865, https://www.sec.gov/litigation/complaints/2018/comp -pr2018-219.pdf.
40 See the April 26, 2019, court-approved settlement at http://prod-upp-image-read. ft.com/1199ee1e-686d-11e9-9adc-98bf1d35a056.
41 Sherman (2019).
42 Associated Press (December 4, 2019). Lawyer: Tesla boss Elon Musk's "pedo guy" tweet forced Thai cave rescue diver Vernon Unsworth to sue.
43 https://www.socialbakers.com/statistics/twitter/profiles/detail/44196397-elonmusk.
44 Stewart (2020).
45 See https://www.businessinsider.com.au/twitter-cracks-down-on-coronavirus-content-that -could-endanger-people-2020-3?r=US&IR=T.
46 Stewart (2020).
47 Gemmell (2019, p. 14).
48 Swan (2019, p. 25).
49 Albrechtsen (2020, p. 10).

50   Editorial (2019, September 17). "Woke" religion filling the void in modern societies. *The Australian*, p. 13.

51   Ibid.

52   Shane (2018, p. 1).

53   Ibid. p. 9.

54   Ibid. p. 3.

55   Lee & Lim (2016); Ellison et al. (2006).

56   Shane (2018, p. 1, p. 9).

57   Castillo (2015).

58   Shane (2018, p. 9).

59   Descriptions of these four categories are drawn from Malhotra & Malhotra (2016, pp. 75–6).

60   O'Leary (2015, p. 229).

61   Hart & Carroll (2013).

62   Hodgkin (2017, pp. 11–12).

63   Available at https://twitter.com/dkhos?lang=en.

64   This has been illustrated in the use of tweets by contemporary Indian political leaders (Antil & Verma, 2019).

65   O'Leary (2015, p. 234).

66   Shane (2018, p. 6).

67   Kelly (2017).

68   Shane, (2018, p. 6).

69   Ibid., p. 7.

70   Ibid.

71   Hodgkin (2017, p. 13).

72   Shane (2018, p. 8).

Chapter 8: Tweets as Propaganda

1   Pollman (2019). Stanford (2019) reported that Uber's "take" is 25% of all revenue. The company uses similar technology in its food-delivery operation, UberEats, launched in 2014.

2   Alang (2019).

3   Stanford (2019).

4   Pollman (2019, p. 712) writes: "From its early days, Uber aimed to challenge and change the law."

5   Lacy (2014).

6   Cook et al. (2018, p. 49).

7   Weiss (2014).

8   della Cava (2017a); Sullivan (2017).

9   Weise (2015).

10   Matousek (2018).

11   della Cava (2017b).

12   Smith (2014).

13   Lovelace Jr. (2017).

14   Email by the Uber News Team, dated August 30, 2017, titled "Uber's New CEO." This was sent to Uber employees on behalf of the company's board of directors. https://www.uber.com/newsroom/ubers-new-ceo-3/.

15   Bensinger (2019).

16   Uber Technologies, Inc. Form S-1 registration Statement under the Securities Act of 1933, pp. 216–17, April 26, 2019, www.sec.gov.

17   Berlin (2019).

18   McNeilage (2018).

19   Uber was permitted to operate during the appeals process (Olson, 2019).

20   Olson (2019).

21 Ibid.
22 Levin (2017).
23 Fowler (2019).
24 Cook et al. (2018, p. 43).
25 Jordan (2017).
26 Ibid., p. 4.
27 Ibid., p. 6.
28 In December 2019, the Supreme Court of Canada heard a case in which Canadian Uber drivers were seeking the right to sue their employer, rather than have their grievances heard by an "[employer] stacked arbitration system based in the Netherlands" (Stanford, 2019).
29 Investopedia defines a "gig economy" as one in which "temporary, flexible jobs are commonplace and companies tend toward hiring independent contractors and freelancers instead of full-time employees." https://www.investopedia.com/terms/g/gig-economy.asp.
30 UberEats worker "sacked for being 10 minutes late." *The Australian*, November 19, 2019, p. 5.
31 Dillet (2020).
32 Rosemain & Vidalon (2020).
33 Stanford (2019).
34 Jordan (2017).
35 Ibid., pp. 6–7.
36 Ibid., p. 7.
37 Ibid., p. 10.
38 Ibid.
39 Trabucchi et al. (2019).
40 Collier et al. (2018).
41 Swan (2019, p. 25).
42 Ibid.
43 Pollman (2019). See also Yablon (2019); Pollman & Barry (2017).
44 Pollman (2019, pp. 712–13, footnotes omitted).
45 The ethical propriety of Uber's business model depends upon one's ideological perspective. An editorial in the *Wall Street Journal* on May 9, 2019, offered a Pollyanna view of Uber: "Uber introduced flexible work arrangements for hundreds of thousands of workers. Drivers who are classified as independent contractors can set their own schedules, use their own vehicles and switch between apps. Dozens of companies have emulated Uber's business model … [which is] a model of America's dynamic economy that has succeeded so far … Investors who buy Uber stock will be betting that business innovation and competitive markets can prevail over the trial lawyer-union-government triumvirate." https://www.usatoday.com/story/tech/talkingtech/2017/06/08/ubers-travis-kalanick-offered-sex-rules-2013-party-report/102646050/.
46 Lasswell (1953, pp. 776–80).
47 Carey (1997, p. 12).
48 Nazaryan (2016); Wallace (2014).
49 These have been described by O'Leary (2015), Antil & Verma (2019), Locander & Ladik (2017), and Shane (2018), among others. For example, O'Leary (2015) describes approaches advocated by Nguyen et al. (2011) involving the "parsing" of tweets. Teufl & Kraxberger (2011) highlight a method that involves representing data extracted from tweets using lists, visualizations, and maps.
50 Locander & Ladik (2017, p. 366); Hwang (2012).
51 These are classified using the approach of Ryan & Bernard (2003).
52 Uber's IPO registration statement dated April 26, 2019, defines "drivers" as "an independent driver or courier who uses our platform to provide Ridesharing services, Uber Eats services, or both." The IPO defines "partner" as "any one of a Driver, restaurant, or shipper, all of whom are our customers."

53 Uber's IPO registration statement discloses that it had "3.9 million Drivers on our platform for the quarter ended December 31, 2018" (p. 5).

54 Scheiber (2019).

55 Ibid.

56 Uber's Initial Public Offering prospectus is accessible at https://www.sec.gov/Archives /edgar/data/1543151/000119312519103850/d647752ds1.htm.

57 The Uber IPO states: "The independent contractor status of Drivers is currently being challenged in courts and by government agencies in the United States and abroad. We are involved in numerous legal proceedings globally, including putative class and collective class action lawsuits, demands for arbitration, charges and claims before administrative agencies, and investigations or audits by labor, social security, and tax authorities that claim that Drivers should be treated as our employees…We believe that Drivers are independent contractors because…they can choose whether, when, and where to provide services on our platform, are free to provide services on our competitors' platforms, and provide a vehicle to perform services …the costs associated with defending, settling, or resolving pending and future lawsuits…could be material to our business" (p. 28). The capitalization of Drivers appears in the original.

58 Uber IPO, p. 28.

59 The "nice surprise" alluded to (by the hashtag #nicesurprise) was a letter Khosrowshahi received from an UberEats customer (attached to his tweet) that commended the Uber CEO and the delivery driver.

60 Pérez (2008, p. 50).

61 Nonetheless, there was some forewarning of Khosrowshai's heart metaphor thinking. In his tweet on September 13 (#6, see appendix D) he claims that it is "the awesome drivers that make @Uber what it is."

62 Shane (2018).

63 Ibid.

Chapter 9: Accounting-Speak

1 CN Annual Report (2018, p. 3). The CN annual reports quoted in this chapter are available at https://www.annualreports.com/Company/canadian-national-railway-company.

2 Many would ponder, for example, how "deferred acquisition cost" could be classed as an asset.

3 Miller (1994, p. 256).

4 This profile of CN is an edited and abridged version of the entry "Canadian National Railway Company (CN)" in *Encyclopædia Britannica Online.* https://www.britannica.com /topic/Canadian-National-Railway-Company. See also Craig & Amernic (2020a).

5 CN Annual Report (2018, p. 65). https://www.annualreports.com/HostedData/ AnnualReportArchive/c/TSX_CNR.TO_2018.pdf.

6 For example, see Boardman et al. (2013, p. 19).

7 For example, see Jason Hall at https://www.fool.com/investing/2019/01/12/the-3-best -railroad-stocks-to-buy-in-2019.aspx.

8 CN Annual Report (2018, p. ii).

9 Ibid., p. iii. In this same location CEO J.J. Ruest claims that CN is a "dynamic organization" with a "talented, experienced and energized" team that it will "continue to raise [its] game to align with new market realities and lead the industry."

10 As of January 1, 2011, almost all Canadian publicly accountable companies had to convert to International Financial Reporting Standards. Some, like CN, converted to, or continued to use, US Generally Accepted Accounting Principles.

11 CN, 2002 Annual Information Form (April 22, 2003, p. 22).

12 Bruce (1997, p. 26).

13 CN Annual Report (2018, p. 1, p. 59).

14 Even companies in the same industry and geographical region are different, and justifiable differences in assumptions, policies, and methods might be expected. Determining what is "justifiable" might be extremely difficult.

15 Mongeau served as CEO of CN from January 1, 2010, to July 1, 2016, succeeding E. Hunter Harrison.

16 CN Takes Issue with Accounting Criticism, *National Post,* March 1, 2006, p. FP 23.

17 Ibid.

18 Major North American railroad companies define FCF in varying ways. CSX Corporation uses *modified* free cash flow (MCF) "as the primary performance target" in its long-term incentive plan (CSX Proxy Statement, fiscal year 2005, p. 26, https://sec.report/Document/0000950144-06-002908/). CSX's calculation of MCF does not include cash flows from business unit sales, real estate sales, taxes, working capital, and some items of discretionary capital spending. Canadian Pacific Railway uses the term "Free Cash" as a performance measure. This is defined as "cash provided by operating activities, less cash used in investing activities and dividends" (Canadian Pacific Railway, Annual Report 2005, p. 29). https://www.annualreports.com/HostedData/AnnualReportArchive/c/TSX_CNR.TO_2005.pdf.

19 CN Annual Report (2004, p. 130). https://www.annualreports.com/HostedData/AnnualReportArchive/c/TSX_CNR.TO_2004.pdf.

20 www.investopedia.com.

21 Ibid.

22 Ibid.

23 See Craig & Amernic (2004) for additional details of how CEO Tellier employed accounting-speak to help lay the rhetorical groundwork for CN's privatization.

24 *Keeping Track, 28*(4), pp. 1–3.

25 Ibid.

26 Ibid.

27 *Keeping Track, 28*(9), p. 3.

28 Canadian National Railways (1995, October 18). *Amended preliminary prospectus,* Montreal.

29 We do not cite a concluding date for this phase because CN's self-eulogizing about the effects of its privatization seems to have no end. In early March, 2021, CN issued a special booklet to "celebrate the 25 years of achievement since privatization." In this booklet, the chair of the CN board of directors, Robert Pace, says that "the privatization sparked the incredible transformation" of CN. He claims "the 25-year transformational journey since privatization has been nothing short of extraordinary." CEO J.J. Ruest inflates the historical significance of the privatization by inviting readers 'to recall where you were when CN was privatized." However, what some observers would regard as "incredible" and "extraordinary" in this booklet is the hyperbolic self-glorification of the corporation. This is facilitated (in part, implicitly) by accounting-speak. The booklet is accessible at https://online.pubhtml5.com/avqf/evrv/#p=1.

30 Lanham (1993).

31 CN Management Proxy Circular for fiscal 1997 (dated March 24, 1998). CN's decision to begin reporting OR based on US GAAP was prompted by the need to facilitate benchmark comparisons with US railroad companies.

32 CN Annual Report (1997, p. 22).

33 CN's 2003 audited financial statements, issued January 27, 2004. https://www.annualreports.com/HostedData/AnnualReportArchive/c/TSX_CNR.TO_2003.pdf.

34 CN Annual Report (2000). https://www.annualreports.com/HostedData/AnnualReportArchive/c/TSX_CNR.TO_2000.pdf.

35 CN Annual Report (2001). https://www.annualreports.com/HostedData/AnnualReportArchive/c/TSX_CNR.TO_2001.pdf.

36 See https://www.businesswire.com/news/home/20040128005350/en/CN-Reports-Strong
-Q4-2003-Performance-Record-Operating.
37 CN Annual Report (2004).
38 Data are drawn from CN Annual Reports available at https://www.annualreports.com
/Company/canadian-national-railway-company.

Chapter 10: Autobiographical Vignettes

1   *English Oxford Dictionary*, https://en.oxforddictionaries.com/definition/vignette.
2   Rinehart (2006, p. 1058).
3   Ibid., p. 1059.
4   For example, by Cunningham (2013).
5   Ricoeur (1984).
6   See also Dalpiaz & Di Stefano (2018).
7   Amernic (1992, p. 1).
8   Morris (1946).
9   Heracleous & Klaering (2017, p. 31).
10 Raban (2009, p. W2).
11 Raban (2009).
12 Schoenberger (2001, p. 279).
13 Fuoli & Paradis (2014, pp. 64–5).
14 BP Annual Report (2010), Letter to shareholders. Available January 2021 at https://www
.bp.com/content/dam/bp/business-sites/en/global/corporate/pdfs/investors/bp-annual
-report-and-form-20f-2010.pdf.
15 Ibid.
16 Maclean et al. (2011, p. 17, p. 36).
17 Ibid., pp. 31–6.
18 Ibid.
19 Tinker (1985, p. 82).
20 Schoenberger (2001, p. 282).
21 Maclean et al. (2011, p. 35).
22 Shamir & Eilam (2005, p. 414).
23 Shaw (2010, p. 104). See also Cavarero (2000).
24 Rinehart (2006, p. 1059; italics added).
25 *English Oxford Dictionary Online*, https://en.oxforddictionaries.com/definition/post-truth.
26 Heracleous & Klaering (2017, p. 32).
27 Lanham (1993).
28 Llewellyn (1999, p. 223).
29 Guerin (2003, p. 264).
30 Amernic & Craig (2000).
31 Boje & Rosile (2008, pp. 164, 170, 171).
32 The company's core business model is claimed to feature low wages, products made in
sweatshops, and brutal exercise of market dominance. See Boje & Rosile (2008).
33 Walmart Annual Report (2008), Letter to shareholders. Available January 2021 at https://
www.annualreports.com/HostedData/AnnualReportArchive/w/NYSE_WMT_2008.pdf.
34 Muilenburg's statement to the US House of Representatives Committee on Transportation
and Infrastructure. Available January 2021 at https://transportation.house.gov/imo/media
/doc/Muilenburg%20Testimony.pdf.
35 See "Boeing Announces Leadership Changes." https://boeing.mediaroom.com/2019-12
-23-Boeing-Announces-Leadership-Changes.
36 https://docs.house.gov/meetings/JU/JU05/20200729/110883/HHRG-116-JU05-Wstate
-BezosJ-20200729.pdf .

37 Barry & Elmes (1997, p. 433).
38 Craig & Amernic (2008, p. 1093).
39 Craig & Amernic (2008).
40 Ibid., p. 1091.
41 The following profile of Harrison is compiled from Foran (2009), McNish (2012), and Kelly (2017).
42 Unless otherwise specified, the information sources for this subsection are contemporary news reports by the Canadian Broadcasting Commission, together with Canadian Autoworkers Union newsletters, and magazines circulating in the Canadian transport industry.
43 Warwaruk (2004, pp. 5–8).
44 Ibid., p. 8.
45 Partridge (2004).
46 Ochs & Capps (1996, p. 32).
47 Cheney (1983).
48 CN Annual Report (2004), Letter to shareholders. Available January 2021 at AnnualReportArchive/c/TSX_CNR.TO_2004.pdf.
49 Schoenberger (2001, p. 277).
50 Guerin (2003, p. 253).
51 Frederick Taylor developed scientific management for efficient work processes in the early twentieth century. https://www.mindtools.com/pages/article/newTMM_Taylor.htm#:~:text=Taylor's%20philosophy%20focused%20on%20the,simplifying%20jobs%2C%20productivity%20would%20increase.
52 CN Annual Report (2005), Letter to shareholders. Available January 2021 at https://www.annualreports.com/HostedData/AnnualReportArchive/c/TSX_CNR.TO_2005.pdf.
53 Ibid.
54 Silberstein (2002); Hart et al. (2005); Guerin (2003).
55 McNish (2012).
56 Näslund & Pemer (2012, p. 106).
57 CN Annual Report (2007), Letter to shareholders. Available January 2021 at https://www.annualreports.com/HostedData/AnnualReportArchive/c/TSX_CNR.TO_2007.pdf.
58 Tinker (1985).
59 Future research could beneficially explore the frequency, nature, and pattern of autobiographical vignettes in CEO letters and whether autobiographical vignettes are used more often by CEOs of successful or struggling companies; by novice or experienced CEOs; during economic upswings or downswings; or by CEOs with particular personalities.

Chapter 11: Narcissism and Hubris

1 Sahadi (2018, November 5).
2 Beheshti (2018, October 19).
3 Coren (2019, March 3).
4 Editorial Board, *Financial Times* (2019, November 19).
5 Kasulis (2018, October 13).
6 See http://www.daedalustrust.com/.
7 Ibid.
8 Chamorro-Premuzic (2016).
9 Ibid.
10 Kellaway (2012).
11 Otazo (2019, p. 194).
12 Banzato (2008). This definition was revised in *DSM-V*, issued in June 2011. The *DSM-IV-TR* definition was current at the time the text analyzed was made public.

13 Miller et al. (2009).
14 Maccoby (2003, p. 39).
15 Kets de Vries & Miller (1985, p. 588).
16 Kets de Vries (1994, p. 84).
17 Kets de Vries & Miller (1985, p. 588).
18 Maccoby (2003, p. xiv).
19 The following paragraphs on constructive narcissism and destructive narcissism are abridged from Amernic & Craig (2010).
20 Kets de Vries & Miller (1985, p. 595).
21 Kets de Vries (2004); Lubit (2002).
22 Glad (2002).
23 Maccoby (2003, pp. 166–92).
24 Ibid., p. 11.
25 Ibid., p. xvii.
26 Kets de Vries (2004, p. 189).
27 Glad (2002).
28 Kets de Vries & Miller (1985, p. 595).
29 Campbell et al. (2004); Chatterjee & Hambrick (2007, p. 351).
30 Brown (1997, p. 672).
31 Schwartz (1991, p. 249).
32 Clements & Washbush (1999, p. 171).
33 Bazerman et al. (2006).
34 Kets de Vries (2004, p. 191).
35 Berglas (2014).
36 *New Webster's Dictionary of the English language* (1975). Consolidated Book, p. 731.
37 http://www.answers.com/topic/hubris#ixzz2Ei6iYaWO.
38 Gabriel (2012, p. 242).
39 Sadler-Smith et al. (2019, p. 8).
40 Roll (1986); Hayward & Hambrick (1997).
41 Li & Tang (2010, p. 51).
42 Button (2012, p. 330).
43 Zeitoun et al. (2019, p. 648).
44 Ibid., p. 655.
45 Sadler-Smith et al. (2019, p. 9).
46 The source is Owen & Davidson (2009) but with slight modification to highlight the five attributes unique to hubris.
47 Ibid., p. 12.
48 Ibid., p. 14.
49 Ibid. The analogy drawn is to preventive medicine.
50 Craig & Amernic (2011).
51 Craig & Amernic (2014; 2018).
52 Several of the following paragraphs draw upon Craig & Amernic (2011, pp. 567–8).
53 Wallace & Baumeister (2002, p. 830, p. 833).
54 Craig & Amernic (2011).
55 Enron Annual Report (2000). https://fliphtml5.com/thnh/cnnm/basic.
56 Wolson (2004).
57 Ridgway (1956).
58 Starbucks Annual Report 2005. https://s22.q4cdn.com/869488222/files/doc_financials/annual/2005/Annual_Report_2005_part1.pdf.
59 The full letter is accessible at https://s22.q4cdn.com/869488222/files/doc_financials/annual/2005/Annual_Report_2005_part1.pdf.
60 Allison (2007).

61 The full letter is accessible at https://www.annualreports.com/HostedData /AnnualReportArchive/g/NYSE_GM_2005.pdf.

62 See Reuters Online Newswire, U.S. Sen. Dodd says CEO should resign, December 7, 2008. Accessible at https://www.reuters.com/article/us-autos-bailout-dodd-sb/u-s-sen-dodd-says-gm-ceo -should-move-on-idUSTRE4B61CZ20081207?mod=related&channelName=businessNews.

63 Holstein (2009, p. 43).

64 For example: Garrard et al. (2014); Craig & Amernic (2014). Akstinaite (2018, p. 13) concludes that that "the high use of impersonal pronouns, the total count of pronouns, auxiliary verbs, common verbs and tentative tone indicate CEO hubris."

65 Craig & Amernic (2014, pp. 84–5).

66 Murphy (2013, p. 57).

67 Owen & Davidson (2009, p. 1398).

68 Boeing Annual Report (2017). https://s2.q4cdn.com/661678649/files/doc_financials /annual/2017/2017-Annual-Report.pdf.

69 On October 29, 2018, Lion Air Flight 610, a Boeing 737 MAX 8, plunged into the Java Sea 13 minutes after takeoff from Soekarno–Hatta International Airport, Jakarta, Indonesia. All 189 people on board died. The aircraft had been delivered to Lion Air two months earlier. On March 10, 2019, Ethiopian Airlines Flight 302, a Boeing 737 MAX 8 crashed six minutes after takeoff from Addis Ababa, Ethiopia, killing all 157 people on board. The aircraft was four months old at the time. Evidence suggested that, at the time of the crashes, both aircraft were configured to dive.

70 DICTION software analyses text in 500-word chunks.

71 The master variables are the five elements that "provide the most robust understanding" of a text and are broadly defined by Hart (2001, p. 43) as follows:

> ACTIVITY: language featuring movement, change, the implementation of ideas and the avoidance of inertia
> CERTAINTY: language indicating resoluteness, inflexibility, and completeness and a tendency to speak *ex cathedra*
> OPTIMISM: language endorsing some person, group, concept, or event or highlighting their positive entailments
> REALISM: language describing tangible, immediate, recognizable matters that affect people's everyday lives
> COMMONALITY: language highlighting the agreed-upon values of a group and rejecting idiosyncratic modes of engagement

72 Owen & Davidson (2009, p. 1398).

73 Short & Palmer (2008, p. 732).

74 The word "safety" is used in the following paragraph which appears near the end of the letter:

> "Our Enduring Values
>   The importance of our purpose and mission demands that we work with the utmost integrity and excellence and embrace the enduring values that define who we are today and the company we aspire to be tomorrow.
>   These core values – integrity, quality, **safety**, diversity and inclusion, trust and respect, corporate citizenship and stakeholder success – remind us all that how we do our work is every bit as important as the work itself" (emphasis added).

Chapter 12: Monitoring CEO-Speak

1 Lakoff & Johnson (1980).

2 Amernic et al. (2007).

3 Amernic & Craig (2004, p. 333).
4 Sayers (2014).
5 Entman (1993).
6 Craig et al. (2001).

Epilogue: Pandemic

1 Salt (2020, p. 20).
2 Paz (2020), writing in *The Atlantic* magazine, provides an "unfinished compendium of Trump's overwhelming dishonesty" during the COVID-19 emergency.
3 An example is the *Deepwater Horizon* crisis (see chapter 6).
4 Cutter & Maloney (2020, p. 20).
5 Examples include Donald Trump (US), Boris Johnson (UK) and Jair Bolsonaro (Brazil).
6 Coronavirus: Outcry after Trump suggests injecting disinfectant as treatment. https://www.bbc.com/news/amp/world-us-canada-52407177.
7 Duncan (2020).
8 Garvey (2020, p. 5).
9 Lopatto (2020).
10 Aten (2020).
11 Chambers & Benson (2020, p. 1).
12 JPMorgan Chase Annual Report (2020), Letter to shareholders (p. 18). https://www.jpmorganchase.com/content/dam/jpmc/jpmorgan-chase-and-co/investor-relations/documents/annualreport-2019.pdf.
13 https://www.cdc.gov/flu/pandemic-resources/1918-pandemic-h1n1.html.
14 Editors of History.com. https://www.history.com/topics/middle-ages/black-death.
15 Floor (2018, p. 3).
16 Moir (2019, October 17).
17 Corbett (2015, April 21).
18 In the Great Depression, "industrial production in the United States declined 47 percent and real gross domestic product fell 30 percent. The wholesale price index declined 33 percent … and the unemployment rate exceeded 20 percent at its highest point. … In America's next worst recession, the Great Recession of 2007–09, the country's real GDP declined just 4.3 percent and the unemployment rate peaked at less than 10 percent." *Encyclopaedia Britannica* online. https://www.britannica.com/event/Great-Depression#ref234439.
19 Investopedia defines a "Black Swan" event as "an unpredictable event that is beyond what is normally expected of a situation and has potentially severe consequences. [Such events] are characterized by their extreme rarity, severe impact, and the widespread insistence they were obvious in hindsight." https://www.investopedia.com/terms/b/blackswan.asp.
20 Berkshire Hathaway Annual Report (2019), Letter to shareholders. https://www.berkshirehathaway.com/letters/2019ltr.pdf.
21 Benoit (2020, April 8).
22 McGee (1980, p. 15).
23 Amernic & Craig (2004, p. 329, p. 334).
24 Ibid., p. 330.
25 Musk's tweets are accessible at https://twitter.com/elonmusk?ref_src=twsrc%5Egoogle%7Ctwcamp%5Eserp%7Ctwgr%5Eauthor.
26 Lopatto (2020).
27 Amernic & Craig (2004, p. 334).

References

Abrahamson, E., & Amir E. (1996). The association between the information contained in the president's letter to shareholders and accounting market variables. *Journal of Business Finance & Accounting, 23*(8), 1157–82. https://doi.org/10.1111/j.1468-5957.1996.tb01163.x.

Acevedo, B. (2013). Portraiture and the construction of "charismatic leadership." In E. Bell, S. Warren, & J. Schroeder (Eds.) *The Routledge companion to visual organization* (Chapter 7). Routledge. https://www.routledgehandbooks.com/doi/10.4324/9780203725610.

Agarwal, L. (2009, April 7). Raju showed fake bank receipts. *ICAI – The Indian Express*. www.indianexpress.com/news/raju-showed-fake-bank-receipts-icai/444183/ (URL no longer valid).

Akstinaite, V. (2018). Use of linguistic markers in the identification and analysis of chief executives' hubris. Ph.D Thesis, University of Surrey.

Alang, N. (2019, October 24). Time for tech to see themselves as they really are. *The Star.* https://www.thestar.com/business/opinion/2019/10/11/time-for-tech-to-see-themselves-as-they-really-are.html.

Albrechtsen, J. (2020, August 11). She won't talk, she tweets – Pericles would wince. *The Australian*, p. 10.

Alli, R., Nicolaides, R., & Craig, R. (2018). Detecting advance fee fraud emails using self-referential pronouns: A preliminary analysis. *Accounting Forum, 42*(1), 78–85. https://doi.org/10.1016/j.accfor.2018.01.003.

Allison, M. (2007, January 2). Union struggles to reach, recruit Starbucks workers. *Seattle Times*. https://www.seattletimes.com/business/union-struggles-to-reach-recruit-starbucks-workers/.

Alvesson, M., & Deetz, S. (2000). *Doing critical management research*. SAGE.

Alvesson, M., & Spicer, A. (2011). *Metaphors we lead by: Understanding leadership in the real world*. Routledge.

Amernic, J. (1992). A case study in corporate financial reporting: Massey-Ferguson's visible accounting decisions 1970-1987. *Critical Perspectives on Accounting, 3*(1), 1–43. https://doi.org/10.1016/1045-2354(92)90013-h.

Amernic, J., & Craig, R. (2000). Accountability and rhetoric during a crisis: An analysis of Walt Disney's 1940 letter to stockholders. *Accounting Historians Journal, 27*(2), 49–86. https://doi.org/10.2308/0148-4184.27.2.49.

Amernic, J., & Craig, R. (2004). 9/11 in the service of corporate rhetoric: Southwest Airlines' 2001 letter to shareholders. *Journal of Communication Inquiry, 28*(4), 325–41. https://doi.org/10.1177/0196859904267121.

Amernic, J., & Craig, R. (2006). *CEO-speak: The language of corporate leadership*. McGill-Queen's University Press.

Amernic J., & Craig, R. (2009). Understanding accounting through conceptual metaphor: Accounting is an instrument? *Critical Perspectives on Accounting, 20*(8), 875–83. https://doi.org /10.1016/j.cpa.2009.06.004.

Amernic, J., & Craig, R. (2010). Accounting as a facilitator of extreme narcissism. *Journal of Business Ethics, 96*(1), 79–93. https://doi.org/10.1007/s10551-010-0450-0.

Amernic, J., & Craig, R. (2017). CEO speeches and safety culture: British Petroleum before the *Deepwater Horizon* disaster. *Critical Perspectives on Accounting, 47*, 261–80.

Amernic, J., Craig, R., & Tourish, D. (2007). The charismatic leader as pedagogue, physician, architect, commander, and saint: Five master metaphors in Jack Welch's letters to stockholders of General Electric. *Human Relations, 60*(12), 1839–72. https://doi.org/10.1177 /0018726707084916.

Amernic, J., Craig, R., & Tourish, D. (2010). *Measuring and assessing tone at the top using annual report CEO letters.* Institute of Chartered Accountants in Scotland.

Anderson, L.B., & Guo, J. (2020). Paradoxical timeliness in Wells Fargo's crisis discourse: Expanding the discourse of renewal theory. *International Journal of Business Communication, 57*, 212–26.

Antil, A., & Verma, H.V. (2019). Rahul Gandhi on Twitter: An analysis of brand building through Twitter by the leader of the main opposition party in India. *Global Business Review,* https:// doi.org/10.1177/0972150919833514.

Antonsen, S. (2009). Safety culture and the issue of power. *Safety Science, 47*(2), 183–91. https:// doi.org/10.1016/j.ssci.2008.02.004.

Apostolides, N. (2010). Exercising corporate governance at the annual general meeting. *Corporate Governance, 10*(2), 140–9. https://doi.org/10.1108/14720701011035666.

Arsenault, A., & Castells, M. (2008). Switching power: Rupert Murdoch and the global business of media politics. *International Sociology, 23*(4), 488–513. https://doi.org/10.1177 /0268580908090725.

Ashforth, B.E., Gioia, D.A., Robinson, S.L., & Trevino, L.K. (2008). Re-viewing organizational corruption. *Academy of Management Review, 33*(3), 670–784. https://doi.org/10.5465/amr .2008.32465714.

Aten, J. (2020). Marriott's CEO shared a video with his team and it's a powerful lesson in leading during a crisis. https://www.inc.com/jason-aten/marriotts-ceo-shared-a-video-with-his -team-its-a-powerful-lesson-in-leading-during-a-crisis.html.

Bachmann, R., Gillespie, N., & Priem, R. (2015). Repairing trust in organizations and institutions: Toward a conceptual framework. *Organization Studies, 36*(9), 1123–42. https://doi.org/10.1177 /0170840615599334.

Baker Report (2007, January). Report of the BP U.S. Refineries Independent Safety Review Panel. www.bp.com.

Balick, A. (2017, July 3). The psychology of Trump's tweets: Signals from a distressed man. *HUFFPOST.* https://www.huffingtonpost.co.uk/.

Bandura, A. (1999). Moral disengagement in the perpetuation of inhumanities. *Personality and Social Psychology Review, 3*(3), 193–209. https://doi.org/10.1207/s15327957pspr0303_3 Medline: 15661671.

Banzato, C.E. (2008). Critical evaluation of current diagnostic systems. *Indian Journal of Psychiatry, 50*(3), 155–7. https://doi.org/10.4103/0019-5545.43621 Medline: 19742240.

Barilli, R. (1989). *Rhetoric.* University of Minnesota Press.

Barry, D., & Elmes, M. (1997). Strategy retold: Towards a narrative view of strategic discourse. *Academy of Management Review, 22*(2), 429–52. https://doi.org/10.5465/amr.1997.9707154065.

Bazerman, M. H., Moore, D. A., Tetlock, P. E., & Tanlu, L. (2006). Reports of solving the conflicts of interest in auditing are highly exaggerated. *Academy of Management Review, 31*(1), 43–9. https://doi.org/10.5465/amr.2006.19379623.

Beheshti, Naz. (2018, October 19). Can a narcissistic CEO destroy their company? *Forbes.* https://www.forbes.com/sites/nazbeheshti/2018/10/19/can-a-narcissistic-ceo-destroy-their -company/#59c246104b02.

Benoit, D. (2020, April 8). JPMorgan's Dimon: A bad recession on cards. *The Australian*, p. 20.

Benoit, W.L. (2001). Framing through temporal metaphor: The "bridges" of Bob Dole and Bill Clinton in their 1996 acceptance speeches. *Communication Studies*, 52(1), 70–84. https://doi.org/10.1080/10510970109388541.

Bensinger, G. (2019, September 26). Sen. Blumenthal assails how Uber and Lyft deal with driver misconduct following Washington Post report. *Washington Post* online. https://www.washingtonpost.com/technology/2019/09/25/sen-blumenthal-assails-how-uber-lyft-deal-with-driver-misconduct-following-washington-post-report/.

Berglas, S. (2014, April 14). Rooting out hubris, before a fall. *HBR Blog Network*. http://blogs.hbr.org/2014/04/rooting-out-hubris-before-a-fall/.

Bergmann, M. (1982). Metaphorical assertions. *Philosophical Review*, 91(2), 229–45. https://doi.org/10.2307/2184628.

Berlin, L. (2019, Sept 6). Mike Isaac's Uber book has arrived. *New York Times*. Book Review. https://www.nytimes.com/2019/09/06/books/review/super-pumped-mike-isaac.html.

Berman, N. (2018, July 6). Ten things you didn't know about Wells Fargo CEO Tim Sloan. *MONEY INC*. https://moneyinc.com/wells-fargo-ceo-tim-sloan/.

Bettman, J.R., & Weitz, B.A. (1983). Attributions in the board room: Causal reasoning in corporate annual reports. *Administrative Science Quarterly*, 28(2), 165–83. https://doi.org/10.2307/2392616.

Bhandari, B., Chintala, P.R., Gombar, V., Jishnu, L., Majumdar, S., & Pandey A. (2009). *The Satyam saga*. New Delhi: Business Standard.

Biel, A.L. (1993). Converting image into equity. In D.A. Aaker & A.L. Biel (Eds.), *Brand equity & advertising: Advertising's role in building strong brands* (pp. 67–82). Erlbaum Associates.

Blazsin, H., & Guldenmund, F. (2015). The social construction of safety: Comparing three realities. *Safety Science*, 71, 16–27. https://doi.org/10.1016/j.ssci.2014.06.001.

Bloomberg News (2009, November 26). Additional fraud at Satyam discovered. *The New York Times*. http://topics.nytimes.com/topics/reference/timestopics/people/r/ramalinga_raju/index.html.

Boardman, A.E., Laurin, C., Moore, M.A., & Vining, A.R. (2013). Efficiency, profitability and welfare gains from the Canadian National Railway privatization. *Research in Transportation Business & Management*, 6, 19–30. https://doi.org/10.1016/j.rtbm.2012.11.011.

Boje, D.M., & Rosile, G.A. (2008). Specters of Wal-Mart: A critical discourse analysis of stories of Sam Walton's ghost. *Critical Discourse Studies*, 5(2), 153–79. https://doi.org/10.1080/17405900801990116.

Bouilloud, J-P., Deslandes, G., & Mercier, G. (2019). The leader as Chief Truth Officer: The ethical responsibility of "managing the truth" in organizations. *Journal of Business Ethics*, 157(1), 1–13. https://doi.org/10.1007/s10551-017-3678-0.

Bournois, F., & Point, S. (2006). A letter from the president: Seduction, charm and obfuscation in French CEO letters. *Journal of Business Strategy*, 27(6), 46–55. https://doi.org/10.1108/02756660610710355.

Breeze R. (2012). Legitimation in corporate discourse: Oil corporations after *Deepwater Horizon*. *Discourse & Society*, 23(1), 3–18. https://doi.org/10.1177/0957926511431511.

Brennan, N., Guillamon-Saorin, E., & Pierce, A. (2009). Impression management: Developing and illustrating a scheme of analysis for narrative disclosures – a methodological note. *Accounting, Auditing & Accountability Journal*, 22(5), 789–8. https://doi.org/10.1108/09513570910966379.

Brown, A.D. (1997). Narcissism, identity, and legitimacy. *Academy of Management Review*, 22(3), 643–86. https://doi.org/10.5465/amr.1997.9708210722.

Bruce, H. (1997). *The pig that flew: The battle to privatize Canadian National*. Douglas & McIntyre.

Button, J. (2012). "Hubris breeds the tyrant": The anti-politics of hubris from Thebes to Abu Ghraib. *Law, Culture and the Humanities*, 8(2), 305–32. https://doi.org/10.1177/1743872110383106.

Campbell, W.K., Goodie, A.S., & Foster, J.D. (2004). Narcissism, confidence, and risk attitude. *Journal of Behavioral Decision Making, 17*(4), 297–311. https://doi.org/10.1002/bdm.475.

Capriotti, P., & Ruesja, L. (2018). How CEOs use Twitter: A comparative analysis of global and Latin American companies. *International Journal of Information Management, 39*, 242–8. https://doi.org/10.1016/j.ijinfomgt.2018.01.003.

Carbone, T. (1975). Stylistic variables as related to source credibility: A content analysis approach. *Speech Monographs, 42*(2), 99–106. https://doi.org/10.1080/03637757509375884.

Carey, A. (1997). *Taking the risk out of democracy: Corporate propaganda versus freedom and liberty.* University of Illinois Press.

Carter, E. (2015). The anatomy of written scam communications: An empirical analysis. *Crime, Media, Culture, 11*(2), 89–103. https://doi.org/10.1177/1741659015572310.

Castillo, M. (2015, August 13). *When candidates try too hard on social media.* CNBC. https://www.cnbc.com/2015/08/13/when-candidates-try-too-hard-on-social-media.html.

Catasús, B., & Johed, G. (2007). Annual general meetings – rituals of closure or ideal speech situations? A dual analysis. *Scandinavian Journal of Management, 23*(2), 168–90. https://doi.org/10.1016/j.scaman.2006.10.009.

Cavarero, A. (2000). *Relating narratives: Storytelling and selfhood.* Routledge.

Chambers, G., & Benson, S. (2020, March 26). We must stick together: PM. *The Australian.*

Chamorro-Premuzic, T. (2016). Why we keep hiring narcissistic CEOs. *Harvard Business Review* (online). https://hbr.org/2016/11/why-we-keep-hiring-narcissistic-ceos.

Chandran, R. (2009, January 13). Satyam saga shows holes in Indian corporate governance. *Thaindian News.* www.thaindian.com/newsportal/business/satyam-saga-shows-holes-in-indias-corporate-governance-say-analysts_100141689.html (URL no longer valid).

Chatterjee, A., & Hambrick, D.C. (2007). It's all about me: Narcissistic chief executive officers and their effects on company strategy and performance. *Administrative Science Quarterly, 52*(3), 351–86. https://doi.org/10.2189/asqu.52.3.351.

Chemical Safety Board (CSB). (2007, May 16). CSB Chairman Carolyn Merritt tells House Subcommittee of "striking similarities" in causes of BP Texas City tragedy and Prudhoe Bay pipeline disaster. www.csb.gov.

Chen, H., Hwang, B., & Liu, B. (2019). The emergence of "social executives" and its consequences for financial markets. https://papers.ssrn.com/sol3/papers.cfm?abstract_id=2318094.

Cheney, G. (1983). The rhetoric of identification and the study of organizational communication. *Quarterly Journal of Speech, 69*(2), 143–58. https://doi.org/10.1080/00335638309383643.

Cheney, G. (1998). "It's the economy stupid!" A rhetorical-communicative perspective on today's market. *Australian Journal of Communication, 25*(3), 25–44.

Churyk, N.T., Lee, C., & Clinton, D. (2009). Early evidence of fraud: Evidence from restatements. *Advances in Accounting Behavioral Research, 22*, 25–40. https://doi.org/10.1108/S1475-1488(2009)0000012004.

Clark, T. (2012). *Stay on message: Poetry and truthfulness in political speech.* Australian Scholarly Publishing.

Clements, C., & Washbush, J.B. (1999). The two faces of leadership: Considering the dark side of leader-follower dynamics. *Journal of Workplace Learning, 11*(5), 170–6. https://doi.org/10.1108/13665629910279509.

Collier, C.B., Dubal, V.B., & Carter, C.L. (2018). Disrupting regulation, regulating disruption: The politics of Uber in the United States. *Perspectives on Politics, 16*(4), 919–37. https://doi.org/10.1017/S1537592718001093.

Collins, J. (2001). *Good to great.* Harper Business.

Colwell, K., Hiscock, C.K., & Memon, A. (2002). Interviewing techniques and the assessment of statement credibility. *Applied Cognitive Psychology, 16*(3), 287–300. https://doi.org/10.1002/acp.788.

Conger, J. (1991). Inspiring others: The language of leadership. *Academy of Management Executive*, 5(1), 31–45. https://doi.org/10.5465/ame.1991.4274713.

Cook, J., Patel, R., & O'Rourke, J.S. (2018). Uber Technologies Inc.: Accountability in corporate culture. *Journal of Organizational Behavior Education*, 11, 33–50. https://doi.org/10.4135/9781526489067.

Cooper, P. (2019, January 16). General Twitter stats. https://blog.hootsuite.com/twitter-statistics/.

Corbett, P.B. (2015, April 21). An unprecedented tsunami of hyperbole. *New York Times* blog.

Coren (2019, March 3). *Quartz*. https://qz.com/1561985/elon-musk-may-not-be-the-narcissist-tesla-needs-right-now/.

Craig, R., & Amernic, J. (2004a). Enron discourse: The rhetoric of a resilient capitalism. *Critical Perspectives on Accounting*, 15(6–7) 813–52. https://doi.org/10.1016/j.cpa.2002.12.001.

Craig, R., & Amernic, J. (2004b). The deployment of accounting-related rhetoric in the prelude to a privatization. *Accounting, Auditing & Accountability Journal*, 17(1), 41–58. https://doi.org/10.1108/09513570410525201.

Craig, R., & Amernic, J. (2008). A privatization success story: Accounting and narrative expression over time. *Accounting, Auditing & Accountability Journal*, 21(8), 1085–115. https://doi.org/10.1108/09513570810918779.

Craig, R., & Amernic, J. (2010). Exploring the public accountability communications of a CEO through "close reading" analysis: A teaching primer. *International Journal of Management Education*, 8(2), 75–82. ISSN 1472-8117.

Craig, R., & Amernic, J. (2011). Detecting linguistic traces of destructive narcissism at-a-distance in a CEO's letter to shareholders. *Journal of Business Ethics*, 101(4), 563–75. https://doi.org/10.1007/s10551-011-0738-8.

Craig, R., & Amernic, J. (2014). Exploring signs of hubris in CEO language. In R.P. Hart, (Ed.), *Communication and language analysis in the corporate world* (pp. 69–88). IGI-Global.

Craig, R., & Amernic, J. (2018). Are there language markers of hubris in CEO letters to shareholders? *Journal of Business Ethics*, 149(4), 973–86. https://doi.org/10.1007/s10551-016-3100-3.

Craig, R., & Amernic, J. (2020a). Autobiographical vignettes in annual report CEO letters as a lens to understand how leadership is conceived and enacted. *Accounting, Auditing & Accountability Journal*, 33(1), 106–23. https://doi.org/10.1108/AAAJ-12-2018-3774.

Craig, R., & Amernic, J. (2020b). The language of leadership in a deadly pandemic. *Strategy & Leadership*, 48(5), 41-7. https://doi.org/10.1108/SL-05-2020-0068.

Craig, R., Garrott, L., & Amernic, J. (2001). A "close reading" protocol to identify perception-fashioning rhetoric in website financial reporting: The case of Microsoft. *Accounting and the Public Interest*, 1(1), 1–16. https://doi.org/10.2308/api.2001.1.1.1.

Craig, R., Mortensen, T., & Iyer, S. (2013). Exploring top management language for signals of possible deception: The words of Satyam's chair Ramalinga Raju. *Journal of Business Ethics*, 113(2), 333–47. https://doi.org/10.1007/s10551-012-1307-5.

Crespo-Fernández, E. (2018). Euphemism as a discourse strategy in U.S. local and state politics. *Journal of Language and Politics*, 17(6), 789–811. https://doi.org/10.1075/jlp.17040.cre.

Crooks E. (2010, July 27). Dudley vows new BP safety culture. *Financial Times*. http://www.ft.com/cms/s/0/ab15d58e-994c-11df-9834-00144feab49a.html?ftcamp=rss.

Cunningham, C. (2005). Section 404 compliance and "tone at the top." *Financial Executive*, 21(5), 6.

Cunningham, L.A. (Ed.) (2013). *The essays of Warren Buffett: Lessons for corporate America*. North Carolina Academic Press.

Cuno, J. (2005). Telling stories: Rhetoric and leadership, a case study. *Leadership*, 1, 210. https://doi.org/10.1177/1742715005051859.

Cutter, C., & Maloney, J. (2020, March 24). How CEOs step up when they can't step out. *The Australian*, p. 20.

Dalpiaz, E., & Di Stefano, G. (2018). A universe of stories: Mobilizing narrative practices during transformative change. *Strategic Management Journal, 39*(3), 664–96. https://doi.org/10.1002/smj.2730.

Dando, C., & Bull, R. (2011). Maximising opportunities to detect verbal deception: Training police officers to interview tactically. *Journal of Investigative Psychology and Offender Profiling, 8*(2), 189–202. https://doi.org/10.1002/jip.145.

della Cava, M. (2017a, March 8). Uber admits its ghost driver "Greyball" tool was used to thwart regulators, vows to stop. *USA Today.* https://www.usatoday.com/story/tech/talkingtech/2017/03/08/uber-stop-using-greyball-target-regulators/98930282/.

della Cava, M. (2017b, June 9). Uber's Travis Kalanick offered sex rules for 2013 party. *USA Today.* https://www.usatoday.com/story/tech/talkingtech/2017/06/08/ubers-travis-kalanick-offered-sex-rules-2013-party-report/102646050/.

Denning, S. (2006). Effective storytelling: Strategic business narrative techniques. *Strategy & Leadership, 34*(1), 42–8. https://doi.org/10.1108/10878570610637885.

Dillet, R. (2020, March 4). Uber driver reclassified as employee in France. *Telecrunch.* https://techcrunch.com/2020/03/04/uber-driver-reclassified-as-employee-in-france/.

Donohue, B. (2013). How to fail at corporate fraud. http://threatpost.com/how-fail-fraud-010813/77378.

Dudley, R. W. (2012, January 13). A safer, stronger BP: Our quest to earn back America's trust. *Vital Speeches of the Day,* March, 93–7. Address by Robert W. Dudley, Group Chief Executive, BP, Economic Club of Chicago.

Duffy, J. (2013, December 3). The ethics of metaphor. *Chronicle of Higher Education.* https://www.chronicle.com/blogs/conversation/2013/12/03/the-ethics-of-metaphor-2/.

Duncan, C. (2020). Coronavirus: How Boris Johnson ignored health advice at his peril before Covid-19 diagnosis. *The Independent.* https://www.independent.co.uk/news/uk/politics/coronavirus-boris-johnson-positive-test-health-advice-shaking-hands-hospital-hancock-a9430231.html.

Dunn, S. (1990). Root metaphor in the old and new industrial relations. *British Journal of Industrial Relations, 28*(1), 1–31. https://doi.org/10.1111/j.1467-8543.1990.tb00350.x.

Edersheim, E.H. (2007, Summer). Peter Drucker's "unfinished chapter": The role of the CEO. *Leader to Leader, 2007*(45), pp. 40–6. https://doi.org/10.1002/ltl.242.

Editorial Board, *Financial Times.* (2019, November 19). https://www.ft.com/content/69343192-ebf0-11e8-8180-9cf212677a57.

Edwards, J.R.D., Davey J., & Armstrong K. (2013). Returning to the roots of culture: A review and re-conceptualization of safety culture. *Safety Science, 55,* 70–80. https://doi.org/10.1016/j.ssci.2013.01.004.

Egan, M. (2012, June 13). Despite resistance, boards shift toward breaking up CEO, Chair roles. www.foxbusiness.com (URL no longer valid).

Elkind P., Whitford, D., & Burke, D. (2011, January 24). BP: An accident waiting to happen. *Fortune.*

Ellison, N.B., Heino, R.D., & Gibbs, J.L. (2006). Managing impressions online: Self-presentation processes in the online dating environment. *Journal of Computer-Mediated Communication, 11*(2), 415–41. https://doi.org/10.1111/j.1083-6101.2006.00020.x.

Emby, C., & Finley, D. (1997). Debiasing framing effects in auditors' internal control judgments and testing decisions. *Contemporary Accounting Research, 14*(2), 55–77. https://doi.org/10.1111/j.1911-3846.1997.tb00527.x.

Entman, R.M. (1993). Framing: Towards clarification of a fractured paradigm. *Journal of Communication, 43*(4), 51–8. https://doi.org/10.1111/j.1460-2466.1993.tb01304.x.

Etter, M., Ravasi, D., & Colleoni, E. (2019). Social media and reputation formation. *Academy of Management Review, 44,* 28–52. https://doi.org/10.5465/amr.2014.0280.

Fanelli, A., & Grasselli, N. (2005). Defeating the minotaur: The construction of CEO charisma and the US stock market. *Organization Studies*, *27*, 811–32. https://doi.org/10.1177/0170840606061070.

Fears, D. (2020, February 12). The toxic reach of *Deepwater Horizon*'s oil spill was much larger – and deadlier – than previous estimates, a new study says. *The Washington Post.* https://www.washingtonpost.com/climate-environment/2020/02/12/toxic-reach-deepwater-horizons-oil-spill-was-much-larger-deadlier-than-previous-estimates-new-study-says/.

Fiol, C.M. (1989). A semiotic analysis of corporate language: Organizational boundaries and joint venturing. *Administrative Science Quarterly*, *34*, 277–303. https://doi.org/10.2307/2989899.

Floor, W. (2018). The Justinian plague (bubonic plague) also attacked the Sasanian lands. *Studies in the history of medicine in Iran*. Mazda Publishers, p. 3.

Foran, P. (2009, September.). CN's Hunter Harrison is the recipient of Progressive Railroading's "Railroad Innovator" award. *Progressive Railroading.* http://www.progressiverailroading.com/canadian_national/article/CNs-Hunter-Harrison-is-the-Recipient-of-Progressive-Railroadings-Railroad-Innovator-Award--21414.

Fowler, G.A. (2019, December 6). Uber CEO Q&A: When rape happens in an Uber, who's responsible? *The Washington Post.* https://www.washingtonpost.com/technology/2019/12/06/uber-ceo-qa-when-rape-happens-an-uber-whos-responsible/.

Fuoli, M., & Paradis, C. (2014). A model of trust-repair discourse. *Journal of Pragmatics*, *74*, 52–69. https://doi.org/10.1016/j.pragma.2014.09.001.

Flitter, E., Appelbaum, B., & Cowley, S. (2018, February 2), Federal reserve shackles Wells Fargo after fraud scandal. *The New York Times.* https://www.nytimes.com/2018/02/02/business/wells-fargo-federal-reserve.html.

Gabriel, Y. (2000). *Storytelling in organisations: Stories, fantasies, and subjectivity.* Oxford University Press.

Gabriel, Y. (2012). Under new management: Subject, objects and hubris, new and old. *Nouvelle revue de psychosociologie*, *13*, 241–64. https://doi.org/10.3917/nrp.013.0241.

Garrard, P., Rentoumi, V., Lambert, C., & Owen, D. (2014). Linguistic biomarkers of hubris syndrome. *Cortex*, *55*, 167–81. https://doi.org/10.1016/j.cortex.2013.08.014 Medline: 24074886.

Garvey, P. (2020, May 5). Doctor wary of Rinehart remedy. *The Australian*, p. 5.

Gemmell, N. (2019, July 20). Coming up for air. *The Weekend Australian Magazine*, p. 14.

Gilbert, D., & Scheck, J. (2014). BP found grossly negligent in *Deepwater Horizon* disaster. *Wall Street Journal.* http://online.wsj.com/articles/u-s-judge-finds-bp-grossly-negligent-in-2010-deepwater-horizondisaster-1409842182 (URL no longer valid).

Girginova, K. (2013). Social CEOs: Twitter as a constitutive form of communication. MA thesis, Georgetown University, Washington, DC.

Glad, B. (2002). Why tyrants go too far: Malignant narcissism and absolute power. *Political Psychology*, *23*, 1–37. https://doi.org/10.1111/0162-895X.00268.

Glazer, E. (2017, October 2). Five things to know about Wells Fargo CEO Timothy Sloan's testimony. *Wall Street Journal.* https://www.wsj.com/articles/five-things-to-know-about-wells-fargo-ceo-timothy-sloans-testimony-1506959479.

Gramm, W.S. (1996). Economic metaphors: Ideology, rhetoric, and theory. In J.S. Mio & A.N. Katz (Eds.). *Metaphors: Implications and applications* (pp. 147–70). Erlbaum Associates.

Gray, A. (2017, October 3). Wells Fargo boss should go, says Elizabeth Warren. *FT.com.* https://www.ft.com/content/78dbb0bc-a852-11e7-ab55-27219df83c97.

Guerin, B. (2003). Language use as social strategy: A review and an analytic framework for the social sciences. *Review of General Psychology*, *7*, 251–98. https://doi.org/10.1037/1089-2680.7.3.251.

Guldenmund, F.W. (2000). The nature of safety culture: A review of theory and research. *Safety Science*, *34*, 215–57 https://doi.org/10.1016/S0925-7535(00)00014-X.

Gupta, S., & Skillicorn, D. (2006). Improving a textual deception detection model. *Proceedings, 2006 conference of the Center for Advanced Studies on Collaborative Research* (p. 29). IBM Corporation.

Guthey, E., & Jackson, B. (2008). Revisualizing images in leadership and organization studies. In D. Barry & H. Hansen (Eds.). *The SAGE handbook of new approaches in management and organization* (pp. 84–92). SAGE.

Hancock, J., Curry, L., Goorha, S., & Woodworth, M. (2007). On lying and being lied to: A linguistic analysis of deception in computer-mediated communication. *Discourse Processes, 45,* 1–23. https://doi.org/10.1080/01638530701739181.

Hanlon, G., & Mandarini, M. (2015). On the impossibility of business ethics: Leader heterogeneity and politics. In A. Pullen & C. Rhodes (Eds.). *The Routledge companion to ethics, politics and organizations* (pp. 462–78). Routledge.

Hargie, O., Stapleton, K., & Tourish, D. (2010). Interpretations of CEO public apologies for the banking crisis: Attributions of blame and avoidance of responsibility. *Organization, 17,* 721–42. https://doi.org/10.1177/1350508410367840.

Harrington, A. (1995). Metaphoric connections: Holistic science in the shadow of the Third Reich. *Social Research, 62,* 357–85.

Hart, R.P. (2001). Redeveloping DICTION: Theoretical considerations. In M. West (Ed.), *Theory, method, and practice of computer content analysis* (pp. 43–60). Ablex.

Hart, R., & Carroll, C.E. (2013). *DICTION 7.0 user's manual.* Digitext.

Hart, R.P., Childers, J.P., & Lind, C.J. (2013). *Political tone: How leaders talk and why.* University of Chicago Press.

Hart, R.P., Jarvis, S.E., Jennings, W.P., & Smith-Howell, D. (2005). *Political keywords: Using language that uses us.* Oxford University Press.

Haukelid, K. (2008). Theories of (safety) culture revisited–An anthropological approach. *Safety Science, 46,* 413–26. https://doi.org/10.1016/j.ssci.2007.05.014.

Hayward, M.L.A., & Hambrick, D.C. (1997). Explaining the premiums paid for large acquisitions: Evidence of CEO hubris. *Administrative Science Quarterly, 42*(1), 103–27. https://doi.org/10.2307/2393810.

Heffernan, M. (2011). *Willful blindness.* Doubleday.

Henry, E. (2008). Are investors influenced by how earnings press releases are written? *Journal of Business Communication, 45,* 363–407. https://doi.org/10.1177/0021943608319388.

Heracleous, L. (2004). Interpretivist approaches to organisational discourse. In D. Grant, C. Hardy, C. Oswick, & L. Putnam (Eds.). *The SAGE handbook of organizational discourse* (pp. 175–92). SAGE.

Heracleous, L., & Klaering, L.A. (2017). The circle of life: Rhetoric of identification in Steve Jobs' Stanford speech. *Journal of Business Research, 79,* 31–40. https://doi.org/10.1016/j.jbusres.2017.05.011.

Hodgkin, A. (2017). *Following Searle on Twitter: How words create digital institutions.* University of Chicago Press.

Holmes, R. (2016). The world's top 100 CEOs on social media: What you can learn. https://www.linkedin.com/pulse/worlds-top-100-ceos-social-media-what-you-can-lear-ryan-holmes.

Holstein, W.J. (2009). *Why GM matters: Inside the race to transform an American icon.* Walker Publishing.

Hopkins, A. (2006). Counteracting the cultural causes of disaster. *Journal of Contingencies and Crisis Management, 7,* 141–9. https://doi.org/10.1111/1468-5973.00107.

House of Commons Culture, Media and Sport Committee. (2012, April 30). *News International and phone-hacking: Eleventh Report of Session 2010–12, Volume I.*

Hwang, S. (2012). The strategic use of Twitter to manage personal public relations. *Public Relations Review, 38,* 159–61. https://doi.org/10.1016/j.pubrev.2011.12.004.

Hyland, K. (1998). Exploring corporate rhetoric: Metadiscourse in the CEO's letter. *Journal of Business Communication, 35*(2), 224–45. https://doi.org/10.1177/002194369803500203.

Iyengar, S. (1990). Framing responsibility for political issues: The case of poverty. *Political Behavior, 12,* 19–40. https://doi.org/10.1007/BF00992330.

Jaques, E. (2002). *Social power and the CEO: Leadership and trust in a sustainable free enterprise system.* Quorum Books.

Johansson, P., Hall, L., Sikstrom, S., Tarning, B., & Lind, A. (2006). How something can be said about telling more than we can know: On choice blindness and introspection. *Consciousness and Cognition, 15*, 673–92. https://doi.org/10.1016/j.concog.2006.09.004 Medline: 17049881.

Jones, M.J., & Shoemaker, P.A. (1994). Accounting narrative: A review of empirical studies of content and readability. *Journal of Accounting Literature, 13*, 142–84.

Jönsson, S. (1998). Relate management accounting research to managerial work! *Accounting, Organizations and Society, 23*, 411–34. https://doi.org/10.1016/S0361-3682(97)00018-4.

Jordan, J.M. (2017). Challenges to large-scale digital organization: The case of Uber. *Journal of Organization Design, 6*, article 11, accessible at https://doi.org/10.1186/s41469-017-0021-2.

Kalmoe, N.P., Gubler, J.R., &. Wood, D.A. (2017). Toward conflict or compromise? How violent metaphors polarize partisan issue attitudes. *Political Communication, 35*, 333–52. https://doi.org/10.1080/10584609.2017.1341965.

Kasulis (2018, October 13). *Boston Globe* (Online). https://www.bostonglobe.com/ideas/2018/10/13/ceo-hubris-costs-millions/lJl5EkGInLg686KRkA1ibL/story.html.

Keila, P.S., & Skillicorn, D.B. (2005). *Detecting unusual and deceptive communication in email.* http://research.cs.queensu.ca/TechReports/Reports/2005-498.pdf.

Kellaway, L. (2012, September 17). One way to prevent corporate crashes: A hubris test for CEOs. *The Globe and Mail.* http://www.theglobeandmail.com/report-on-business/careers/careers-leadership/one-way-to-prevent-corporate-crashes-a-hubris-test-for-ceos/article4549620/.

Kelly, B.E. (2017, March 27). It shouldn't take a $300 million man. *Railway Age.*

Kendall, J.E. (1993). Good and evil in the chairman's "boiler plate": An analysis of corporate visions of the 1970s. *Organization Studies, 14*, 571–92. https://doi.org/10.1177/017084069301400406.

Kets de Vries, M. (1994). The leadership mystique. *Academy of Management Executive, 8*(3), 73–89. https://doi.org/10.5465/ame.1994.9503101181.

Kets de Vries, M. (2004). Organizations on the couch: A clinical perspective on organizational dynamics. *European Management Journal, 22*, 183–200. https://doi.org/10.1016/j.emj.2004.01.008.

Kets de Vries, M., & Miller, D. (1985). Narcissism and leadership: An object relations perspective. *Human Relations, 38*, 583–601. https://doi.org/10.1177/001872678503800606.

Knapp, M.L., Hart R.P., & Dennis, H.S. (1974). An exploration of deception as a communication construct. *Human Communication Research, 1*, 15–29. https://doi.org/10.1111/j.1468-2958.1974.tb00250.x.

Kodish, S. (2017). Communicating organizational trust: An exploration of the link between discourse and action. *International Journal of Business Communication, 54*, 347–68. https://doi.org/10.1177/2329488414525464.

Lacy, S. (2014, October 22). The horrific trickle down of asshole culture: Why I've just deleted Uber from my phone. *PandoDaily.* https://pando.com/2014/10/22/the-horrific-trickle-down-of-asshole-culture-at-a-company-like-uber/.

Lakoff, G. (1993). The contemporary theory of metaphor. In A. Ortony (Ed.), *Metaphor and thought* (pp. 202–51). Cambridge University Press.

Lakoff, G. (1996). *Moral politics: How liberals and conservatives think.* University of Chicago Press.

Lakoff, G., & Johnson, M. (1980). *Metaphors we live by.* University of Chicago Press.

Landau, M. (1961). On the use of metaphor in political analysis. *Social Research, 28*, 331–53.

Lane, A. (2011, August 1). Hack work. *The New Yorker.*

Lanham, R.A. (1993). *The electronic word: Democracy, technology, and the arts.* University of Chicago Press.

Larcker, D., & Tayan, B. (2010). Financial manipulation: Words don't lie. http://papers.ssrn.com/sol3/papers.cfm?abstract_id=1678058.

Larcker, D., & Zakolyukina, A.A. (2010). Detecting deceptive discussions in conference calls. *Stanford GSB Research Paper No. 2060*. Rock Center for Corporate Governance, working paper No. 83.

Larcker, D., & Zakolyukina, A. (2012). Detecting deceptive discussions in conference calls. *Journal of Accounting Research, 50*, 495–540. https://doi.org/10.1111/j.1475-679X.2012.00450.x.

Lasswell, H.D. (1953). The theory of political propaganda. In B. Bardson & M. Janowitz (Eds). *Reader in public opinion and communication*. Free Press.

Lee, J., & Lim, Y. (2016). Gendered campaign tweets: The cases of Hillary Clinton and Donald Trump. *Public Relations Review, 42*, 849–55. https://doi.org/10.1016/j.pubrev.2016.07.004.

Lei, L., Li, Y., & Luo, Y. (2019). Production and dissemination of corporate information in social media: A review. *Journal of Accounting Literature, 42*, 29–43. https://doi.org/10.1016/j.acclit.2019.02.002.

Leone, M. (2009, January 16). Satyam overlooked oversight. *CFO*. http://www.cfo.com/article.cfm/12960159/1/c_2984287?f=archives (URL no longer valid).

Levin, S. (2017, June 28). Uber's scandals, blunders and PR disasters: The full list. *The Guardian*. https://www.theguardian.com/technology/2017/jun/18/uber-travis-kalanick-scandal-pr-disaster-timeline.

Li, J., & Tang, Y. (2010). CEO hubris and firm risk taking in China: The moderating role of managerial discretion. *Academy of Management Journal, 53*, 45–68. https://doi.org/10.5465/amj.2010.48036912.

Llewellyn, S. (1999). Narratives in accounting and management research. *Accounting, Auditing & Accountability Journal, 12*, 220–37. https://doi.org/10.1108/09513579910270129.

Locander, W.H., & Ladik, D.M. (2017). CEO tweet behavior: The use of metaphors and gendered communication style. *Journal of Managerial Issues, XXIX*, 365–79.

Lopatto, E. (2020, May 7). Was Elon's Tesla Twitter meltdown illegal? An investigation. *This Week in Elon*. https://www.theverge.com/2020/5/1/21244747/elon-musk-tesla-tweets-shares-sec-settlement-stock.

Loughran, T., McDonald, B., & Yun, H. (2009). A wolf in sheep's clothing: The use of ethics-related terms in 10-K reports. *Journal of Business Ethics, 89*, 39–49. https://doi.org/10.1007/s10551-008-9910-1.

Lovelace, B. Jr. (2017, August 21). *Cramer: I don't get former GE CEO Jeff Immelt's possible move to Uber*. CNBC. www.cnbc.com/2017/08/21/cramer-i-dont-get-jeffreyimmelts-possible-move-to-uber.html (URL no longer valid).

Lubit, R. (2002). The long-term organizational impact of destructively narcissistic managers. *Academy of Management Executive, 16*, 127–138. https://doi.org/10.5465/ame.2002.6640218.

Lye, J. (1997). *Ideology: A brief guide*. https://academic.uprm.edu/laviles/id218.htm.

Lyons, L.E. (2011). "I'd like my life back": Corporate personhood and the BP oil disaster. *Biography, 34*(1), 96–107. https://doi.org/10.1353/bio.2011.0012.

Maccoby, M. (2003). *The productive narcissist: The promise and peril of visionary leadership*. Broadway.

Maclean, M., Harvey, C., & Chia, R. (2011). Sensemaking, storytelling and the legitimization of elite business careers. *Human Relations, 65*, 17–40. https://doi.org/10.1177/0018726711425616.

Mahadeo, S. (2006, Nov/Dec.). How management can prevent fraud by example. *Fraud*. http://www.acfe.com/fraud/view.asp?ArticleID=625 (URL no longer valid).

Malhotra, C.K., & Malhotra, A. (2016). How CEOs can leverage Twitter. *MIT Sloan Management Review*, Winter, 73–9.

Mallick, H. (2011). Lack of knowledge an asset for the Murdochs. *The Star*. http://www.thestar.com/news/world/article/1027278--mallick-lack-of-knowledge-an-asset-for-the-murdochs.

Martin, J. (1990). Deconstructing organizational taboos: The suppression of gender conflict in organizations. *Organization Science 1*, 339–59. https://doi.org/10.1287/orsc.1.4.339.

Matousek, M. (2018, January 11). Uber reportedly disrupted government investigations for almost 2 years with a "secret" system called "Ripley." *Business Insider*. https://www.businessinsider.com.au/report-uber-system-disrupted-government-investigations-2018-1.

McCloskey, D.N. (1985). *The rhetoric of economics*. University of Wisconsin Press.

McGee, M.C. (1980). The "ideograph": A link between rhetoric and ideology. *The Quarterly Journal of Speech, 66*, 1–16. https://doi.org/10.1080/00335638009383499.

McGill, A. (2016, August 10). Is Trump's campaign locking him out of Twitter? *The Atlantic*. https://www.theatlantic.com/politics/archive/2016/08/donald-trump-twitter-iphone-android/495239.

McLannahan, B. (2016, October 15). Wells Fargo turns to no-nonsense professional Tim Sloan. *FT.com*. Document FTCOM00020161014ecae007hi

McNeilage, A. (2018). Uber's underpayment of drivers keeping it afloat, report finds. *The Guardian* (Australian edition). https://www.theguardian.com/technology/2018/mar/07/ubers-underpayment-of-drivers-keeping-it-afloat-report-finds.

McNish, J. (2012, December 7). CP's Hunter Harrison: There is a new sheriff in town. *The Globe and Mail*.

Men, L.R., & Tsai, W.-H.S. (2016). Public engagement with CEOs on social media: Motivations and relational outcomes. *Public Relations Review 42*, 932–42. https://doi.org/10.1016/j.pubrev.2016.08.001.

Merkl-Davies, D.M., & Brennan, N.M. (2007). Discretionary disclosure strategies in corporate narratives: Incremental information or impression management? *Journal of Accounting Literature, 26*, 116–94.

Miller, P. (1994). Accounting and objectivity: The invention of calculating selves and calculable spaces. In A. Megill (Ed.), *Rethinking Objectivity* (pp. 239–64). Duke University Press.

Miller, J. D., Gaughan, E.T, Pryor, L.R., Kamen, C., & Campbell, W. K. (2009). Is research using narcissistic personality inventory relevant for understanding narcissistic personality disorder? *Journal of Research in Personality, 43*, 482–8. https://doi.org/10.1016/j.jrp.2009.02.001.

Moir, M. (2019, October 17). Hyperbole creeps into the use of "unprecedented." *Christian Science Monitor*.

Morris, C.W. (1946). *Signs, language and behaviour*. Prentice-Hall.

Morris, J.A., Brotheridge, C.M., & Urbanski, J.C. (2005). Bringing humility to leadership: Antecedents and consequences of leader humility. *Human Relations, 58*, 1323–50. https://doi.org/10.1177/0018726705059929.

Morrow, R. (2008). Psychopathic storytelling: The effect of valence on self and time in psychopathic language use. http://ecommons.cornell.edu/bitstream/1813/12930/1/Morrow,%20Rebecca%20-%20Honors%20Thesis.pdf.

Murphy, A.C. (2013). On true portraits of letters to shareholders and the importance of phraseological analysis. *International Journal of Corpus Linguistics, 18*, 57–81. https://doi.org/10.1075/ijcl.18.1.06mur.

Nag, K. (2009). *The double life of Ramalinga Raju*. Harper Collins.

Näslund, L., & Pemer, F. (2012). The appropriated language: Dominant stories as a source of organizational inertia. *Human Relations, 65*, 89–110. https://doi.org/10.1177/0018726711424322.

Navarro, J. (2010, August 30). Deciphering the CEO deception study. *Psychology Today*. http://www.psychologytoday.com/blog/spycatcher/201008/deciphering-the-ceo-deception-study.

Nazaryan, A. (2016, July 12). Jeff Bezos wants to rule the world. *Newsweek*.

Newman, M.L., Pennebaker, J.W., Berry, D.S., & Richards, J.M. (2003). Lying words: Predicting deception from linguistic styles. *Personality and Social Psychology Bulletin, 29*, 665–75. https://doi.org/10.1177/0146167203029005010 Medline: 15272998.

Nguyen, T-M, Koshikawa, K., Kawamura, T., Tahara, Y., & Ohsuga, A. (2011). Building earthquake semantic network by mining human activity from Twitter. In *Proceedings 2011 IEEE International Conference on Granular Computing* (pp. 496–501). IEEE.

Nicolaides, R., Trafford, R., & Craig, R. (2018). Helping auditors identify signs of deception through psycholinguistics. *Journal of Financial Crime, 25*, 1062–76. https://doi.org/10.1108 /JFC-05-2017-0042.

Obama B. (2010, June 15). Remarks by the President to the nation on the BP oil spill. http:// www.whitehouse.gov/the-press-office/remarks-president-nation -bp-oil-spill (URL no longer valid).

Oberlechner, T., & Mayer-Schoenberger, V. (2002). Through their own words: Towards a new understanding of leadership through metaphors. Working Paper. John F. Kennedy School of Government, Harvard University.

Ocasio, W. (2005). The opacity of risk: Language and the culture of safety in NASA's space shuttle program. In W.H Starbuck & M. Farjoun (Eds.) *Organization at the limit: Lessons from the Columbia Disaster* (pp. 101–21). Blackwell.

Ochs, S.M. (2016, October 6). The leadership blind spots at Wells Fargo. *Harvard Business Review.* https://hbr.org/2016/10/the-leadership-blind-spots-at-wells-fargo.

Ochs, E., & Capps, L. (1996). Narrating the self. *Annual Review of Anthropology, 25*, 19–43. https:// doi.org/10.1146/annurev.anthro.25.1.19.

OFHEO (Office of Federal Housing Enterprise Oversight) (2006, May). *Report of the Special Examination of Fannie Mae.* www.ofheo.gov (URL no longer valid).

O'Leary, D.E. (2015). Twitter mining for discovery, prediction and causality: Applications and methodologies. *Intelligent Systems in Accounting, Finance and Management, 22*, 227–47. https:// doi.org/10.1002/isaf.1376.

Olson, P. (2019, November 27). Uber loses London licence amid fake drivers scandal. *The Australian*, p. 22.

Oswick, C., Putnam, L., & Keenoy, T. (2004). Tropes, discourse and organizing. In D. Grant, C. Hardy, C. Oswick, & L. Putnam (Eds.). *The SAGE handbook of organizational discourse* (pp. 105–28). SAGE.

Otazo, K. (2019). Preventing and curing hubris in leaders. In P. Garrard (Ed.), *The leadership hubris epidemic: Biological roots and strategies for prevention* (pp. 193–221). Palgrave Macmillan.

Ott, B.L. (2017). The age of Twitter: Donald J. Trump and the age of debasement. *Critical Studies in Media Communication, 34*, 59–68. https://doi.org/10.1080/15295036.2016.1266686.

Owen, D. (2011). Psychiatry and politicians – afterword: Commentary on ... "Psychiatry and politicians." *The Psychiatrist Online, 35*, 145–8. https://doi.org/10.1192/pb.bp.110.031708.

Owen, D., & Davidson, J. (2009). Hubris syndrome: An acquired personality disorder? A study of US presidents and UK prime ministers over the last 100 years. *Brain, 132*, 1396–406. https:// doi.org/10.1093/brain/awp008 Medline: 19213778.

Palmer, I., King, A.W., & Kelleher, D. (2004). Listening to Jack: GE's change conversations with shareholders. *Journal of Organizational Change Management, 17*, 593–614. https://doi.org /10.1108/09534810410564578.

Paparone, C.R. (2008, Nov.-Dec.). On metaphors we are led by. *Military Review*, 55–64.

Partridge, J. (2004, March 24). CN estimates strike cost as much as $40-million. *The Globe and Mail.* https://www.theglobeandmail.com/report-on-business/cn-estimates-strike -cost-as-much-as-40-million/article18262191/.

Paz, C. (2020, April 9). All the president's lies about coronavirus. *The Atlantic.* https://www .theatlantic.com/politics/archive/2020/04/trumps-lies-about-coronavirus/608647/.

Peltz, J.F. (2018, May 9). Wells Fargo launches ad campaign to leave accounts scandal behind. Not everyone is buying it. *Los Angeles Times.* https://www.latimes.com/business/la-fi-wells-fargo -ad-campaign-20180509-story.html.

Pennebaker, J.W., Mehl, M.R., & Niederhoffer, K.G. (2003). Psychological aspects of natural language use: Our words our selves. *Annual Review of Psychology*, *54*, 547–77. https://doi.org /10.1146/annurev.psych.54.101601.145041 Medline: 12185209.

Perelman, C., & Olbrechts-Tyteca, L. (1969). *The new rhetoric: A treatise in argumentation*. University of Notre Dame Press. (Original work published 1958).

Pérez, R.G. (2008). A cross-cultural analysis of heart metaphors. *Revista Alicantina de Estudios Ingleses*, *21*, 25–56. https://doi.org/10.14198/raei.2008.21.03.

Peshkin, A. (2001). Angles of vision: Enhancing perception in qualitative research. *Qualitative Inquiry*, *7*(2), 238–53. https://doi.org/10.1177/107780040100700206.

Petersoo, P. (2007). What does "we" mean? National deixis in the media. *Journal of Language and Politics*, *6*(3), 419–36. https://doi.org/10.1075/jlp.6.3.08pet.

Picornell, I. (2013). Analysing deception in written witness statements. *Linguistic Evidence in Security, Law and Intelligence*, *1*(1), 41–50. https://doi.org/10.5195/LESLI.2013.2.

Pollman, E. (2019). Corporate disobedience. *Duke Law Journal*, 68, 709–56.

Pollman, E., & Barry, J. (2017). Regulatory entrepreneurship. *Southern California. Law Review*, *90*(3), 383–448.

Porter, S., & Brinke, L. (2010). The truth about lies: What works in detecting high-stakes deception? *Legal and Criminological Psychology*, *15*(1), 57–75. https://doi.org/10.1348 /135532509X433151.

Postman, N. (1996). *The end of education*. Vintage Books.

Prasad, A., & Mir, R. (2002). Digging deep for meaning: A critical hermeneutic analysis of shareholder letters to shareholders in the oil industry. *Journal of Business Communication*, *39*(1), 92–116. https://doi.org/10.1177/002194360203900105.

Purda, L., & Skillicorn, D. (2014). Accounting variables, deception, and a bag of words: Assessing the tools of fraud detection. *Contemporary Accounting Research*, *32*(3), 1193–223. https://doi .org/10.1111/1911-3846.12089.

Putnam, L., & Boys, S. (2006). Revisiting metaphors of organizational communication. In S. Clegg, C. Hardy, T. Lawrence, & W. Nord (Eds.). *The SAGE handbook of organizational studies* (pp. 541–576). SAGE.

Raban, J. (2009, January 10–11). All the presidents' literature. *Wall Street Journal*, pp. W1–W2.

Raghavan, A. (2009). The Satyam saga–The business ethics perspective. *Journal for Decision Makers* (Colloquium), *34*(1), 81–3.

Raskin, R., & Shaw, R. (1988). Narcissism and the use of personal pronouns. *Journal of Personality*, *56*(2), 393–404. https://doi.org/10.1111/j.1467-6494.1988.tb00892.x Medline: 3404383.

Rasmussen, J. (2011). Enabling selves to conduct themselves safely: Safety committee discourse as governmentality in practice. *Human Relations*, *64*(3), 459–78. https://doi.org/10.1177 /0018726710380976.

Reilly, W.K. (2010, November 8-9). National Commission on the BP *Deepwater Horizon* oil spill and offshore drilling. Minutes of 5th meeting, Washington, DC.

Reuters. (2009, June 9). India's Satyam head arrested and board scrapped. http://uk.reuters.com /article/2009/01/09/us-satyam-idUKBOM17776820090109 (URL no longer valid).

Ricoeur, P. (1984). *Time and narrative*. University of Chicago Press.

Ridgway, V.F. (1956). Dysfunctional consequences of performance measurements. *Administrative Science Quarterly*, *1*(2), 240–7. https://doi.org/10.2307/2390989.

Rinehart, R.E. (2006). The "Eddie Scissons syndrome" and fictionalized public confessionals. *Qualitative Inquiry*, *12*(6), 1045–66. https://doi.org/10.1177/1077800406293237.

Rittenhouse, L. (2019, May 19). Can Boeing be safe and profitable? *Forbes*. https://www.forbes.com /sites/laurarittenhouse/2019/05/19/can-boeing-be-safe-profitable-and-wise/#1b9af4627383.

Rohrer, T., & Vignone, M. (2012). The bankers go to Washington: Theory and method in conceptual metaphor analysis. *Nouveaux cahiers de linguistique française*, *30*, 5–38.

Roll, R. (1986). The hubris hypothesis of corporate takeovers. *Journal of Business*, *59*(2), 197–216. https://doi.org/10.1086/296325.

Ron, A. (2008). Power. A pragmatist, deliberative (and radical) view. *Journal of Political Philosophy*, *16*(3), 272–92. https://doi.org/10.1111/j.1467-9760.2008.00305.x.

Rosemain, M., & Vidalon, D. (2020, March 4). Top French court deals blow to Uber by giving driver "employee" status. *Reuters*. https://af.reuters.com/article/companyNews/idUSL8N2AX52U (URL no longer valid).

Russell, G. (2011). Psychiatry and politicians: The "hubris syndrome." *The Psychiatrist Online*, *35*(4), 140–5. https://doi.org/10.1192/pb.bp.110.031575.

Ryan, G.W., & Bernard, H.R. (2003). Techniques to identify themes. *Field Methods*, *15*(1), 85–109. https://doi.org/10.1177/1525822X02239569.

Sadler-Smith, E., Robinson, G., Akstinaite, V., & Wray, T. (2019). Hubristic leadership: Understanding the hazard and mitigating the risks. *Organizational Dynamics*, *48*(2), 8–18. https://doi.org/10.1016/j.orgdyn.2018.05.007.

Sahadi. (2018, November 5). *CNN Business*, https://www.cnn.com/2018/11/05/success/narcissist-ceo/index.html.

Salancik, G.R., & Meindl, J.R. (1984). Corporate attributions as strategic illusions of management control. *Administrative Science Quarterly*, *29*(2), 238–54. https://doi.org/10.2307/2393176.

Salt, B. (2020, April 2). Galvanised for post-virus action. *The Australian*, p. 20.

Salter, M.S. (2008). *BP innovation corrupted: The origins and legacy of Enron's collapse*. Harvard University Press.

Sayers, J. (2014). Technology. In B. Burgett, & G. Hendler (Eds.). *Keywords for American cultural studies*. New York University Press. http://hdl.handle.net/2333.1/rr4xh08x

Scheff, T.J. (1997). *Emotions, the social bond, and human reality: Part/whole analysis*. Cambridge University Press.

Scheiber, N. (2019, May 14). Uber drivers are contractors, not employees, labor board says. https://www.nytimes.com/2019/05/14/business/economy/nlrb-uber-drivers-contractors.html.

Schein E. (2004). *Organizational culture and leadership*. Wiley.

Schneider, M.J. (1998). The Wal-Mart annual meeting: from small-town America to global corporate culture. *Human Organization*, *57*(3), 292–9. https://doi.org/10.17730/humo.57.3.l8km2555679qg024.

Schoenberger, E. (2001). Corporate autobiographies: The narrative strategies of corporate strategists. *Journal of Economic Geography*, *1*(3), 277–98. https://doi.org/10.1093/jeg/1.3.277.

Schön, D.A. (1993). Generative metaphor: A perspective on problem-solving in social policy. In A. Ortony (Ed.), *Metaphor and thought* (pp. 137–163). Cambridge University Press.

Schwartz, H.S. (1991). Narcissism project and corporate decay: The case of General Motors. *Business Ethics Quarterly*, *1*(3), 249–68. https://doi.org/10.2307/3857613.

Scott, M.B., & Lyman, S.M. (1968). Accounts. *American Sociological Review*, *33*(1), 46–62. https://doi.org/10.2307/2092239 Medline: 5644339.

Segars, A.H., & Kohut G.F. (2001). Strategic communication through the World Wide Web: An empirical model of effectiveness in the CEO's letter to shareholders. *Journal of Management Studies*, *38*(4), 535–56. https://doi.org/10.1111/1467-6486.00248.

Shamir, B., & Eilam, G. (2005). "What's your story?" A life-stories approach to authentic leadership development. *Leadership Quarterly*, *16*(3), 395–417. https://doi.org/10.1016/j.leaqua.2005.03.005.

Shane, T. (2018). The semiotics of authenticity: Indexicality in Donald Trump's tweets. *Social Media and Society*. July-September, 1–14. Accessible at https://journals-sagepub-com.ezphost.dur.ac.uk/doi/abs/10.1177/2056305118800315 (URL no longer valid).

Shaw, J. (2010). Papering the cracks with discourse: The narrative identity of the authentic leader. *Leadership*, *6*(1), 89–108. https://doi.org/10.1177/1742715009359237.

Sheeder, F. (2005). What exactly is "tone at the top", and is it really that big of a deal? *Journal of Health Care Compliance*, *7*(3), 35–8.

Sherman, E. (2019, July 30). Elon Musk's latest tweet may land him back in SEC crosshairs. *Fortune*. https://fortune.com/2019/07/30/elon-musk-tweet-solar-sec-consent-decree/.

Short, J. C., & Palmer, T. B. (2008). The application of DICTION to content analysis research in strategic management. *Organizational Research Methods*, *11*(4), 727–52. https://doi.org/10.1177/1094428107304534.

Silberstein, S. (2002). *War of words: Language, politics and 9/11*. Routledge.

Silbey, S.S. (2009). Taming Prometheus: Talk about safety and culture. *Annual Review of Sociology*, *35*(1), 341–69. https://doi.org/10.1146/annurev.soc.34.040507.134707.

Simons, H.W. (1994). "Going meta": Definition and political applications. *Quarterly Journal of Speech*, *80*(4), 468–81 https://doi.org/10.1080/00335639409384088.

Sims, R.R., & Brinkmann, J. (2002). Leaders as moral role models: The case of John Gutfreund at Salomon Brothers. *Journal of Business Ethics*, *35*(4), 327–39. https://doi.org/10.1023/A:1013826126058.

Sindreu, J. (2019, December 26). Why Boeing's CEO had to go. *The Australian*, p. 16.

Sissell, K. (2010, March 22/29). Looking back at BP Texas City. *Chemical Week*, p. 39.

Slagell, A.R. (1991). Anatomy of a masterpiece: A close textual analysis of Abraham Lincoln's second inaugural address. *Communication Studies*, *42*(2), 155–71. https://doi.org/10.1080/10510979109368330.

Smith, B. (2014, November 17). Uber executive suggests digging up dirt on journalists. *Buzzfeed*. https://www.buzzfeednews.com/article/bensmith/uber-executive-suggests-digging-up-dirt-on-journalists.

Smith, R., & Eisenberg, E. (1987). Conflict at Disneyland: A root-metaphor analysis. *Communication Monographs*, *54*(4), 367–80. https://doi.org/10.1080/03637758709390239.

Smith, M., & Taffler, R. (2000). The chairman's statement: A content analysis of discretionary narrative disclosures. *Accounting, Auditing & Accountability Journal*, *13*(5), 624–46. https://doi.org/10.1108/09513570010353738.

Stanford, J. (2019). Bring your own equipment and wait for work. Working for Uber is a lot like being a dock worker a century ago. *The Star*. Available at https://www.thestar.com/business/opinion/2019/11/17/bring-your-own-equipment-and-wait-for-work-working-for-uber-is-a-lot-like-being-a-dock-worker-a-century-ago.html.

Staw, B.M., McKechnie P.I., & Puffer, S.M. (1983). The justification of organizational performance. *Administrative Science Quarterly*, *28*(4), 582–600. https://doi.org/10.2307/2393010.

Steffy, L.C. (2011). *Drowning in oil: BP and the reckless pursuit of profit*. McGraw-Hill.

Steger, T. (2007). The stories metaphors tell: Metaphors as a tool to decipher tacit aspects in narratives. *Psychology*, *19*(1), 3–23. https://doi.org/10.1177/1525822X06292788.

Stewart, E. (2020, March 26). Elon Musk's coronavirus journey: A timeline. *Vox*. https://www.vox.com/recode/2020/3/19/21185417/elon-musk-coronavirus-tweets-panic-ventilators-chloroquine-tesla-factory.

Stolee, G., & Caton, S. (2018). Twitter, Trump, and the base: A shift to a new form of presidential talk? *Signs and Society*, *6*(1), 147–65. https://doi.org/10.1086/694755.

Sullivan, J. (2017, March 8). An update on "greyballing": Uber newsroom. https://www.uber.com/newsroom/an-update-on-greyballing/.

Swan, D. (2019, 28/29 December). Reeling from the Zuckerberg punch. *The Weekend Australian*, p. 25.

Sydserff, R., & Weetman, P. (2002). A texture index for evaluating accounting narratives: An alternative to readability formulas. *Accounting, Auditing & Accountability Journal*, *12*(4), 459–88. https://doi.org/10.1108/09513579910283503.

Tenbrunsel, A.E., & Messick, D.M. (2004). Ethical fading: The role of self-deception in unethical behavior. *Social Justice Research*, *17*(2), 223–36. https://doi.org/10.1023/B:SORE.0000027411.35832.53.

Teufl, P., & Kraxberger S. (2011). Extracting semantic knowledge from Twitter. In E. Tambouris, A. Macintosh, & H. de Bruijn (Eds). *Electronic participation*. Lecture Notes in Computer Science, vol. 6847 (pp. 48–59). Springer.

The most followed accounts on Twitter. https://www.brandwatch.com/blog/most-twitter
-followers/.

Thornton, D.B. (1988). Theory and metaphor in accounting. *Accounting Horizons, 2*(4), 1–9.

Tinker, T. (1985). *Paper prophets.* Praeger.

Tinker, T. (1986). Metaphor or reification: Are radical humanists really libertarian anarchists?
Journal of Management Studies, 23(4), 363–84. https://doi.org/10.1111/j.1467-6486.1986
.tb00423.x.

Tourish, D., & Hargie, O. (2012). Metaphors of failure and the failures of metaphor: A critical
study of root metaphors used by bankers in explaining the banking crisis. *Organization
Studies, 33,* 1045–1069. https://doi.org/10.1177/0170840612453528.

Tourish, D., & Vatcha, N. (2005). Charismatic leadership and corporate cultism at Enron: The
elimination of dissent, the promotion of conformity and organizational collapse. *Leadership,
1*(4), 455–80. https://doi.org/10.1177/1742715005057671.

Trabucchi, D., Talenti, L., & Buganza, T. (2019). How do big bang disruptors look like? A business
model perspective. *Technological Forecasting and Social Change, 141,* 330–40. https://doi.
org/10.1016/j.techfore.2019.01.009.

Turner, N., & Gray, G.C. (2009). Socially constructing safety. *Human Relations, 62*(9), 1259–66.
https://doi.org/10.1177/0018726709339863.

Tversky, A., & Kahneman, D. (1981). The framing of decisions and the psychology of choice.
Science, 211(4481), 453–58. https://doi.org/10.1126/science.7455683 Medline: 7455683.

Van Dijk, T.A. (2006). Ideology and discourse analysis. *Journal of Political Ideologies, 11*(2), 115–40.
https://doi.org/10.1080/13569310600687908.

Vartapetiance, A., & Gillam, L. (2012). Deception detection for the tangled web. *Computers and
Society, 42*(1), 34–47. https://doi.org/10.1145/2422512.2422517.

Vignone, M.J. (2012). Family, buildings, and wars: Organizational conceptual metaphors. *OD
Practitioner, 44,* 34–7.

Vo, T.T. (2010). To be or not to be both CEO and board chair. *Brooklyn Law Review, 76,* 65–129.

Vohra, N. (2009). The Satyam story: Many questions and a few answers. *Vikalpa: The Journal for
Decision Makers (Colloquium), 34,* 69–71. https://doi.org/10.1177/0256090920090106.

Vrij, A. (2008). *Detecting lies and deceit.* Wiley.

Vrij, A., Edward, K., Roberts, K., & Bull, R. (2000). Detecting deceit via analysis of verbal and
nonverbal behaviour. *Journal of Nonverbal Behavior, 24,* 239–63. https://doi.org/10.1023
/A:1006610329284.

Vrij, A., Ennis, E., Farman, S., & Mann S. (2010). People's perceptions of their truthful and
deceptive interactions in daily life. *Open Access Journal of Forensic Psychology, 2,* 6–49.

Wallace, B. (2014, July 15). Kara Swisher is Silicon Valley's most feared and well-liked journalist.
How does that work? *New York Magazine.* https://nymag.com/intelligencer/2014/07/kara
-swisher-silicon-valleys-most-powerful-snoop.html.

Wallace, H. M., & Baumeister R. F. (2002). The performance of narcissists rises and falls with
perceived opportunity for glory. *Journal of Personality and Social Psychology, 82*(5), 819–34.
https://doi.org/10.1037/0022-3514.82.5.819.

Walters-York, L.M. (1996). Metaphor in accounting discourse. *Accounting, Auditing &
Accountability Journal, 9*(5), 45–70. https://doi.org/10.1108/09513579610367242.

Warwaruk, E. (2004). The Americanization of CN. *Canadian Dimension 38,* p. 3. https://
canadiandimension.com/articles/view/the-americanization-of-cn.

Weick, K., & Sutcliffe, K. (2007). *Managing the unexpected: Resilient performance in an age of
uncertainty.* Jossey Bass.

Weise, K. (2015, June 24). How Uber took over Portland. *Bloomberg News.* https://www
.bloomberg.com/news/features/2015-06-23/this-is-how-uber-takes-over-a-city.

Weiss, G. (2014, January 27). Uber acknowledges nasty ploy to sabotage a competitor. https://
www.entrepreneur.com/article/231058.

Wells, W.D. (1993). Brand equities, elephants, and birds: A commentary. In D.A. Aaker & A.L. Biel (Eds.), *Brand equity & advertising: Advertising's role in building strong brands* (pp. 343–355). Erlbaum Associates.

Werth, P. (1994). Extended metaphor – a text-world account. *Language and Literature, 3*(2), 79–103. https://doi.org/10.1177/096394709400300201.

Westphal, J.D., & Zajac, E.J. (1998). The symbolic management of stockholders: Corporate governance reforms and shareholder reactions. *Administrative Science Quarterly, 43*(1), 127–53. https://doi.org/10.2307/2393593.

Williams, R. (1976). *Keywords: A vocabulary of culture and society*. Fontana.

Wolson, P. (2004, February 14/15). America's grandiose persona under Bush. *Counterpunch*. https://www.counterpunch.org/2004/02/14/america-s-grandiose-persona-under-bush/.

Yablon, C.M. (2019). The lawyer as accomplice: Cannabis, Uber, Airbnb, and the ethics of advising "disruptive" businesses. *Minnesota Law Review, 104*(1), 309–84.

Young, J.J. (2013). Devil's advocate: The importance of metaphors. *Accounting Horizons, 27*(4), 877–86. https://doi.org/10.2308/acch-10369.

Zeitoun, H., Nordberg, D., & Homberg, F. (2019). The dark and bright sides of hubris: Conceptual implications for leadership and governance research. *Leadership, 15*(6), 647–6. https://doi.org/10.1177/1742715019848198.

Zhou, L., Burgoon, J.K., Nunamaker, J.F., & Twitchell, D. (2004). Automating linguistics-based cues for detecting deception in text-based asynchronous computer mediated communications. *Group Decision and Negotiation, 13*(1), 81–106. https://doi.org/10.1023/B:GRUP.0000011944.62889.6f.

Zuckerman, M., DePaulo, B.M., & Rosenthal, R. (1981). Verbal and nonverbal communication of deception. In L. Berkowitz (Ed.), *Advances in Experimental Social Psychology, 14*, 1–57.

Index

Lightning Source UK Ltd.
Milton Keynes UK
UKHW010741120921
390399UK00004B/83/J